SCIENCE FOR
PRIMARY AND EARLY YEARS

Developing Subject Knowledge

Second Edition

Ways of knowing: language, mathematics and science in early years

This book forms part of The Open University course *Ways of knowing: language, mathematics and science in early years* (E230). This is a 30 point course at level 2 and is part of the Foundation Degree in Early Years.

Details of this and other Open University courses can be obtained from the Student Registration and Enquiry Service, The Open University, PO Box 197, Milton Keynes MK7 6BJ, United Kingdom: tel. +44 (0)845 300 60 90, email general-enquiries@open.ac.uk.

Alternatively, you may visit The Open University website at http://www.open.ac.uk where you can learn more about the wide range of courses and packs offered at all levels by The Open University.

SCIENCE FOR PRIMARY AND EARLY YEARS

Developing Subject Knowledge

Second Edition

Jane Devereux

SAGE Publications

Los Angeles · London · New Delhi · Singapore

The Open University

The Open University
Walton Hall
Milton Keynes
MK7 6AA
United Kingdom
www. open. ac uk

 A SAGE Publications Ltd
1 Oliver's Yard
55 City Road
London EC1Y 1SP

SAGE Publications Inc
2455 Teller Road
Thousand Oaks, California 91320

SAGE Publications India Pvt Ltd
B1/I1 Mohan Cooperative Industrial Area
Mathura Road,
New Delhi 110 044
India

SAGE Publications Asia-Pacific Pte Ltd
33 Pekin Street #02–01
Far East Square
Singapore 0487 63

British Library Cataloguing in Publication data

A catalogue record for this book is available from the British Library

ISBN 978-1-4129-4611-7
ISBN 978-1-4129-4612-4(pbk)

Library of Congress Control Number: 2006940074

Typeset by Pantek Arts Ltd, Maidstone, Kent
Printed and bound in Great Britain by The Cromwell Press, Trowbridge, Wilts
Printed on paper from sustainable resources

Contents

List of Figures

Acknowledgements

This text draws heavily upon the subject knowledge chapters in *Open University Course-S624-Primary Teachers Learning Science.*

Workbook   1   Life Diversity and Evolution

                 2   Materials: Chemical and Physical Change

                 3   Forces and Energy

                 4   Electricity: Making Connections

                 5   The Planet Earth

                 6   Ecosystems

I would like to thank all those in the course team for generously allowing their text to be used as a basis for parts of this text. Special thanks to Sandra Amos, Frank Banks and Richard Boohan who acted as critical readers providing thoughtful and candid comment at all stages. I would also like to thank the External Assessors for their thoughtful and constructive feedback that has helped to shape this text.

Finally my sincere thanks to June Down for her patience and forbearance in typing this document.

Introduction

The aim of this text is to develop your subject knowledge in science for your work in primary schools and early years settings. Many students are apprehensive about teaching science because their own experiences of science education may not have all been positive. This book is intended for all those needing to develop their subject knowledge in primary science, not only those on ITT courses but also teachers in school and others working with young children in a variety of contexts. It can be used in a number of ways, for example:

▶ As self-study material.

▶ As pre-course study material.

▶ As course material at the very start of your course.

▶ At stages throughout your course as you meet specific science topics, perhaps on school placements.

This text covers the three basic sciences, biology, physics and chemistry. It deals with ideas rather than areas of science but works through broad topics and concepts. It uses the requirements for primary teaching laid out in *Qualifying to Teach* (2006), The Training and Development Agency for Schools, and more than covers the science knowledge needed to teach the Foundation Stage, Key Stage 1 and Key Stage 2.

The text is divided into two parts. Part 1 has four chapters. The first explores the nature of science and the skills and knowledge that are developed through science and scientific processes. The three other chapters aim to develop your understanding of the key ideas of particles, forces and energy. These ideas underpin most areas of science and are fundamental in building a firm basis to your subject knowledge.

Part 2 builds on these core ideas by applying them to specific science topics such as life and living processes, continuity and change, ecosystems and electricity and magnetism, Earth in space, light and sound.

How to use this book

Throughout the whole book it is assumed that you will take an active part in your learning. Used sequentially this book will provide a comprehensive grounding in the science national curriculum and meet the requirements of the Foundation Stage. Everyone may not need to study all parts of the book. However, it is advisable that you read or work through Part 1 followed by the topics identified by your audit as needing development. Reading or working through Part 1 will confirm your confidence in these key areas or provide a chance to build a firm foundation.

Each section incorporates activities and questions for you to work through, which are designed to extend and challenge your current knowledge. Each activity is followed by a commentary where the scientific phenomena and experiences are discussed to aid your understanding. The book is designed for self-study but at times you may wish to share ideas with friends or colleagues in your setting or on your course. Keeping your subject knowledge up to date is an important part of being an effective teacher or practitioner.

In working through the book you will need a certain amount of equipment to help you explore ideas. These are listed near the beginning of each chapter. Most of the equipment needed is everyday items you would find in most households. However there is some specialist equipment such as prisms that you may need to borrow from your placement school, feeder secondary or maybe your Local Authority (LA) Teachers' Centre.

Matters of Health and Safety are dealt with in general terms in Part 1, Chapter 1 and specific aspects are highlighted as necessary throughout the book. It is important that you work in a safe environment and use equipment that is sturdy enough for the task.

The Association for Science (ASE) Booklet entitled *Be Safe* (2001) should be read and put into practice at all stages of your work, and when working in school. Details are given in the Bibliography.

It is hoped that as you work through these sections you will enjoy the experience of studying science and deepening your knowledge so you can be an exciting, enthusiastic and effective teacher of children.

PART 1

Chapter 1 aims to give you a brief introduction to the nature of science and to explore some of the key skills, processes and understandings that underpin what it means to be a scientist and work scientifically. If you would like more detail or wish to explore issues further there are several books listed in the Bibliography. Chapters 2, 3 and 4 look specifically at three key areas that underpin all other areas of science, namely, particles, forces and energy.

1 The Nature of Science and Science Processes

The nature of science

Defining the nature of science is a matter for great debate. Science has changed over the years and reflects the society and culture of our times. It is important here that we consider very briefly what we understand at this stage, about science.

Resources

For your activities in this section you need:

▶ two or three different gloves

▶ four small fizzy drink bottles

▶ four different fabrics

▶ thermometer

▶ notebook and pencil and a timer.

Describing science	Activity 1

Write down a list of words or phrases that you think describe your understanding of science.

Commentary

Your list probably included some of the following ideas:

Science is a set of discrete disciplines.
Physics, chemistry and biology.
It has a clearly defined body of knowledge.
It has a set of facts that are true.
It is a way of looking at the world.
It is about exploring and investigating the world around us.
It involves research and exploration into new ideas.
Scientists are curious, studious and systematic.

This list could go on but a clear, universally agreed definition is not easy to find. Each of these statements, if used singly, provides a very narrow and limiting description of what science might be. Collectively they still do not give a rounded definition of what science is all about. Discussion on the nature of science has been part of our history and has influenced the way scientists have and do work. Everybody is affected by science in their everyday lives. How we are influenced is determined by our own experiences of science as pupils, but also as citizens and the ways it impinges on us.

The following list of continuums about science provided by Nott and Wellington (1993) suggests some interesting dimensions to the nature of science to extend your thinking on how you see science.

- Relativism *vs* positivism – truth as being relative or absolute.

- Inductivism *vs* deductivism – generalising from observations to general laws versus forming hypotheses and testing observable consequences.

- Contextualism *vs* decontextualism – science interdependent with or independent of cultural context.

- Process *vs* content – science characterised mainly by processes or by facts and ideas.

- Instrumentalism *vs* realism – science as providing ideas which work versus a world independent of scientists' perceptions.

You may find it useful to discuss with colleagues/friends where along the various continuums you feel your ideas are situated. Each of these continuums highlights key tenets of science. It is important that you think about these ideas, alongside your own on the nature of science, especially if you intend to work as a teacher. Your own ideas on the nature of science will influence how you approach your work. It is important for you to understand the place of science in society and the way in which it influences our lives both directly and indirectly so that you can help others to make informed decisions about issues.

As the bounds of science and technology stretch wider it is important to be aware of the many ethical issues that surround some work in the science field.

The current debate on genetically modified crops is an example of an issue that raises many fears and anxieties. Different groups of people such as farmers, parents and politicians have wide-ranging opinions about the research into genetically modifying plants to enhance particular effects. Much of the anxiety is related to the different results that have been published and the interpretation of these results. There is concern as to whether we have the moral right to manipulate and change the genetic make-up of organisms. Where will it stop? Public pressure has encouraged supermarket chains to stop using GM materials in any of their own products until further notice.

This issue is an example of the way science and scientific research can have dramatic changes on our lives as citizens. It highlights how important it is for us to keep up to date with new ideas and developments. This enables us to make informed decisions as and when necessary, e.g. voting at elections.

Jenkins (1997) identifies several significant features about science that define the role it plays in citizenship. This includes how one views the risks involved, how it affects other aspects of our lives, how we make sense of the information and which social group we belong to.

The Association for Science Education (ASE, 1990) says that science content should have human and philosophical significance along with scientific and personal significance. They define human and philosophical significance as how science:

- contributes to the learner's understanding of the world

- illuminates the way that scientific ideas are developed over time

- shows the impact of scientific ideas on the way we live.

Scientific significance, they say, shows how:

- the content should aim to show how scientists model the world in order to understand it

- ideas should suggest explanations and lead to fruitful development

- the range of ideas chosen should include those currently being used by the scientific community and reflect the history of science.

Personal significance of science content should include:

- ideas which are immediately accessible

- preparation for the future as a citizen in a technological world

- development of ideas within appropriate social, personal and industrial contexts.

Science involves us in making moral and ethical judgements about different research, its methodology and outcomes. In order to be able to do this, it is important to develop the public understanding of science. Developing scientific literacy is a complex and wide-ranging issue that is summarised in the lists above. It shows the interactions that are so important in our roles as citizen, worker and family member.

Science essentially is about understanding. It involves reaching possible conclusions, exploring relationships and explanations between ideas and events. It includes the testing of ideas and the proposal of new theories and questions. These ideas are subject to change all the time as our ideas, skills and knowledge are developed through new research and evidence. As Reiss (2002) states, science is a 'body of knowledge about the world. The facts that comprise this knowledge are derived from accurate observations and careful experiments that can be checked by repeating them and as time goes on, scientific knowledge steadily progresses'. Science, being essentially a human endeavour, relies on the imagination and inventiveness of people to push out the boundaries of science. It involves collaboration and co-operation between individuals and groups and is a creative and stimulating area to work in.

Yet there are key ideas which seem to span the centuries and help us to understand the world in which we live. These basic, simple understandings that underpin many branches of science are developed in Part 1, Chapters 2, 3 and 4 of this book. The next section will look at what is involved in carrying out a scientific investigation and provide a context to reflect on your understanding.

In this section we have seen that:

▶ Science is about the way our world works.

▶ We all have roles to play, as citizens, in scientific endeavour and ideas.

Planning, carrying out and evaluating investigations

What is involved in a scientific investigation? What is the difference between investigations and experimenting? Why is it so important to work in a systematic way?

In this section you are to look at what is involved in carrying out an investigation. It will include an experiment using a range of fabrics. This will provide the context for analysing the scientific process and the skills knowledge and attitudes needed. The investigation will be divided into sections to enable us to explore the process as you progress through the task.

Activity 2	Posing useful questions

(a) Thinking about choosing a suitable fabric to make gloves to wear in cold conditions provides a suitable context for raising questions and investigating some of them. You may choose this or provide your own topic for investigation. But not all questions raised are suitable for investigation. Working on your own or with another person write down as many questions as you can about the collection of gloves/fabric that you have.

(b) Look carefully at your list of questions. Can you group them into those that are: more a comment or expression of interest, those that are asking for straight information, those that are more philosophical and those that lend themselves to investigation (Harlen, 2000)?

Commentary

Harlen (2000) categorises questions into the four types listed in (b) above, and this provides a useful way to classify questions into investigations or those that just need an answer or further observation or discussion.

Which glove is the best?
Which glove will keep my hand warmest?
What are the characteristics that make a good glove?

These are all questions that could lead into an investigation. Investigations cover a wide range of activities and do not have to include experimenting. They could include all or some of the following:

▶ research into current ideas using secondary sources

▶ modelling ideas

▶ observing

▶ hypothesising and experimenting to test ideas.

Investigating what would be the best fabric to make a glove may involve looking closely at the structure of the fabrics, exploring how gloves are made and what properties the fabric needs as well as carrying out experiments to test some of these properties.

The kind of question posed will define the breadth of the investigation but not all questions lead to an investigation. The question 'Which fabric will make the best glove for winter?' is one of those that supports investigative work and has the potential for lots of practical experimenting with the fabrics. Alsop et al. (2002) regard asking such questions and testing these ideas in reliable and valid ways as the basis of science.

Defining what is meant by best is an obvious starting point to explore these questions further and may give rise to a range of activities before any decisions are made about testing the fabrics to see which is suitable.

Characteristics such as whether or not they are windproof or they keep your hands warmest will need to be considered before experimenting. These discussions and decisions are what you as the person in control of the experiment must make. It should determine how you plan, carry out and evaluate the experiment. It is important that when you report your findings you include these decisions and ideas in your report as it will determine how the reader views your findings and interprets the results.

Planning an investigation

Having raised a suitable question to investigate it is important to find a way to do this that will answer the question posed. This is not always easy. Many scientific investigations have been criticised because the methodology chosen did not allow the question posed to be answered. It is important to define what you mean by 'best' for the glove. In this investigation, having looked at the important properties of a glove and the way they are made, we have chosen one characteristic of the fabrics to test. This will involve us carrying out an experiment to see which fabric retains most heat. We may devise more than one experiment to investigate the fabrics' properties in this area. For this exercise we are doing just one experiment to test our idea and that will now influence all that we do.

Hypothesising and predicting

Predicting and hypothesising are often linked together but they do have distinctive features. Predicting is saying what you think will happen or in our case which will be the best fabric for keeping our hands warm. In predicting this we may also include a hypothesis, i.e., a reason why we think this, based on our previous knowledge, research and experience. Often people have ideas about why they have predicted what they have, even if they do not articulate these to you. Hypothesising is very much about using previous knowledge, evidence and observations to formulate tentative theories about why things happen in the way they do. It is an important skill to develop and helps us to make sense of our understanding of the world as we transfer this knowledge from one situation to another.

Activity 3	Which material will be the best fabric to use for a glove to wear in cold weather?

Our set of materials is made up of three kinds of fabric, suitable to make gloves. One is woollen, one is cotton and the other plastic. Your collection may be different but that will not affect the way you work through the task.

Look carefully at your fabrics and order them from best to worst for allowing heat to pass through them.

Note down your ideas as to why you think this is so. We will return to these at the end of the investigation, when we evaluate our findings. There is no need for a commentary at this stage.

Planning

The next step is to plan and order our work so that we gather the information we need to answer the question posed. What kind of evidence do we need to be able to do this? First we may need to consult resources such as books and collect together appropriate apparatus to help us decide what to do and in what order.

Our investigation will use warm water in small plastic drink bottles to represent the warmth of the hand. Each bottle will be covered with a chosen fabric and one will be left uncovered. The temperature of each bottle will be taken at regular intervals and recorded.

What kind of investigation are we undertaking? The AKSIS Project (Association for Science Education and King's College Investigations in Schools [Goldsworthy, 1998]) lists six types of investigation with sample questions from the project included to exemplify the kind of investigation and type of question to be answered.

1 *Fair testing*. These investigations are concerned with exploring relations between variables or factors, e.g.:

What affects the rate at which sugar dissolves?
What makes a difference to the time it takes for a paper spinner to fall?
Which is the strongest bag?

2 *Classifying and identifying.* Classifying is a process of arranging a large range of objects or events into manageable sets. Identifying is a process of recognising objects and events as members of particular sets, possibly new and unique sets, and allocating names to them.

What is this chemical?
How can we group these invertebrates?

3 *Pattern seeking.* These investigations involve observing and recording natural phenomena or carrying out surveys and then seeking patterns in the findings.

Do dandelions in the shade have longer leaves than those in the light?
Where do we find most snails?
Do people with longer legs jump higher?

4 *Exploring.* Pupils either make careful observations of objects or events, or make a series of observations of a natural phenomenon occurring over time.

How does frogspawn develop over time?
What happens when different liquids are added together?

5 *Investigating models.* These are investigations that explore models.

How does cooling take place through insulating materials?
Does the mass of a substance increase, or decrease, during combustion?

6 *Making things or developing systems.* These investigations are usually technological in nature, but have a high scientific content.

Can you find a way to design a pressure pad switch for a burglar alarm?
How could you make a weighing machine out of elastic bands?

You can see from the list the variety of ideas there are for practical activity in science. The emphasis in our investigation of making sure it is a fair test will place it within the fair testing category with strong links to number 5 above – investigating models.

It is important now to ask some key questions in order to make our test fair – so that we are comparing like with like and not changing more than one variable at a time.

The list of questions one needs to ask at this stage includes some or all of the following:

What do we need to measure?
What shall we use to measure?
What do we need to change?
What do we need to keep the same?
How will we measure the changes as they occur?
How often will we measure?
How will we record this data?
Shall we use a table or chart to record the results?
If so what will it look like?

It is important in an investigation to remember that it will involve you in changing something to test the effect and measure the change.

Activity 4	List some changes

List all the possible things you could change in the glove investigation.

Commentary

Your list might have included some of the following:

▶ different types of fabric

▶ temperature of water

▶ amount of warm water

▶ size/shape of container

▶ size of glove closeness of fabric to bottle

▶ thermometer.

The factors that you could change are called **independent** variables. It is important to decide on your key variable and only change that one keeping everything else constant. The independent variable here is going to be the different types of fabric. We are going to measure the temperature of the water in each bottle at intervals over a period of time. This second variable is the **dependent** variable as it relates to or is dependent on the change we have made by using different fabrics. The set-up for the apparatus is shown in Figure 1.

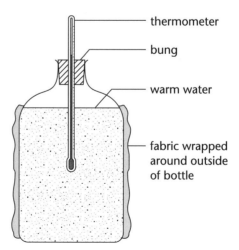

Figure 1 Apparatus to test fabrics for making a glove

It is essential to keep all the other possible variables constant. So factors such as using same size piece of fabric, same size of bottle and same type of thermometer are important. These are the **control** variables.

Using the list of questions on page 9 design your experiment, working out what order you are going to do things in and what changes you are going to make. How will you measure these? As you now work through the activity note any redesigning or adjustments you have to make to your initial plan.

At each stage try to list the skills and knowledge and understanding you have had to use to complete the investigation.

How to record, analyse and interpret findings

Collecting and recording data

We could use several ways of collecting and recording data, including a chart, a prepared table or a computer spreadsheet. If we had the equipment we could use a sensor attached to a computer so that readings are automatically recorded each time we measure. Depending on where you are doing this work you will have to select the most appropriate means to collect and record data. A possible table could look like that in Table 1.

Table 1 Temperature readings

	Start	3 mins	6 mins	9 mins	12 mins	15 mins
Bottle A Cotton						
Bottle B Wool						
Bottle C Plastic						
Bottle D No fabric						

Looking at the data, can you see any patterns or make links between the factors you were testing? It may be that you wish to display the information in another format that will help you to look more specifically at the results for each fabric. In this case drawing a line graph, with all three fabrics being represented on one graph, will enable you to make comparisons of the rate of cooling for each.

Figure 2 shows a graph of possible results from such an investigation.

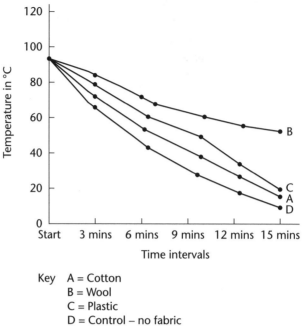

Figure 2 A graph to show results of testing fabrics

Using the graph as your resource, list as many questions as you can about the kind of connections you could make with the results as displayed.

Commentary

Some of the more obvious questions you might use to interrogate the graph are given below.

Interpreting results

Which bottle cooled the quickest? Which one took the longest to cool? What happened to the bottle with no cover? Did the cooling for each fabric follow similar patterns? Are the line graphs similar shapes? Are there other factors you want to investigate further? Can you draw any conclusions from this one test?

Evaluation

You might want to repeat the investigation several times to see if the pattern repeats itself. The more evidence one gathers to support the outcome the more sure you can be of any conclusions that you draw.

At this point look back at your predictions and hypotheses. Were the results as you expected? Can you support your reasons for the choices you made?

Do you need to explore more avenues to be able to speak with more authority about which material is best for keeping things warm?

Now return to the notes you made during your investigation. Did you have to modify or adjust procedures and equipment as you went along? If you did, it is possible this was because you had not identified all the possible variables or needed to change the information you needed to gather. This is a quite common part of the scientific process. It is important, all the time you are working, to question your workings and to evaluate whether or not what you are doing will provide the data required.

Having gained some results and drawn some conclusions it is important to evaluate the work, to decide how rigorous your working and findings were. This will help you decide whether you should repeat the experiment or redesign your investigation before starting again.

What skills, knowledge, attitudes and values did you use as you worked? Table 2 adapted from *Progression in Primary Science* (Hollins and Whitby, 1998) is a list of the key process skills alongside a more detailed breakdown of what each might involve. Compare your notes with this detailed list and you will see that you have probably been involved in more activities than you have listed. Carrying out investigations is a very important way of developing skills and understanding of the scientific process. It is only by doing activities that we understand the finer detail and the need to constantly evaluate our ways of working. It also provides a very real context to develop our thinking and relate our previous knowledge to new experiences.

Table 2 Key process skills

Observing	Looking closely at similarities and differences
	Comparing and contrasting
	Regularities and irregularities
	What do you notice about … type of questions
	Describing patterns
	Ordering and sequencing events
Raising questions	Raising questions whilst working
	Restructuring questions into useful ones for investigation
	Defining testable questions
Measuring	Selecting appropriate measuring techniques
	Recognising when to use estimating
	Using measuring devices with accuracy
	Recognising arbitrary nature of units
	Recognising need to repeat and check measurements
	Recognising variability and reliability of measurement

continues

Hypothesising	Attempting to explain observations in terms of concepts or principles Recognising the fact that there are several possibilities to explain phenomena Applying knowledge already required Using the explanation to make predictions of something that can be observed or tested
Planning	Defining the problem Identifying which variables are to be controlled Identifying the independent and dependent variable Considering how observations made will be used to solve problems Selecting appropriate equipment, materials Giving careful consideration to order of working Considering methods of recording findings
Interpreting	Eliciting what can be deduced from the observations and measurements taken Recognising sets and subsets Making use of keys or taxonomies Appreciating the tentative nature of conclusions Making generalisations Making and justifying inferences Making predictions based on patterns
Communicating	Following verbal instructions Describing activity orally Using diagrams/drawings and writings to tell about findings Following written and diagrammatic instructions Using tables and graphs, models etc. to represent information Selecting appropriate ways of presenting information Responding to a range of audiences, selecting appropriate methods of communication Listening to reports/ideas of others and responding to them Contributing to group discussion Using secondary sources to acquire information Using information technology as appropriate

Source: Hollins and Whitby, 1998.

Close observation of Table 2 shows the wide range of skills and experiences that make up a scientific investigation. It is important that we are able to identify which aspects of these skills we are using in a particular investigation.

In this section we have seen that:

- Not all questions lead to investigations.

- There are different dimensions to and processes involved in an investigation.

- There is a need to identify the dependent and independent variables when carrying out an experiment.

Health and safety considerations

This final section is concerned with health and safety issues in science particularly as they apply to primary schools. Sections 7 and 8 of the Health and Safety at Work Act (1974) are most pertinent to work in science and the ASE booklet *Be Safe* (2001) is an important document that should be in all schools alongside any locally agreed safety advice.

There are three important dimensions to health and safety in science. The first of these is the legal requirements that must be obeyed. The second is awareness and assessment of the risks in any practical activity. Clear policies and procedures for when an accident or incident does occur is the third important strand of health and safety.

The Health and Safety at Work Act (1974) which is concerned with the health, safety and welfare of all people at work was a landmark. This included protecting people at work from risks to health and safety as well as the risks associated with the use, possession and acquisition of dangerous substances, linked directly to the workplace. Most education employers have followed advice given in COSHH (Control of Substances Hazardous to Health Regulations 2002) and the Approved Code of Practice that is given with the Management of Health and Safety at Work Regulations 1992. These encourage employers who control a number of similar workplaces containing similar activities to provide a basic model risk assessment that highlights the core hazards and risks associated with particular activities. Every employee has to take reasonable care of the health and safety of themselves and other people with whom they work. They are also obliged to follow any procedures laid down by the organisation or by law. Section 8 of the Act requires employees not to interfere or alter any safety precautions or equipment provided. The reality in school is that any teacher must ensure that everything they do in the course of their teaching takes account of the risks to the pupils. Therefore assessing any science activity for risk is vital.

Be Safe (ASE, 2001 (3rd Edition)) address all aspects of health and safety in the primary classroom in a manner which is sensible rather than alarmist and Ofsted Inspectors (1996) are encouraged to be familiar with the latest edition. It provides clear guidance on hazards associated with most areas of science.

This last section of this chapter highlights some key areas, identifying possible hazards and suggesting ways to minimise risk.

First some general common sense advice.

- Plan for a safe working environment by giving clear advice about safe ways of working and procedures to follow if an incident occurs.

- Protective clothing and apparatus, such as goggles and disposable gloves, must be worn if there is any risk of contamination or of objects jumping, falling, slipping or spitting. If such equipment is not available then the activity should not be attempted.

- Never use the mains electricity for investigations – dry batteries and rechargeable batteries are suitable sources of power. Make sure electrical goods are in good working order.

- Give clear guidance and training on the correct and safe use of any equipment including tools and glues. 'Super glues' should not be used at all and be aware of solvent misuse. Always supervise the use of glue guns, if your LA allows their use in school.

- Make sure people are aware of the safety issues.

The following short sections highlight some more specific areas of risk and suggest ways of working. These are not exhaustive and it is important to consult other resources such as *Be Safe* and LA guidelines.

Ourselves

It is important, when working within this topic, to be sensitive to the differences between children. Situations that put individuals under physical, emotional or mental stress must be avoided. Be aware of any allergies or other medical conditions that could place pupils under stress.

The strictest hygiene practices should be followed when using food for investigations and experiments. Ensure that all equipment and surfaces are clean. Disinfect all equipment that is to be used by others.

Food and hygiene

Any food activities must be done with great care and attention to health and hygiene. Store any food correctly and be aware of those individuals with specific allergies to food and food additives. Be aware of cultural and religious requirements about food.

Do not let people taste food or other substances unless you are sure it is safe and have given permission.

Animals

There are various regulations about keeping animals in school that must be followed. Wild birds and mammals, venomous animals or plants should not be brought into school. Rare plants and animals are often protected by law; flowers such as wild orchids and cowslips should not be collected at all.

Some people may have allergic reactions to particular animals and plants. This must be taken into account when keeping animals such as mice or hamsters in school.

The RSPCA (Royal Society for the Prevention of Cruelty to Animals) provides excellent information and guidance on all matters concerning having live animals in schools.

Heating

If heating or cooking substances make sure the cooker or heat source is safely sited, with good access and ease of use. Do not use spirit burners, picnic stoves, portable bottle gas burners or hot paint strippers as a heat source. Suitable sources of heat include warm water, candles, night lights, hair dryers and kilns.

Wear goggles if there is danger of spitting when heating.

Heat substances in containers that are safe and appropriate for the task. Any glass containers, such as test tubes, should be heat resistant. Stand candles/night lights in a sand tray.

Any burns should be flooded with cold water for at least ten minutes to cool the skin and medical help sought if necessary.

Chemicals

Do not use any corrosive or flammable materials. Many household chemicals should not be used at all. The list below, taken from ASE *Be Safe* (1994), identifies the main ones:

bleach	fireworks, sparklers and party poppers
caustic soda	some plant growth substances, e.g. rooting powder
de-rusting solutions	hydrogen peroxide
dishwasher detergent	lavatory cleaners
disinfectants	Milton
dry-cleaning fluids	pesticides, scale removers, weedkillers
some fertilisers	oven cleaners, paint strippers.

Make sure that clear procedures are given for handling chemicals so that they are not contaminated or spilt.

Outside activities

When working outside it is important that:

▷ clear expectations of behaviour are given

▷ children are supervised effectively

▷ local regulations of staff/pupil ratios are met

- protective clothing is worn, e.g. gloves when collecting litter or pond animals
- correct apparatus and methods are used to collect small animals, e.g. pooters and paintbrushes
- all hazards have been assessed.

This list applies to all science activities, inside and outside the classroom, but it is very important when working outside that they are considered early in the planning process.

The CLEAPSS School Science Service provides an excellent service to schools and local education authorities. This includes a help line if you are not sure about an activity or need advice. There is a list of publications that advise on good practice and offer evaluations of resources. A regular newsletter gives up to the minute advice and guidance on ways of working. Contact details are given at the end of the book.

Many other agencies also provide guidance and support that will advise you about such things as keeping animals in school, e.g. the RSPCA.

Science is an exciting and challenging subject. Careful preparation and assessment of the risks will help science to remain a stimulating experience for all.

In this section we have seen that:

- It is necessary to carry out a risk assessment for all investigations.
- There are legal requirements regarding health and safety.
- There is a need for a clear set of procedures to be followed if an accident happens.

2 Materials and their Properties

What is stuff made of and how is it changed?

Materials is an exciting and interesting area, but it is a vast topic. This section will concentrate on the underlying scientific ideas that help us to explain structure and changes in materials. The story of materials is found in **chemistry**, so we start by considering what is meant by chemistry and continue with a study of solids, liquids and gases. We then look in detail at what happens when materials change – either from one form to another or by combining with another substance to form a new material. Along the way you will gain an insight into how a scientific **theory** is developed and you will also be able to think about your own learning in this area of science.

Chemistry is the study of the way one substance can be changed into another – how it happens and why it happens; so during your study you will be involved in studying chemistry. Much of our modern world is dependent upon the conversion of raw materials into useful products. Whether the products are processed food in the supermarket, clothing, cars or medicines, all exist because we have learned how to change less useful substances into more useful ones. Chemistry is exciting, relevant and central to modern life.

There is also another important aspect of studying 'change'. Some of the world's most pressing environmental problems are caused by undesirable changes – depletion of the ozone layer and acid rain are just two examples. These changes are complex and it is chemists who are among the first to research and understand the changes and propose solutions to the problems.

Resources

For the activities in this section on materials and change you will need the following equipment and materials:

- three or four different shower gels
- notebook and pencil
- a stopwatch
- small containers
- tubing
- a funnel
- hand lens

- candles
- iron nails
- water
- oil.

Materials

The Earth and everything on it are made of materials: natural materials like rocks and air, materials that have been made from other materials; those that we think of as 'chemicals'; and those that make up living things. In this section we start with the different forms in which we find materials and investigate the relationship between the use we make of them and their properties.

Activity 1   Materials

List as many different materials as you can think of. You might want to start this activity by just looking around you; then consider other materials with different uses outside the home or at work.

Commentary

Activity 1 is not a trivial task; it has an important purpose in that it allows you to explore your understanding of the term 'material'. So what does the word 'material' really mean? The *Concise Oxford Dictionary* definition is 'matter from which a thing is made'. This is a very broad definition. It means that everything around us – solid, liquid or gas – is a material. Did your list contain gaseous and liquid materials as well as solids? Are there any other materials you could add now?

We often find it difficult to acknowledge that the term 'material' applies to liquids and gases as well as solids – this may be because in everyday speech its use is often restricted to fabrics used for making things. All living things are made of the same basic materials.

Activity 2   Solid, liquid or gas

Return to the list you compiled for Activity 1. Make a note by each item to indicate whether it is a solid, a liquid or a gas. Think about and record the criteria you are using to classify each item. You may wish to come back to these criteria later.

As you classify, highlight any items that seem to be problematic.

Commentary

Some materials are hard to classify, for example, toothpaste, plasticine, jelly, hair mousse and non-drip paint. Do you have any others? Many materials are mixtures of substances – which is why they are not easily classifiable. Look back at your criteria. In which group would you place the five items listed above? While most materials can be classified as solid, liquid or gas, some do not fall into such clear-cut groups. Figure 3 shows a way of arranging materials that may be helpful.

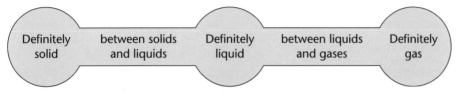

| Definitely solid | between solids and liquids | Definitely liquid | between liquids and gases | Definitely gas |

Figure 3 A way of grouping solids, liquids and gases

Useful definitions   **Activity 3**

Use the criteria you devised in Activity 2 to answer these three questions:

1   What is it about a solid that makes it solid?

2   What is it about a liquid that makes it a liquid?

3   What is it about a gas that makes it a gas?

Keep your responses to return to later.

Commentary

Classification involves first deciding on the goal of a particular classification. This determines what characteristics are chosen. If these prove to be inadequate for the purpose, new criteria must be used. Remember that classifications are artificial constructions; we invent them to help us make sense of the world.

Activities 2 and 3 should have helped you to begin to define the characteristic properties of solids, liquids and gases, and begin to make sense of the enormous range of materials.

Using materials

In classifying the materials in your list you undoubtedly considered their characteristics. Each material has its own characteristics and these are important when we try to distinguish between materials and choose materials for particular purposes. The uses we can make of materials depend upon their properties. This idea – materials being chosen for specific uses according to their characteristics – is an important one. The physical form of a material affects its use. For example, wood is used not only for furniture but also for cooking utensils, and its inherent properties make it a useful material for a wide variety of objects.

The next series of activities gives you an opportunity to think about how the properties of a particular material make it useful for a particular purpose. The example chosen here is a washing product – a shower gel – but you could devise similar work with other products. You will be exploring the properties of this product through a series of investigations, which should consolidate the scientific process described in Chapter 1.

Activity 4	Exploring the properties of a gel

Examine a collection of three or four commercial shower gels to decide on the required characteristics of such a product. List the properties you think are important for a shower gel. Which gel do you prefer? What reasons do you have for this choice?

Commentary

No doubt you will have identified some or all of the following properties that are important for a shower gel:

- thickness (**viscosity**)
- opacity/opalescence
- 'latherability' (how easily it foams; what the foam is like; how much it foams)
- pH (acid or alkaline)
- 'uniformness' (homogeneity).

Let's take *one* of these properties, viscosity, and examine it in detail. For a shower gel, the viscosity of the final product is critical – can you suggest why?

Viscosity – what is it?

Viscosity is usually thought of as a property of a liquid that has something to do with its 'thickness'. Look back to your own definition of a liquid. Three of the most characteristic properties of liquids are:

- the ability to flow (which is shared by gases)
- the possession of a sharply defined surface (which distinguishes them from gases)
- the tendency to vaporise into the space above and to exert a vapour pressure.

Viscosity – synonymous with 'internal friction' – is a measure of resistance to flow. The higher the viscosity the slower the flow.

Cooking oils, treacle, salad cream, sauces, household cleaners, household bleaches, paint and toothpaste are just a few substances where viscosity represents an important property.

In the development of a shower gel, viscosity is a critical property that the manufacturer needs to consider.

If the viscosity of the gel is too low then it will pour out of the container too quickly; if the viscosity is too high the gel will not come out of the container at all. So tomato ketchup and salad cream, with high viscosity, have to be shaken to encourage the substance to flow.

The gel has to maintain its viscosity over quite a large range of temperatures – possibly from **freezing point** (0°C) in winter to over 25°C in summer, and when in use to a temperature of around 37°C. Viscosities of most liquids decrease with increasing temperature, so it is important to manufacture the product with a fairly constant viscosity over a very wide temperature range.

Measuring shower gel viscosity	Activity 5

For this investigation you will need some everyday equipment with which to make a comparative measure of viscosity – namely a watch, small containers, tubing and a funnel, plus a small sample of shower gels.

Look at the samples of the commercial gels and try to predict whether their viscosity will be the same or different. How can you find out which one has the highest viscosity? Using your everyday equipment, design an experiment to measure the relative viscosities of the sample gels. How does the viscosity of the gels compare with water? Refer back to the questions in Chapter 1 as you devise your experiment. Don't forget to make it as fair as possible.

Commentary

Simple tests to make a comparative measure of viscosity could include:

▶ Will the substance in question pour?

▶ What does it look like when it is stirred?

▶ What diameter pipe will it flow through?

▶ How long does it take for a given volume to flow through a tube?

▶ How fast does a particular object (such as a ball-bearing) fall through a given depth of the substance?

▶ What is the diameter of one squirt of the substance on a particular surface?

Review what you have achieved through this series of activities. Make a note of the exploration skills, the planning process and the procedure you have used. You could refer to Chapter 1 for guidance.

Commentary

Reviewing and reflecting on progress is an essential part of learning. But reflection alone is insufficient unless it involves us in challenging and critically evaluating our views, without which the temptation is merely to reinforce our existing tendencies and ways of thinking.

Investigating a material in detail helps us to confirm our ideas about the properties and nature of materials in a more general way. Are you now certain where you would place a gel product in a classification grouping of solids, liquids and gases? How would you justify your decision?

The particulate theory of matter

The particulate theory of matter underpins much of our understanding about materials and the way in which they behave. In this section we consider some of the simpler aspects of the theory – but even these involve complex ideas concerning atomic structure, energy and force. Do not expect to be able to understand all these ideas immediately – take time to think about how they can help you to understand the way things appear and why things happen in the world around you.

Think of an object and draw a series of sketches to show what you think the object is made of. Construct your views so that they appear at different magnifications, for example as seen by the eye, using a hand lens, and through an imaginary powerful microscope that enables you to see the fundamental structure of the substance. Don't forget to label your sketches and keep them to refer to later.

Commentary

This activity takes us so far inside the object to see what it is made of, but we need to go further to really understand why different materials behave as they do. If you had a piece of charcoal that would fit comfortably into a teaspoon, how many times would you have to divide this up before you arrived at the smallest unit – a single carbon particle? Cutting the piece of charcoal evenly nine times into two would result in pieces of carbon each with a mass of about 0.02 grams. These are the size of crumbs, and at this stage the cutting process would become quite difficult. Each further division into two produces even tinier pieces. But at last, after about another 70 divisions you finally get there – your last cut gives you two solitary, separate, carbon particles. Obviously this would be an impossible operation to perform by hand! In 12 grams of carbon, there are about six hundred thousand million, million, million particles – 600,000,000,000,000,000,000,000. It is difficult to comprehend numbers of this scale but, if *everyone* on the planet were to count these particles at the rate of one particle per second, it would take over two million years to complete the task.

Because particles are so small (around 0.00000000001 metres in diameter), some kind of model is needed to represent them and, moreover, to show the relationship between the particles. Your sketches for Activity 7 represent such a model. The next activity asks you to develop your particle model to help explain the different properties of solids, liquids and gases.

Why are solids, liquids and gases different	Activity 8

Think back to the different materials you identified as solids, liquids and gases in Activities 1 and 2 and to the idea developed above that all substances can be thought of as assemblies of particles.

Water vapour, water and ice differ in appearance but are the same substance.

Try to explain, using labelled diagrams, your answers to the questions below:

1   Is there anything between the particles?

2   Does anything hold the particles together?

3   Do the particles move?

If you are working with friends, compare your model with theirs. Are there common elements?

Commentary

According to the particulate theory of matter, the particles in the solid, liquid and gaseous forms of a pure substance are the same, they are arranged and move differently.

Solids

In solids, the particles are packed closely together in regular patterns and have small spaces between them, rather like rafts of polystyrene spheres.

There is nothing between the particles – just empty space.

There are strong forces between neighbouring particles, allowing vibration in all directions about a fixed position but no other movement.

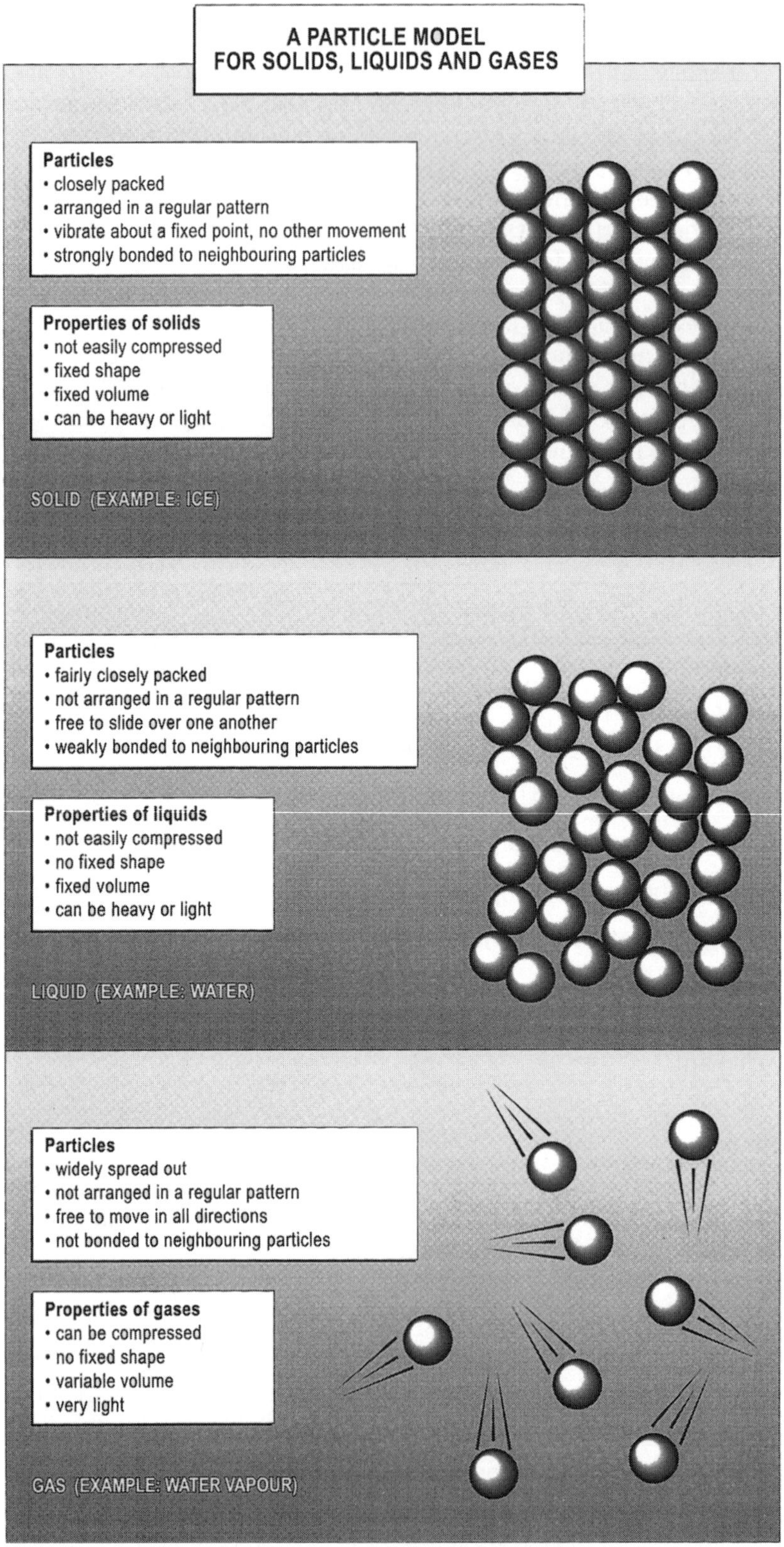

A PARTICLE MODEL FOR SOLIDS, LIQUIDS AND GASES

Particles
- closely packed
- arranged in a regular pattern
- vibrate about a fixed point, no other movement
- strongly bonded to neighbouring particles

Properties of solids
- not easily compressed
- fixed shape
- fixed volume
- can be heavy or light

SOLID (EXAMPLE: ICE)

Particles
- fairly closely packed
- not arranged in a regular pattern
- free to slide over one another
- weakly bonded to neighbouring particles

Properties of liquids
- not easily compressed
- no fixed shape
- fixed volume
- can be heavy or light

LIQUID (EXAMPLE: WATER)

Particles
- widely spread out
- not arranged in a regular pattern
- free to move in all directions
- not bonded to neighbouring particles

Properties of gases
- can be compressed
- no fixed shape
- variable volume
- very light

GAS (EXAMPLE: WATER VAPOUR)

Figure 4 Summarising the different states of matter

Liquids

In liquids, the particles:

 ▶ are a little less closely packed than in solids (except in water – which is why ice is less dense than water)

 ▶ are not arranged regularly

 ▶ have small empty spaces between them

 ▶ are free to slide over each other at random

 ▶ move faster.

Since particles of liquids can move around each other and do not remain in fixed positions like those of solids, they can flow and change their shape. This is because the forces or 'bonds' holding the particles together are weaker than in a solid. Particles in a liquid move by sliding over each other. The more viscous the liquid the more difficult it is for particles to slide over one another.

Gases

Particles of gases are widely and randomly spaced out compared with particles in liquids (Figure 4). There are very weak forces between particles so they are able to move about more freely. They collide with each other and any container or barrier

Figure 4 provides a pictorial model of these differences between solids, liquids and gases.

Changing from one state to another

So far, a model has been developed to help us understand and explain the nature and properties of solids, liquids and gases. You can no doubt think of a number of examples of materials that can change from one state to another (and back again) quite easily. Water and chocolate are just two common examples. If you want to change a block of ice to water and then to water vapour, you would normally need to heat it.

Energy is needed to make things happen

When something is heated or cooled, **energy** is transferred from one place to another so as to cause a change in temperature. Energy moves from hot to cold objects spontaneously, so that the temperature of the latter increases while that of the former decreases. If the energy that is transferred is great enough, materials can be made to change from a solid to a liquid and then to a gas.

To explain why this happens we can use the particle model (Figure 5). We have seen that particles in solids, liquids and gases all move, so they all have energy (energy that is associated with movement is called kinetic energy). In the solid state, particles are vibrating but they are held in

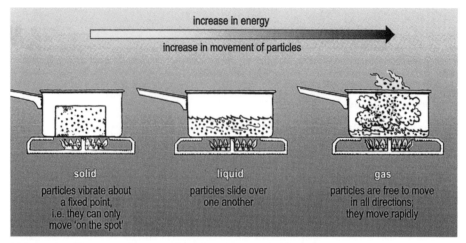

increase in energy

increase in movement of particles

solid	liquid	gas
particles vibrate about a fixed point, i.e. they can only move 'on the spot'	particles slide over one another	particles are free to move in all directions; they move rapidly

Figure 5 Change of state showing increase in energy

position by strong forces. If the amount of energy in the material is increased by heating, the movements become greater. Eventually the particles move so vigorously that they are no longer fixed in relation to one another and a liquid is formed.

Transferring more energy to the materials causes the particles to move around even more vigorously and to move further apart, and eventually a gas is formed.

Energy is difficult to define and explain because we cannot see it or take it off the shelf to show someone. It is an abstract idea used to explain what we see happening in the world around us.

Activity 9	Heating substances

Try these two different activities:

(a) Heat some chocolate in a bowl standing in a dish of warm water. Watch what happens as it melts. Leave it to cool.

(b) Heat a pan of water until it boils and leave to simmer for a few minutes. Watch closely what you see happening. If possible take the temperature of the water at different times.

A **change of state** requires energy to be transferred to or away from the substance. When a solid is changing to a liquid, or when a liquid is changing to a gas, the temperature usually remains constant whilst the change is happening. This is the case for a pure substance, but most materials (which are mixtures) change state over a range of temperature. This is because the energy transferred to the substance during change of state is involved in overcoming the forces of attraction between particles. A change from a liquid to a gas is usually achieved by heating the liquid. As you transfer energy to the liquid its temperature rises, but will it keep on rising for ever? When you heat a saucepan of water the temperature rises from room temperature as you supply energy, and it keeps on rising until the water starts to boil (that is, turns from a liquid to a gas). Under normal conditions (at atmospheric pressure) water boils at 100°C. But if you keep on adding energy by leaving the heat on, the temperature of the water does not rise any further

Physical change

Changing from one state to another is called a physical change. For water this is quite easy to recognise, but how would you recognise such a change in an unfamiliar material? If you refreeze liquid water, it will turn back into solid ice. A physical change is usually easy to reverse. So what changes?

▶ The energy each particle has.

▶ The distance between particles.

▶ The effect of the forces between particles.

▶ The volume of the substance.

▶ The shape of the substance.

And what stays the same?

▶ The particles.

▶ The shape and volume of the particles.

▶ The number of particles.

▶ The mass of the substance.

▶ The temperature of the substance (at the moment of change).

Although water is the most common liquid we come across in our daily lives, it has some properties that are unusual when compared with other liquids. A substance usually has a larger volume when it is a liquid than in its solid form – in their solid state most substances occupy the minimum amount of space possible. However, with water the opposite is true. A given mass of ice (solid water) occupies a greater volume than an identical mass of liquid water.

You can see the results of this phenomenon in winter when some people are unfortunate enough to suffer burst pipes. What happens is that in the cold the liquid water freezes in the pipe, occupies a greater volume (that is, expands) and causes the pipe to burst. When the temperature rises the ice turns back into liquid water and runs out of the hole in the pipe.

Figure 6 summarises in diagrammatic form all the changes described.

On Earth, water is very important and is constantly being recycled. The **water cycle** describes the way in which water may be transported and illustrates the dependence of this cycle on the interconversion between the gas, liquid and solid forms of water. We will use the water cycle to explore evaporation and condensation. Figure 55 on page 139 may help with the next activity.

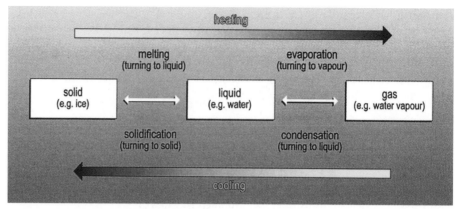

Figure 6 The three states of matter

Activity 10	Explaining evaporation and condensation

Use the particle model to explain the different processes taking place within the water cycle. How the particles are behaving at different points in the cycle is important. In particular, make sure you explain what is happening when evaporation and condensation are taking place.

Commentary

Evaporation occurs as energy is transferred from the surroundings, enabling particles of the liquid to move around more vigorously and further apart – eventually forming a gas. Warm temperatures, large surface areas of water and moving air (that is, wind) are conducive to evaporation.

Condensation represents the process in reverse. When energy is transferred from a gaseous substance its particles move less vigorously, becoming more closely packed and a liquid is formed.

Evaporation takes place at or near the surface of a liquid. **Boiling** is different in that large bubbles of vapour form continuously throughout the liquid. As the bubbles rise to the surface the particles move into the space above. For boiling to start and be maintained you need a continual input of energy. The temperature at which liquid boils is called the **boiling point** of the liquid (Figure 7).

Conversely, the freezing point of a substance is the temperature at which the liquid is seen to solidify, that is, turn from a liquid to a solid. Water freezes and changes into ice (solid water) at 0 °C. This is also the temperature at which ice melts and turns into water, so it is also known as the melting point.

Changes of state represent reversible changes in the arrangement of the particles – the particles themselves do not change.

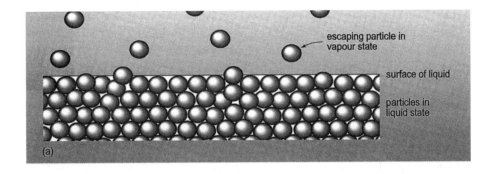

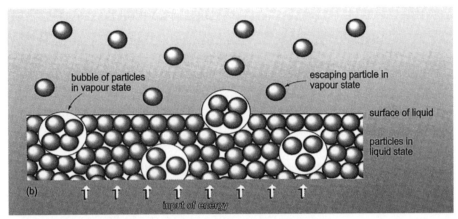

Figure 7 Modelling (a) evaporation and (b) boiling

Recognising chemical changes

We have been concerned with physical changes, but much of chemistry is concerned with ways in which materials can be transformed into new substances. These changes are known as chemical changes; the ability to recognise a chemical change and distinguish it from a physical change is important.

A chemical change occurs when new substances are formed. But what is meant by the term 'new substance' and how can you tell when new substances are being formed? Think what happens when you cook an egg. The yolk and white of a raw egg are both liquids. Heat will change them to solids but no amount of cooling will cause the egg to revert to its original form. New substances have been formed and a chemical change has taken place.

Observations of some other changes are shown in Table 3.

Table 3 Some examples of change

Process	Observations
Striking a match	The match burns, giving out heat and yellow light. A spent match cannot be reused
Ripening a green tomato	The tomato turns red. Once ripe, its colour will not revert to green
Adding liver salts to water	The solution fizzes. Some matter is released as gas, so the mass of the remaining solution decreases
Adding boiling water to instant coffee powder	A brown solution is formed. The coffee powder can be recovered by evaporating the water from the solution
Firing clay to form pottery	The clay hardens and becomes impervious to liquids. The pot will not revert to clay
Passing an electric current through a coil of wire	A magnetic field is produced, but this disappears as soon as the electric current is turned off

Activity 11 — Chemical and physical change

Look at Table 3 and consider the following questions as you read through:

What characteristics are associated with a chemical change?
What characteristics are associated with a physical change?

Commentary

A chemical change can involve a change in energy or colour. New substances, such as gases, may be easily recognisable. There may appear to be an apparent loss in mass – it is not an actual loss. The changes are hard to reverse. A physical change may be easy to reverse and no new substances are formed.

The difference between chemical and physical change is by no means clear cut. The **dissolving** of instant coffee powder in water described in Table 3 seems to be a physical change. But in most cases dissolving is accompanied by an energy change, and most chemists consider dissolving to be a sort of chemical change, even though it is possible to recover the original components by physical means.

To understand this we need to find out more about how these particles are involved in change.

In this section you have seen that:

▶ Matter can be solid, liquid or gas.

▶ Evaporation and condensation are important aspects of the water cycle.

▶ Changes can be physical or chemical.

▶ Physical changes can be reversed.

▶ Chemical changes cannot normally be reversed.

What are particles made of?

So far we have thought of particles as solid spheres, like tiny billiard balls. We now need to look at matter in more detail and regard it as more than a collection of single particles. We need to recognise that all particles are in fact made up of **atoms**, the building blocks of matter. The idea was first considered by the ancient Greeks.

John Dalton, the English chemist, revived ideas about atoms in the early nineteenth century. In his atomic model, he regarded atoms as the smallest indivisible particles of **elements**, rather like tiny, hard spheres. He used atomic theory to explain the results of experiments in which he investigated the composition of the products of some chemical reactions.

Atoms	Activity 12

Look at the diagrams in Figure 8.

How many different types of atom are shown?

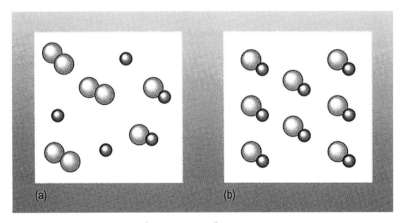

Figure 8 Ways atoms can be arranged

Figure 8(a) includes some particles that contain only one type of atom represented by small or large circles. Substances that only contain one type of atom are known as **elements**.

In Figure 8(b) two types of atom are joined together, in fixed proportions, as a result of a chemical reaction. This substance is called a **compound**.

There are about 100 different kinds of atom in the universe and therefore about 100 elements.

Elements include **hydrogen**, which has its own unique **hydrogen atoms**, **oxygen**, which has its own unique oxygen atoms, and, an element that you can see, **gold**, which has its own unique **gold atoms**. If you hold a piece of pure gold in your hand, the lump of yellow metal contains nothing but identical atoms of the element gold.

Elements in the body

Table 4 gives the ten most common elements in the human body, which together make up 99.80% of the total number of atoms present in the body.

In addition to the 92 naturally occurring elements, scientists have managed to make about 20 others. Some elements occur on Earth in great abundance, others are very rare. Each element is made from atoms that are chemically similar, but that are different from the atoms of every other element.

Each element has its own characteristic chemical and physical properties. Some elements are solid at room temperature and pressure, others are liquids or gases. Some elements are necessary for life, others are poisonous. You can probably identify some that you know to be metals, whilst others you will recognise as non-metals.

Table 4 The ten most common elements in the human body and the approximate percentages of each (of the total number of atoms in the body)

Element	%
Hydrogen	63.0
Carbon	9.5
Oxygen	25.2
Nitrogen	1.4
Calcium	0.31
Phosphorus	0.22
Potassium	0.06
Sulphur	0.05
Chlorine	0.03
Sodium	0.03

It is surprising that of the 92 naturally occurring elements, only four – carbon, oxygen, hydrogen and nitrogen – are present in those components of food that account for most of its mass. Carbohydrates and fats are composed of just carbon, oxygen and hydrogen; proteins are compounds of all four elements.

However, other elements are also essential for life and must therefore be present in the diet, even though the amounts needed are small. Calcium and phosphorus account for 75% of the mass of the eight 'mineral elements' present in human beings (little more than 15 g in total); the other 25% comprises potassium, sulphur, sodium, chlorine, magnesium and iron (about 5 g in an average male). Finally there are the trace elements: copper, zinc, manganese and molybdenum.

If elements are made of atoms of the same kind, what do we mean by the terms **mixture** and **compound**?

Mixtures and compounds

A mixture contains more than one substance. Instant coffee is a mixture of the chemicals in coffee granules and hot water. You might also add milk and sugar. How much of these ingredients you choose to add depends on personal taste – the drink remains, unmistakably, coffee. Adding more coffee powder will make the drink taste more bitter. Adding more sugar will make the drink taste sweeter. A mixture can have a variable composition and its properties are those of its components. It is possible to separate a mixture using physical techniques such as filtration and evaporation. In the case of instant coffee, you could boil away the water and get the solid coffee back again.

A compound is made of more than one element but the amount of each element is a fixed proportion of the compound. Making a compound involves a chemical change. Water is a compound of hydrogen and oxygen.

Using words is a long-winded way of describing the nature of mixtures and compounds. Scientists tend to explain such ideas in terms of models that can be represented pictorially. Look back at the diagrams in Figure 8.

There are eight particles in each diagram and Figure 8(a) is the mixture and Figure 8(b) the compound. There are three types of particle in the mixture and one type of particle in the compound. The compound contains two different atoms; this grouping of atoms is known as a **molecule**.

In Figure 8(b), the molecule consists of two different atoms, but it is possible to have molecules of an element (e.g. a molecule of oxygen) or of a compound (e.g. molecule of water). The point to remember is that molecules always consist of two or more atoms bonded together.

Each of the particles, or molecules, in the compound is identical – the compound is a pure substance. On the other hand, the three types of particle in the mixture represent different substances, which can be separated by physical methods and which can be present in any proportions.

A simple atomic model

So far we have thought of the atom as a tiny solid sphere. This has been sufficient to explain simple phenomena and to describe elements, compounds and mixtures. There has been no need to worry about the internal structure of atoms. However, such a simple model is not detailed enough to describe how atoms join together.

Because atoms are so small, scientists have not yet been able to look inside them to see what they are like, but the results of many experiments have allowed us to develop a good working model of atomic structure. Scientific models are not necessarily the 'truth' or the 'right answer'. They owe their credibility to their success at explaining our observations of the physical world, allowing us to make predictions and guiding our thinking in productive directions.

Many chemical and nuclear processes can be explained by a model in which atoms are thought to be made of three types of sub-atomic particles: **protons**, **neutrons** and **electrons**. Protons and neutrons form the nucleus (or centre) of the atom and the electrons move around it. The electrons are arranged in layers, somewhat like the layers in an onion. Scientists call these layers-shells. Figure 9 illustrates this simple model.

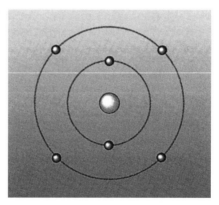

Figure 9 A simple model of the structure of an atom (not to scale)

The nucleus is tiny compared with the volume occupied by the electrons. If you imagined the atom to be the size of Wembley Stadium, the nucleus would be the size of a golf ball on the centre spot!

Inside the atom

Given the extremely small size of an atom, you may find it difficult to visualise any of the smaller sub-atomic particles inside it, namely, the protons, neutrons and electrons. However, you may already be familiar with some of the *effects* of one of these – the electron. It is the build-up of electrons that causes certain types of clothing to stick together, crackle and even spark when you take them out of a tumble-dryer.

Each electron carries a minute but standard amount of **negative charge**. Conventionally, scientists speak of an electron as having a charge of minus 1. The units do not matter in this case as the '–1' is just a comparative amount: one electron has a charge of –1, two electrons a charge of –2 and ten electrons have the charge of –10.

Most objects – clothes, people or atoms – do not usually have any net charge at all. They are described as electrically neutral. Some things can have negative, positive or zero charge.

Atoms are neutral particles; that is, they carry no net charge. But there must be some particles carrying a positive charge to balance the negative charge of the electrons. Moreover, the total negative charge of the electrons must just be balanced by the total positive charge in the positive particles, so that the whole atom has a net charge of zero.

These positive particles are the protons that we mentioned earlier. Each one carries the same amount of charge as an electron but has the opposite sign: plus 1. Since they have the same charge, but opposite signs, there must be the same number of protons as electrons.

The simplest element possible is hydrogen: it has just *one* proton and *one* electron. Oxygen contains eight protons and eight electrons. In fact, the 100 or so different elements contain atoms with, progressively, one up to 100 protons.

The third type of sub-atomic particle that we mentioned – the neutron – is electrically neutral and does not affect the chemistry of elements. Some of the properties of protons, neutrons and electrons are summarised in Table 5.

Protons and neutrons have equal masses, and are much more massive than electrons. (Actually the masses of protons and neutrons are very slightly different.)

Table 5 Some properties of sub-atomic particles

Particle	Mass on relative atomic mass scale	Relative charge	Location
Proton	1	+1	In nucleus
Neutron	1	0	In nucleus
Electron	0.00055	–1	Around nucleus

Although most of the mass of an atom is concentrated in its nucleus, the electrons are far from insignificant. When atoms combine chemically, it is the electrons on the outside that interact with one another

Figure 9 is a very simple representation of the atom and cannot help us to understand how electrons interact with each other. A better model would show electrons in their shells surrounding the nucleus, so in three dimensions the shells would be like a squash ball inside a football – the number of shells depending on the element.

Remember that a model can help us understand the behaviour of electrons but may not represent the 'real' situation that exists in an atom.

The chemical behaviour of an atom is thus determined by the number of electrons in the outermost shell – and it is these electrons we will be considering as we look at the way atoms join together.

How are atoms joined together?

In his atomic theory in 1808, Dalton suggested that two atoms could be bound together. When Rutherford, over 100 years later, described the atom as being made up of electrically charged particles, the major problem was to understand how this bonding could take place.

In nature, very few atoms ever exist entirely on their own. Most atoms are found joined to other atoms by some kind of bonding. We now know that there are two ways in which this bonding together of atoms can occur. One kind is called **covalent bonding** and the other is called **ionic bonding**. Both depend on 'interactions' between the outermost shells of electrons.

Covalent bonding

This is when two or more atoms are held together by sharing electrons, thus forming a molecule. Water consists of covalent molecules that contain two hydrogen atoms and one oxygen atom (see Figure 8(b)).

Another common compound you may be familiar with is carbon dioxide, which consists of covalent molecules that contain one atom of carbon and two of oxygen. You have also met some gaseous elements that exist as covalent molecules. The oxygen gas in the air does not exist in the form of free individual oxygen atoms, but as *pairs* of oxygen atoms joined together by covalent bonds to give oxygen molecules. The same applies to the nitrogen of the air. In fact, elements that exist as free, solitary atoms are quite rare.

Before going on, let us state three crucial points concerning molecules, about which it is easy to make mistakes.

1   It is possible to have molecules that are elements (e.g. a molecule of oxygen) and molecules that are compounds (e.g. a molecule of water).

2   Molecules always consist of two or more atoms bonded together (e.g. two oxygen atoms bond together to make an oxygen molecule; two hydrogen atoms and one oxygen atom bond together to make a water molecule).

3   This kind of bonding in molecules is *always* covalent. If a compound or an element exists as *molecules*, the bonding *has to be* covalent.

At first, it may seem that atoms combine in a quite arbitrary way, but in fact they obey fairly strict rules as to how they interconnect with other atoms. In particular, there is almost always a set *number* of covalent bonds that a given atom can form.

The number of covalent bonds that are normally formed by hydrogen, carbon, nitrogen and oxygen are summarised in Table 6. Two other elements have been added to the table, namely, sulphur and chlorine.

Table 6 The usual number of covalent bonds formed by some elements

Element	Usual number of bonds
Hydrogen	1
Carbon	4
Nitrogen	3
Oxygen	2
Sulphur	2
Chlorine	1

This idea of 'electron sharing' in covalent bonds is an important one in chemistry.

Chemical language

Chemistry has a language all of its own that uses a shorthand language of symbols for the names of the elements. Table 7 shows the symbols for a few of the more common elements, along with the origins of the element's name.

Table 7 Names, their origins and symbols for some elements

Element name	Origin of name	Symbol	Relative mass
Hydrogen	From the Greek: water forming	H	1
Carbon	From the Latin: charcoal	C	12
Nitrogen	From the Latin or Greek: soda	N	14
Oxygen	From the Greek: acid-forming	O	16
Sodium	From the English term: soda	Na	23
Magnesium	From Magnesia, a district in Thessaly	Mg	24
Chlorine	From the Greek, *chloros*: yellowish green	Cl	35

continued

Element name	Origin of name	Symbol	Relative mass
Potassium	From the English term: potash	K	39
Calcium	From the Latin, *calyx*: lime	Ca	40
Iron	Anglo-Saxon name for the metal; the Romans called it ferrum	Fe	56
Gold	Anglo-Saxon name for the metal; the Romans called it aurum	Au	197

In Table 7 the elements are listed in order of increasing **relative mass**. The mass of individual atoms is very small, so, instead of expressing their mass in grams, it is easier to express them *relative to something that has a similar mass*. They are all expressed relative to the simplest atom – the hydrogen atom. Hydrogen is taken as having a mass of 1 (H = 1) and the other elements are expressed as multiples of the mass of the hydrogen atom.

By using symbols, elements and compounds can be represented much more conveniently and much more briefly. Let's look further into this idea using the familiar compound water again. Recall what atoms there are in a water molecule.

Activity 13	Chemical formulae

What symbols would you use to represent the water molecule?

Commentary

It is conventional to add up all the atoms of one type in a molecule, so water is written as H_2O, where the subscript 2 indicates that there are two hydrogen atoms and the absence of a subscript indicates that there is only one oxygen atom. Such a representation is known as a chemical formula. Unfortunately there is no obvious rule to indicate which element should be written down first in a **chemical formula**. Do we write H_2O or O_2H? You know the answer, of course: we write H_2O. The reason is, essentially, a matter of convention: that's the way chemists do it. Remember that the subscript always refers to the symbol that *directly precedes it*.

The chemical formula of a covalent compound shows the number of each type of atom in one molecule of the compound. It is written using the symbols for the elements.

We have examined the naming of elements, their symbols and the formulae of compounds, but what about the names of compounds? The scientific name of a compound reflects the elements found in the compound. Where a compound contains just two elements, the name of the second element is usually modified slightly so that it ends in the letters *-ide* (pronounced as in '*side*'). Thus, the compound HCl is hydrogen chlor*ide* not hydrogen chlor*ine*. Similarly CO_2 is carbon dioxide not carbon dioxygen. The *di-* prefix indicates that there are two oxygen atoms and the *-ide* ending confirms that only two elements are involved in it. Scientists have grouped the elements in a special way called the **periodic table of the elements**, which has recently been expanded to include new elements. This classification is related to the electron shells.

Ionic bonding

Now let's return to how chemicals are joined in chemical reactions. What is the main difference between the covalent compounds you have already met and ionic compounds? Ionic compounds are formed by transferring electrons from metal atoms to non-metal atoms.

When an atom loses or gains electrons it becomes electrically charged and is known as an **ion**. A positive ion is a cation and a negative ion is called an anion. Joining ions together is known as **ionic bonding**. Only elements at opposite sides of the periodic table will form ionic bonds. For example, sodium chloride is an ionic compound. It contains positively charged sodium ions (metal) and negatively charged chloride ions (non-metal). Ions with opposite charges are pulled towards each other and this is known as electrostatic attraction.

Changing what?

When we considered **change of state** it was clear that in such a change the particles themselves do not alter. Thus when solid ice, in which the particles are held together by strong forces, becomes liquid water, what changes is the effect of the forces between the particles. You now know that these particles of water are actually molecules, each containing two atoms of hydrogen and one atom of oxygen. Forces are also responsible for holding the atoms together within the molecules and these forces are stronger than the forces holding the molecules together to form solid ice. When energy is transferred to solid water (ice) the molecules gain enough energy to overcome the attraction of other molecules and are able to move away from each other. But, the atoms making up the molecule are not affected chemically, that is, they do not separate into oxygen atoms and hydrogen atoms. This effect of transferring energy also means the change is reversible. Changing ice to water and back again does not change the substance, water.

The oxygen and hydrogen atoms in a molecule of water can be separated, but it is a different process to a change of state. If you pass an electric current through water the molecules of water break down into molecules of hydrogen and oxygen, which are given off as hydrogen and oxygen gases.

However the constituents of the molecules of a compound are changed, the change taking place is called a chemical change and the process by which it takes place is a **chemical reaction**.

You have also seen that atoms combine in one of two ways – by covalent or ionic bonding. Thus a chemical reaction involves the original constituents bonding to form new products.

Exothermic reaction

When materials react with each other to form new substances, the energy stored in the molecules of the new substances is often less than the energy that was stored in the molecules of the original materials. Thus energy is available for transfer to the material's surroundings. These are called **exothermic reactions**. One common example of an exothermic reaction is burning (or combustion). Another is the reaction that occurs when you mix plaster of Paris; if you have done this you may have noticed that the container becomes warm. Here the reaction takes place without any initial heating from outside.

Endothermic reaction

Not all reactions are exothermic. In some reactions, energy is transferred from the surroundings to the reacting materials, that is, in an opposite direction to an exothermic reaction. These reactions take in energy and are called **endothermic reactions**. An endothermic reaction that you may be familiar with takes place during photosynthesis. Plants use energy from the Sun's light to enable a reaction to take place between carbon dioxide and water that results in sugars and oxygen (Figure 10).

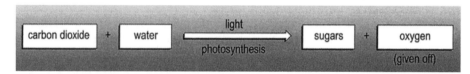

Figure 10 An endothermic reaction

Explaining chemical change

We now turn our attention to explaining what happens in a chemical change. We will use as examples of chemical change the processes that occur during combustion, rusting and pottery-making.

Combustion

| Activity 14 | Observing burning |

Place a candle in a small tin. Light the candle, watch carefully what happens and try to answer the following questions.

1 When the candle burns, what happens to the wax around the wick?

2 Does the candle get smaller as it burns?

3 What is burning?

4 Where do you think the wax is going?

5 Could you collect it again?

6 Is this the same process as water evaporating?

7 If not, how is it different?

8 Would the candle burn if there was no air around it?

9 Is air (or part of the air) used up when a candle burns?

10 Try to explain what happens when a candle burns, using the idea that there are oxygen molecules in the air, and wax molecules in the candle.

Commentary

Before we review what is happening as the candle burns, we need to consider what combustion is. Combustion is the process of burning a substance in air or oxygen so that it forms new chemical compounds with oxygen. When burning takes place the molecules of the fuel are broken down and energy is transferred to the surroundings, usually in the form of heat and light. It is therefore a chemical change. Oxygen is essential for complete combustion. In most circumstances ordinary air provides an adequate supply of oxygen for complete combustion.

If the energy transferred can be gathered in some way and transmitted, it can provide power. For example, in an oil-fired power station, oil (the fuel) is burnt to provide heat energy, which is used to vaporise water, turning it into steam. The steam is used to provide mechanical energy to drive turbines, which produce electrical energy.

In many chemical reactions, an initial input of energy is required to start the reaction. This input of energy causes the temperature to rise, and when the temperature is high enough, the material burns. Different materials start to burn at different temperatures. Once a material is burning, sufficient energy is transferred to maintain the reaction and the outside source of energy is no longer required.

In Activity 14 the wax melts and then vaporises and it is the wax vapour that burns. The candle gets smaller as wax is 'used up'. The 'products' of the reaction are probably gases, which escape. It would not be easy to get the candle back from the products, so this is a chemical change. If there was no air, the candle would go out. Thus two ingredients are needed for this reaction – wax and oxygen. The wick helps the wax to burn more efficiently (see Figure 11).

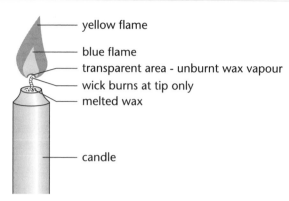

yellow flame
blue flame
transparent area - unburnt wax vapour
wick burns at tip only
melted wax

candle

Figure 11 A candle burning

Rusting

A second chemical change that you will be familiar with is the rusting of iron.

Activity 15	What happens when iron rusts?

Before you begin the practical part of this activity, record your own ideas about rusting. For example, can you name things that rust? Do they have anything in common? Can you predict what will rust? What causes things to rust? How could you investigate what causes rusting? Can you use the particle model to explain what happens when something rusts?

If you can, plan and carry out an investigation or series of investigations to find out what causes things to rust and what happens when things rust. How might you prevent rusting? Think about what you want to find out, the equipment and materials you will need and how you will record and evaluate the results. If you can't carry out an investigation, collect some rusty items and examine them carefully and consider the questions above.

Commentary

Rusting is a chemical change. Both water and oxygen are required for iron to rust. Rusting can be considered to take place in two stages. First, atoms of iron react with atoms of oxygen to form a new compound, iron oxide:

Iron + oxygen = iron oxide

Molecules of iron oxide then combine with molecules *of* water to form hydrated iron oxide. The term hydrated means having water.

Pottery-making

The third example involving change relates to pottery. Pottery is made from clay, but what type of reaction enables wet, shapeless clay to be transformed into pottery?

Clay consists mainly of aluminium, silicon and oxygen atoms bonded together in separate layers. When the clay is wet, water molecules get between the layers and allow them to slide over one another. In this state the clay can be moulded to whatever shape you want.

When you are happy with your pot, you put it into a kiln and 'fire' it (heat it to a very high temperature) to drive out all the water molecules. Atoms in one layer then form bonds with atoms in another to form a rigid structure. Fired pottery cannot be easily converted back into clay and so this represents a chemical change.

In this section we have seen that:

▶ All substances are made of atoms.

▶ Atoms contain protons, neutrons and electrons.

▶ Atoms can combine to form larger particles.

▶ Materials can be classified into one of three categories: elements, compounds and mixtures.

▶ These categories can be distinguished by using a model of atoms as tiny spheres:

    (a) elements contain only one type of atom; compounds and mixtures contain more than one type of atom

    (b) compounds contain atoms that have combined in fixed proportions as a result of a chemical reaction; all the particles in a compound are identical

    (c) the particles in a mixture are not identical and can be present in any proportions.

3 Forces

Forces and energy

Forces and energy are each large areas of science in their own right. Because they are both concerned with motion they are often connected, but they are actually quite different and it is important to understand clearly the aspects of each of them. We deliberately study them separately, starting with forces.

Resources

In this section you will need some toy cars, a smooth surface, a collection of objects (see Figure 12), a newtonmeter and a spring balance (if you can obtain the last two).

Forces

What are forces? **Forces** cannot be seen and sometimes cannot be felt, although we may be aware of their effects. Since we cannot see forces it is not surprising that we do not tend to think about them on a day-to-day basis. Here we aim to describe what forces are.

Activity 1	Forces

Write down your ideas, using diagrams if you can, about what a force does. Try to give some everyday examples of when you encounter forces. From your description, try to define what a force is.

Commentary

In describing what a force does you may have included some of the following effects:

▶ makes stationary objects move

▶ makes moving objects speed up

▶ makes moving objects slow down

▶ makes moving objects stop

▶ makes moving objects change direction

▶ changes the shape of objects.

Figure 12 shows a variety of situations where forces are acting. Try to put in arrows to show the forces. Can you order the drawings from the biggest to the smallest force? Try some of the activities. Can you feel the force(s)?

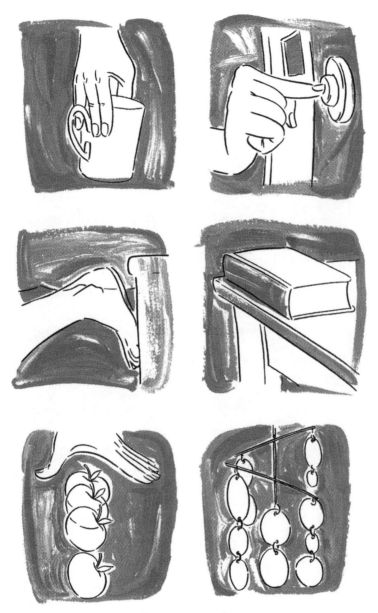

Figure 12 Situations where forces are acting

From the effects that you have described you may have arrived at a definition of a force that includes some of these words: 'push', 'pull', 'twist' and 'squeeze'.

You may also have noted that there are forces all around, some of which we do not notice because they are there all the time (for example **gravity** and **friction**). For the present, we can think of forces as pushes and pulls. Pushes and pulls can change size and direction, and thus a force has two characteristics – size and direction – and can cause changes in movement or shape. Whenever any change to the speed, direction of movement or shape of an object occurs it is because a force is acting on it.

We are familiar with some of the forces that our own bodies can produce and feel because we have to put in some physical effort to lift a box and other activities. It is important to realise that inanimate objects are capable of exerting forces.

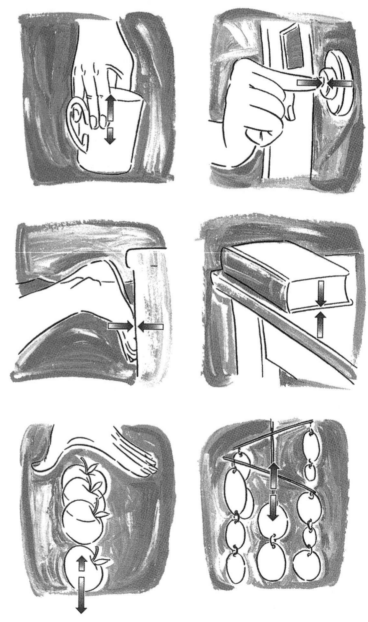

Figure 13 Forces acting on objects. The arrows show the direction and relative strength of the forces

Figure 13 shows how the forces are acting in the situations illustrated in Figure 12. The main forces acting on the objects are shown using arrows to represent the size and direction of the forces. This is a convenient and conventional way to represent forces acting on any object. The direction of the arrow shows the direction of the force, and the length of the arrow indicates the relative size of the force. You may like to have a go at identifying forces yourself in everyday situations using this idea.

Many factors will affect which of the objects has the biggest force. If you compare our results with colleagues' then you may find your order varies. This will reflect your different experiences, and also the criteria you have applied to define a strong force. In order to measure forces so that we can make comparisons and so that we know we are comparing like with like we use a newtonmeter. Forces are measured in **newtons**. The next sections will expand on this.

'Weighing' the objects

When you were doing Activity 1 you probably used words such as 'weight', 'heavy' and 'light' as you put the objects in order. It is important to appreciate that **weight**, with which we are familiar, is simply a force. From everyday experience we know that falling is a natural process and that if things are to be prevented from falling they must have some kind of support. It is not surprising that many of us fail to realise that it is a force that causes objects to fall. This pulling force is known as **gravity**. Weight is the pull of the Earth's gravity on the mass of an object.

Questions such as 'Why do apples fall to the ground?' 'Why does the Moon orbit the Earth?' 'Why do planets move around the Sun?' are ones that may be asked in schools – they have been of importance for centuries. In 1687, Isaac Newton set out three universal laws of motion and a theory of universal gravitation in the book known as his *Principia*. The framework of ideas established by Newton has enabled scientists to answer such questions. Newton was able to say that the forces acting on an apple falling from a tree, and on the Moon in orbit round the Earth, are of the same type: the force of gravity.

Newton demonstrated that gravity operates in the same way for the Sun, the Moon, planets, apples and indeed for every other object regardless of its size. From this work he concluded that all objects attract one another and the force of attraction that they exert depends on their **mass**. Between small objects the force of attraction is so small as to be negligible: our senses certainly cannot detect it. But in the case of the Earth, which has an enormous mass, the force of attraction between it and other objects is noticeable. Thus it is *mass* that is responsible for **gravitational forces**. You are attracted to the Earth because you and the planet each have mass. The force of attraction depends on your mass and the mass of the Earth. The *weight* of any object is the amount of pulling force that the Earth exerts on that object (see Figure 14).

'So in science it's newtons, and in life it's grams'

The types of spring measurers used for **newtonmeters** are identical in construction to spring balances that you may have come across for measuring in grams. So what is the difference? Or rather, what is the connection?

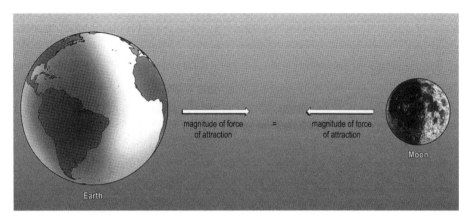

Figure 14 The force attracting the Earth to the Moon and vice versa is the force of gravity

'Weight' is a word that is commonly used in everyday language, but it has a very specific meaning in science. As you have already discovered, weight is the force of gravity acting on an object, and as a force it should be measured in newtons. The newton is the standard measure of force, named after the famous scientist.

However, in everyday life we talk about 'weighing' ourselves and measuring 'weight' in grams or kilograms. These units are in fact a measure of *mass*. The mass of an object tells us how much material (matter) it contains, irrespective of whether gravity is pulling it or not.

For example, a bag of sugar contains 1 kg of sugar. It would contain 1 kg of sugar even if it were taken up in a spacecraft, where it would appear to be 'weightless', or to the Moon, where gravity is about one-sixth of the strength of that on the Earth. If somebody threw the bag of sugar across the spacecraft at your head, it would hurt as much as if it were thrown at you on Earth – you would certainly know that there was 1 kg of sugar there! So its mass is constant, but what if you tried to measure its weight (i.e., how much it stretched the newtonmeter)?

On the Earth, gravity pulls on every 1 kg with a force of about 10 newtons. You can check this yourself with a newtonmeter. We know that on the Moon, gravity is only about one-sixth as strong, so it pulls every 1 kg with a force of approximately 1.7 newtons. In the spacecraft, where gravity is negligible, there will be no force pulling on the bag of sugar so nothing will register on the newtonmeter. The results are shown in Figure 15.

Remember on Earth gravity pulls every 1 kg of mass with a force of about 10 newtons. Although our meters are, strictly speaking, measuring a force in newtons, we know that a force of 10 newtons must have come from a mass of 1 kg, or a force of 1 newton must have come from a mass of 100 g. So we can calibrate our newtonmeters directly into grams or kilograms.

The difference between mass and weight is not an easy concept, but it is important to you. 'Weighing' at this day-by-day, ordinary level is generally done in grams or kilograms.

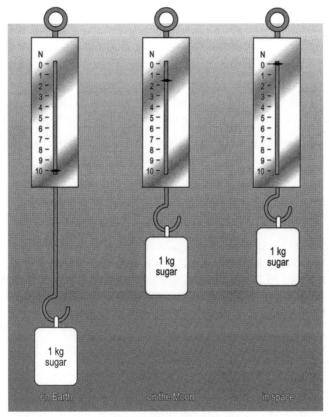

Figure 15 Newtonmeters weighing bags of sugar

In this section we have seen:

▶ Forces are pushes and pulls.

▶ A force has two characteristics: size and direction.

▶ When forces act they can change the shape of the things they act on. There is a bigger change from a bigger force.

▶ We can use the change to provide a quantitative measure of forces.

▶ Forces can be measured using a spring balance or newtonmeter in units called newtons.

- An object's weight is the force of gravity acting on it, thus weight is a force.

- The mass of an object is a measure of the amount of matter in it. It is constant and does not change.

- All objects exert a force of gravity on each other: the size of the force depends upon their masses.

- The force of gravity is smaller on the Moon than on Earth because there is less matter in the Moon than in the Earth.

Forces on the move

We will consider some situations where forces are acting, first to describe the situation and second to analyse it in terms of the forces acting.

Gravity is not the only force that affects us. We are surrounded by forces acting in all directions and having a wide range of effects. Many of these forces we take for granted and others affect us without us really knowing they exist.

Isaac Newton was a great scientist because he observed closely, asked himself questions about what he saw, used his imagination, and tried to look for patterns and rules even when they weren't immediately obvious. As you have already seen, the patterns and rules he discovered are still the basis of much of our scientific understanding about forces today, and you will have noticed that even the unit of force is named after him. Let us now look at some of his ideas.

Activity 2	Getting started

To complete this activity you will need:

- a toy car or buggy that runs quite freely

- a hard, smooth, level surface, e.g. a large table or the floor.

Stand the car on the surface and take a step back.

Would you expect it to start moving?

Now give the car a push to send it moving across the floor, and as you do so watch carefully and answer these questions:

When is the car actually 'speeding up'?
What happens once you let go?
How could you make it 'speed up' more?

Now start the car moving across the floor and then do something to change its course, e.g. nudge it to one side.

What makes the car change direction?

Commentary

Hopefully you may have thought or written down some of the following:

▶ A force is needed to start something moving.

▶ An object will speed up (accelerate) only when a force is acting on it.

▶ The bigger the force, the bigger the acceleration.

▶ A force is needed to make moving objects change direction.

These results may seem obvious, but it does help to take a simple situation and describe and analyse it in this way. The findings will be important in developing some less obvious ideas later on.

These statements about moving objects can all be derived from the first two of the three laws of motion that were formulated about 300 years ago by Sir Isaac Newton to explain the effects of forces.

We will deal with Newton's first law later. Here we look at your observations from Activity 2 in relation to his second law, which states:

> a force causes a mass to accelerate in the direction of that force, and the greater the mass of the object, the more force required to produce the same acceleration.

A consequence of applying a force to a *stationary* object is that it *starts* to move (in scientific terms, it accelerates). Consequences of applying a force to a *moving* object are that it moves faster, it slows down or it changes direction. Activity 3 gives you an opportunity to think about some of these statements.

Putting on the brakes	Activity 3

To complete this activity you will need the same toy car and hard surface as in Activity 2 and the assistance of a co-operative, equally observant friend.

Give the car a strong push and ask your friend to stop the car instantaneously about half a metre after you let go.

Now try again, but this time stop the car more gradually, say over a distance of about 20 cm.

And a third time, stopping the car even more gradually (the distance will depend on how freely the car runs).

Describe and discuss how the strengths of the forces needed to stop the car differed in each case.

Commentary

What conclusions did you arrive at? According to **Newton's laws of motion**, a force is needed to slow something down and the quicker something is slowed down, the more force is needed.

You may find this slightly less easy to accept. After all, wouldn't the car have slowed down to a stop anyway? Slowing down is such a natural event that it is easy to assume that it takes place without any forces being involved.

What if the statement about always needing a force to slow things down were true? Let us imagine taking this last activity to its extreme. Gradually we use less and less force to stop the car until we just *don't* use any force at all. Assuming our statement is right, if we are not providing the force to slow the car down then something else must be! Although it is not an obvious force, this stopping force is widely recognised – it is **friction**. It can be caused by many different things, but we usually encounter it where two surfaces rub together. For example, the axles of the toy car rubbing against their casing, or the tyres of the toy car or a real car on the road surface (Figure 16).

muscular force ⭢   ⭠ frictional forces

Figure 16 The muscular force provided by the person 'competes' against frictional forces within the car and between the tyres and the road

Some surfaces produce more of a frictional force than others. For instance, an ice hockey puck will slide much further across the ice than it would over concrete. There are also many different ways of increasing and decreasing the effects of friction.

Try this practical example. Place your hand *gently* on the table and push your hand slowly away from you. Try to feel the force of friction between the table and your hand resisting your movement. Now press your hand *firmly* down on the table and try again.

Commentary

You will have noticed how much more difficult it is to get your hand sliding. In a similar way, the friction between a cardboard box and the floor will depend on what is in the box. And whenever two surfaces move relative to one another, even when an object moves through air, there is always friction.

Friction does get a bad press! We have to put oil in our car engines to stop the engine parts rubbing against each other. Heavy objects would be far easier to move if we could just slide them across the floor. Imagine if we could get rid of friction completely – in theory our toy car could go on rolling for ever!

Friction is useful. The best way to tackle this is to think of situations in which a problem arises when friction is suddenly drastically reduced:

▶ a bicycle hitting a patch of ice on the road, particularly on a corner (don't forget that forces are needed in order to change direction)

▶ a splash of oil dropped on the kitchen floor

▶ a car stuck in mud (the wheels spin but cannot grip).

We know that an object needs a force to start moving. What happens when we take a step forwards? Our muscles push against the friction between the floor and our feet. Our legs try to push backwards, but in fact the friction reacting against this propels us forwards. Again, consider what happens when this friction is missing. When we try to walk on ice our feet just seem to go from under us, or else we gently make the most of what little friction there is and progress *very slowly*. (Don't forget, a small force will only let us speed up gradually.)

Friction is so important in sport that fortunes are spent on research into the best soles for sports shoes. In motor racing different tyres are used for different conditions so that the car has the optimum grip on the road. Exercise bikes use friction to increase resistance.

We have seen the importance of friction to things moving on land, but what about things that move in water or through the air? In these cases again, friction can be a good thing or bad thing. If you have ever tried to run through water, or felt the force of the air as you pedalled a bicycle into the wind, you will appreciate the amount of resistance that both air and water can produce. Objects moving through air experience the frictional force of the air, which acts in the opposite direction to their movement. This is called **air resistance** and it acts against gravity on falling objects. The air offers a greater resisting force to objects that have a large surface area. The mass of air that has to be moved out of the way accounts for much of the resisting force.

Animals that live or move in air or water tend to be streamlined to reduce the effects of this friction as far as possible. However, they still need to push against something to get them moving, and this is where resistance in the air or water is important to them. Birds push the wide surfaces of their wings against the air for maximum resistance to push them forward or upward. Fish 'wiggle', briefly turning the wider parts of their body from side to side to maximise the push against this resistance.

So, friction is a force that acts to slow things down: it is always present when two surfaces move over one another. But how does friction arise?

If you were to examine any surface (even one that looks very smooth) under a microscope, you would see that it is really quite rough, with many bumps and hollows. If two 'flat' surfaces are in contact, these bumps and hollows tend to lock together: so when a force acts to move one object over another their surfaces tend to stick together. This is what causes friction.

The forces needed to overcome friction raise the temperature of the objects. As you moved your hand across the table top you may have sensed warmth, and we frequently rub our hands together to warm them up.

Balanced and unbalanced forces

One of the simplest ways of looking at the way that forces act together is to think of a tug-of-war. Each person in the team is pulling with a particular force on the rope, and all those forces add up to the team's total force (Figure 17).

Figure 17 Total team forces balance so there is no net movement

If the forces on each end of the rope are equally matched then there is stalemate and the rope does not move. We could say that the overall 'effective' or 'net' force on the rope is zero, as the rope is behaving as if there were no force acting on it at all – even though everyone is pulling as hard as they can!

If, however, there is a bigger force on one end then the rope begins to move in the direction of the strongest force, and the 'effective' force is equal to the difference between the two forces pulling in opposite directions. If the forces are similar size, then the difference is not very great and the rope would gather speed slowly. If one force were a great deal bigger than the other though, the rope would rapidly speed up and there would soon be an outright winner.

So forces can combine, either to pull or to push together, or act against each other. The combined forces make up a resultant net force.

1   Think of some examples of forces acting together to produce a bigger force.

2   Now think of some examples of forces that act against each other to reduce the overall effect of the force.

Commentary
One example of 1 is pushing a car down a slope – gravity acting on the car adds to the pushing force so the car will move faster.

One example of 2 is pushing a car up a slope – not only are we having to push against the forces of friction in the car, but we are also having to push against gravity. Occasionally gravity wins!

Thus when forces act together they may either reinforce or work against one another, causing an object to slow down or speed up as a result of a net force.

Pushes and pulls on a parachute

We can see forces acting against each other when we look at a parachute in action. As the parachutist falls through the sky she gets faster and faster as gravity accelerates her towards the Earth. But there is another force that comes into play as the parachutist speeds up – air resistance. There comes a point when the air resistance force is so great that it *exactly* balances the force of gravity pulling down. So the effective or net force on the parachutist is zero (Figure 18).

Recapping on what we already know about forces:

▶   a force is needed for an object to accelerate (speed up)

▶   a force is needed for an object to slow down (decelerate).

So, at a particular speed, when the forces on the parachutist exactly balance each other, the parachutist is neither speeding up nor slowing down – she has reached a steady speed, sometimes known as the **terminal velocity**. It is not easy to think of an object moving without any net force acting on it, but we have to remember that it is *because* it is moving that there is any air resistance at all. In fact, parachutes are

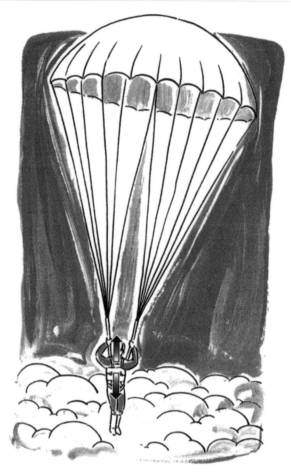

Figure 18 Pushes and pulls on a parachute

designed so that this terminal velocity is reached at comparative slow speeds, i.e., they have a high air resistance. This idea is the substance of Newton's first law of motion, which says that, once moving, an object continues to move in the same way unless something happens to change it, such as a force being applied.

Activity 6	An interesting problem – why don't raindrops kill us?

Think of a raindrop falling from a cloud approximately 1 mile high. It accelerates towards the Earth under the force of gravity. It is possible to calculate that if gravity were the only force acting on it, the raindrop would hit us on the ground at a speed of approximately 400 miles per hour! However, our own experience tells us that this is definitely not the case. Try to explain why, using the same argument as for the parachutist.

Commentary

As with the parachutist, gravity is not the only force acting on the drop. As the drop speeds up as it falls through the air, resistance gets greater and greater until it just balances the pull of gravity. At this point the effective or net force on the raindrop is zero – so it cannot go any faster or any slower – it just stays at the same steady speed.

All these examples involve motion. What we need to do is to explain motion in terms of the forces acting. 'Acceleration' is a term we often use when talking about speed, but scientifically the term 'acceleration' refers to *rate of change* of speed, i.e., how speed changes with time. (Strictly speaking, acceleration is the rate of change of *velocity*, which also involves direction. However, if we confine ourselves to thinking about movement in a straight line, the difference between speed and velocity need not concern us here.) Speed is calculated from measurements of distance and time.

If an object is speeding up, what can you say about the forces acting? When faced with this situation, many of us explain speeding up by talking about an applied force getting something going and keeping it going. But what we need to focus on is the net force, recognising when it starts to act, when it changes and when it ceases to act. This involves us in thinking not only about the *net* force but also about friction and the direction of the force of friction. The bigger the net force the bigger the changes in a given time. So, when an object is speeding up there must be a net force acting on the object and causing it to change speed. A bigger net force in the direction of motion causes a bigger acceleration.

When we now come to deal with a moving object that is slowing down what can we say about the net force? In this situation, the net force is in the opposite direction to motion and acts on the object causing the change in speed. The bigger the net force in the opposite direction to motion, the bigger the deceleration.

Many of us find the ideas associated with constant speed quite problematic, probably because we tend to think that a force causes speed, and that acceleration needs an increasing force. However, again what we need to do is to consider the different forces acting and to combine these to give a net force that has size and direction. If a net force in the direction of motion causes speeding up and net force in the opposite direction to motion causes slowing down, then zero net force results in neither speeding up nor slowing down – that is, constant speed.

In this section we have seen that:

▶ Forces are pushes or pulls and can be measured in newtons.

▶ Gravity is the force that holds you down to the planet Earth.

▶ The size of the gravitational force between two objects (e.g. you and the Earth) depends on their masses. This force is always attractive.

▶ On the Earth every kilogram is pulled by gravity with a force of around 10 newtons towards the centre of the Earth.

▶ The weight of an object is simply another name for the gravitational force that acts on it in a certain region (e.g. your weight on Earth is the gravitational force that acts on you on Earth).

▶ There is a distinction between mass and weight. Mass is an intrinsic property of an object – no matter where you are, you always have the same mass. Your weight is, however, quite a different thing – it is the gravitational force that acts on you. Your weight acts downwards, towards the centre of the Earth.

▶ Mass and weight have different units. Mass is measured in grams and kilograms, whereas weight (a force) is measured in newtons.

▶ Friction is a force that resists movement.

▶ A force is needed to start something moving, speed it up, or slow it down or change its direction.

▶ The bigger the force, the greater the acceleration (or deceleration).

▶ When no overall force is acting on an object it will remain stationary or continue at a steady speed in a straight line.

4 Energy

In this chapter we consider the concept of energy and how we might describe it. The focus is on how energy is transferred from one object or system to another, and how we can think of different forms of energy. It is an important concept as it is found in most aspects of science and as such is a key idea alongside forces, what things are made of and physical and chemical changes. Very few resources are needed and are listed in individual activities.

What is energy?

Energy is a word that is in common usage in everyday language:

'I haven't enough energy today.'
'We must save energ.'
'She is far more energetic than I am.'

We know what we mean when we say these things, but it is much more difficult to give a scientific definition for the word 'energy'. Activity 1 should help you to think about what you mean by 'energy' and to try to define the term.

Energy circus   Activity 1

Below are ten simple situations that you could set up but you may just want to imagine them. Think carefully about each and ask yourself two questions:

(a) What happened?
(b) What was needed to make it happen?

Record your thoughts, using the questions as headings; limit your entries to key words such as:

   movement, light, heat, electricity, muscles/food, height, fuel, elastic …

If none of these words fits your ideas then think of your own.

1 *Snooker*

   Place a marble or a snooker ball on a table. Now hit it by rolling a second ball towards it.
   What happened to the first ball?
   What was needed to make it happen?

2 *Time for tea*

   Half-fill an electric kettle with water. Plug it in and switch in on for a few minutes.

What happened to the water?
What was needed to make it happen?

3 *Leap frog*

Crouch down and then suddenly straighten your legs (i.e., jump).
What happened to your body?
What was needed to make it happen?

4 *Off to work*

Start your car engine, put it into gear, take off the brake and gradually press the accelerator.
What happened to the car?
What was needed to make it happen?

5 *Brrm!*

Take a small battery-powered car or a small buggy made from Legotechnic (or something similar). Switch it on and put it on the table or floor.
What happened to the car?
What was needed to make it happen?

6 *Lights please*

Turn a torch on.
What happened to the bulb?
What was needed to make it happen?

7 *Ramp racer*

Place a toy car at the top of a ramp and let go.
What happened to the car?
What was needed to make it happen?

8 *Dynamo*

Ride a bicycle with a lamp that is dynamo powered.
What happened to the lamp when you started peddling?
What was needed to make it happen?

9 *Next floor*

Step in a lift and press the button for the top floor.
What happened to the lift?
What was needed to make it happen?

10 *Numbers*

Switch on a solar-powered calculator.
What happened to the display?
What was needed to make it happen?
Look carefully at each of your entries in the two lists.

Commentary

In each case you identified what was needed to make it happen.

For example: the movement of one object can be used to make another object gain movement (snooker); electricity can cause light (torch) and light can be used to make electricity (solar-powered calculator); electricity can power a lift to give it height and height can cause a car to move as it rolls downhill.

The terms that you have used in the lists are all terms relating to energy and this leads us to a useful working definition of energy.

Energy is needed to make things happen.

But things don't just happen because an object contains energy. For example, a tank of petrol has potential energy, but left on its own not very much will happen. We have seen that the terms in our lists can be interchangeable between the two columns.

So we can now extend our definition of energy to include this idea:

Energy is needed to make things happen – but things will happen only when energy is transferred from one place to another.

Energy transfer

Imagine you have just woken up. Perhaps it is a holiday and there is no rush. You lie still and look around you. What do you see that tells you the room is real and not just a colour photograph? Above all, you will see movement: the breeze moving the trees outside; a bee on the window pane; steam rising from a cup of tea; the movement of your own limbs. As well as movement, you'll feel the warmth of your body and of the sunlight falling on the bed. You'll also see the light from the Sun and perhaps from a nearby lamp. You'll hear sound: the drone of the bee; the rustle of leaves in the breeze. Finally, movement again as you galvanise your muscles and force yourself to get out of bed and move across the room. All these things are manifestations – observations through our senses – of *energy being transferred from one place to another.*

The concepts of energy and energy transfer are very much part of everyday speech and everyday thinking. That coal, oil, hydro electricity and wind are all related to energy is taken for granted in newspaper articles and on the television. The idea that food provides energy is routine in advertisements for chocolate bars and glucose drinks. So also is the idea that energy from food is used when you move your body: 'I'll have to run a mile to work off this cake.'

So how can we use our definition to help us in our understanding? You are probably aware that the man struggling to push-start the car in Figure 16 is using energy from his muscles to make the car move. Put into the technical jargon of physics – as he pushes it, he is said to be *doing work* on the car. Other examples might include: a crane doing work on a crate by lifting it; a locomotive doing work on the coaches attached to it by pulling them along the rail track; wind doing work by turning the sails of a windmill, a shopper lifting a bag of vegetables.

You met some example of energy being transferred in the waking-up scene. You met other examples when you considered push-starting a car, and in the descriptions of cranes, trains and windmills. People often describe energy as existing in a variety of forms. However, this is just for convenience when considering energy in different situations. Energy doesn't really come in a range of different forms; it is moved about or transferred. Let us look into this idea more carefully.

We can use money as an analogy. Money comes in many forms that are all interconvertible. Someone going on a world tour might draw £10,000 from the bank. As the journey progresses, some would become French francs, some dollars, some pesetas, etc. If the traveller visited Hong Kong or the markets of Saudi Arabia, she might transform some of her money into small gold bars to bring home again. If she visited some isolated corner of the world, she might find that the local currency is salt or rare shells. All of it is money – recognised 'units of purchasing power – but all of it is in different forms that can readily be transferred from one into another.

One way to help you understand this idea more is to think 'energy is energy'. There are not really different forms of energy but there are different forms of energy calculation. For instance, there is a formula for calculating kinetic energy and another for potential energy.

This is in the same way that if you had water in a cubic container you would use a formula to work out the volume, and if you poured it into a cylinder you would use a different formula to work out the volume, but it would still be the same water.

Activity 2 presents similar ideas to the energy circus in Activity 1 but the aim here is to identify some of the different situations where energy is being transferred.

Activity 2	Describing energy

These two experiments are simple. Complete both, record your observations and answer questions 1–5.

Experiment 1

Screw a piece of paper about the size of a bus ticket into a tight ball. Put it on to the table in front of you and flick it with your finger. Repeat the experiment, flicking more vigorously this time. What did you see when you flicked the paper ball? What did you hear? Now answer these questions:

Question 1 You did work on the ball with your finger. Immediately after you had flicked the ball, what form of energy did it have? You may not know a technical term for this, in which case just write a few words explaining your idea. If you hadn't thought of the moving ball as having any energy, picture a moving cannon ball made of iron!

Question 2 Where do you think the energy of your flick came from?

Experiment 2

Put a sheet of A4 paper flat on the table in front of you. Hold the paper steady with one hand. With the other, rub one finger to and fro on the paper while pressing down fairly hard (but not so hard as to ruck or move the paper). Do this as fast as you can for a few seconds. Put the tip of that finger to your lips: what do you notice about its temperature? What did you hear as you did the experiment? Repeat the experiment several times, rubbing faster and harder. Again, what do you notice about your finger temperature? What about the temperature of the paper where you have been rubbing?

Question 3 What everyday term would you use instead of the stars in this sentence: 'When * is given to an object, it gets hotter; when * is lost by an object, it becomes colder'?

Question 4 Bearing in mind how the temperature of the paper changed when you rubbed, in what way does the amount of * it possesses change as it is rubbed? (Note that the star represents the same word as it does in question 3.)

Question 5 Bearing in mind that rubbing your finger caused the temperature of the paper and your fingertip to rise, where do you think that energy came from?

Now that you have completed the experiments and answered the questions, what conclusions can you draw about the different forms of energy involved and the ways in which energy is transferred?

You may like to repeat the experiments but this time describe what happens in terms of the forces acting and relate this to the section on forces.

Commentary

Regarding question 1, the moving paper ball has energy simply because it is moving; the technical term applied to this is **kinetic energy** (movement energy). Cannon balls, cricket balls, avalanches and torrents of water have plenty of it. Even a single molecule in air has some kinetic energy, albeit a very small amount. Once again, this is because the molecules (of oxygen, nitrogen, water and so on), as mentioned in the section on particles, are moving around, rather like very small cannon balls.

Question 2 focuses on the source of the energy that was given to the paper pellet. Some of the chemical energy of the fuel within the cells of the muscles of your flicking finger was changed into the kinetic energy of the paper pellet. You may have heard of the process called *aerobic respiration*. This is the name given to the reactions inside cells by which fuels such as glucose are converted to carbon dioxide and water with the release of energy.

The second experiment introduced you to the idea that increasing the energy of an object makes it hotter: a hot object has more energy than a cold one. The energy is 'stored' inside the hot body – scientists refer to this as 'internal energy', and in everyday speech we often call it 'heat'. So, the star in Questions 3 and 4 could be 'energy' or 'internal energy' or you may have said 'heat'. In fact 'heat' energy is actually kinetic energy, because heat consists of the vibration of the particles of which everything is made: the hotter the thing is, the faster the vibration. As we have already discussed, friction, the force that opposes motion, is a very common and important phenomenon. Whether in the bearings of rotating wheels, in drilling into wood or in rubbing a piece of paper, increasing friction always leads to an increased amount of kinetic energy.

Question 5 asked you to consider where the kinetic energy (and hence 'heat' energy) in Experiment 2 came from. Once again, the answer is from the chemical energy of the fuels within your muscles.

We can now begin to construct a diagram that shows the different situations in Experiments 1 and 2 where we can identify energy changes. Look at Figure 19. This shows – in the boxes with solid lines – the energy changes discussed so far; ignore the dotted boxes for the moment.

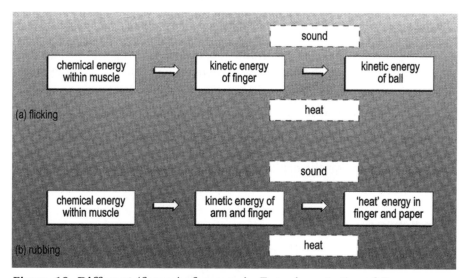

Figure 19 Different 'forms' of energy in Experiments 1 and 2

Now think carefully about what else is going on in these two experiments. There are other energy changes that have not yet been entered on the diagram. The next few paragraphs ask you to think more about these and to make additions to Figure 19 so that it is complete.

When the paper pellet lands on the table, that too becomes very slightly warmer. Draw an arrow on Figure 19(a) to show the energy change involved when the ball lands on the table.

The muscle that did the flicking and rubbing would also have become warm. Heat is always a by-product of muscular effort. This is very obvious if you run or move vigorously for any length of time. Indeed, unless the body gets rid of this heat, overheating would result – and this is why exercise leads to noticeable sweating. As far as muscle is concerned, only part of the energy released in the respiration process:

glucose + oxygen → carbon dioxide + water + energy

becomes kinetic energy. The rest (often more than half of the total) appears as heat. Draw arrows (a) and (b) on Figure 19 to show the energy transfers.

Incidentally, if you exercise for a long time, your muscles may be forced – through lack of oxygen – to switch to **anaerobic respiration**. Glucose is anaerobically converted to a substance called lactic acid. This acid builds up in the muscles, leading to discomfort and cramp.

What else did you observe that has not yet been discussed? You heard things in both experiments – the flick itself, the slight sound of the pellet landing, the noise of rubbing. What do these observations mean? In both experiments there is another 'form' of energy involved: sound. If you imagine standing next to a large drum or gong that is being struck vigorously, then the idea that energy is carried by sound is very believable! Draw arrows (a) and (b) on Figure 19 to show this energy transfer.

Energy chains

The activities and exercises you have completed in this section focus on the idea that energy can be changed from one form to another. We can look at any of these events and try to trace them back to find out where the energy came from in the first place, in the same way as in Figure 19. Putting all the links and transformations in place gives us an energy chain.

From the energy circus in Activity 1 take the example of the 'ramp racer'.

The car at the top of the ramp rolled down the ramp because it had energy due to its position. This is called **potential energy.**

The car had potential energy because I lifted it up to the top of the ramp using my muscles.

My muscles got their energy from my food.

My food (e.g. cereal) got its energy from the Sun.

The Sun originally got its energy from ... ? (An age-old question!)

By continually asking ourselves the question 'Where did the energy come from?' we can build up an energy chain.

Energy chain	Activity 3

1   Complete an energy chain for the ramp racer.

2   Try an energy chain for filling and boiling a kettle of water.

Commentary

1 In words the chain is: movement energy ← potential energy ← muscle energy ← chemical energy ← solar (light) energy. Alternatively, you could use diagrams to illustrate this chain. (You may have noticed a similarity to food chains. In fact, a food chain is just a special type of energy transfer.)

2 Chemical energy → movement energy → electrical energy → movement energy → heat energy.

Activity 4	Energy changes

Choose one of the following examples and describe the energy changes taking place.

1 Describe the cycle of energy changes that take place as someone bounces up and down on a trampoline.

2 A small boy fires a stone with a catapult and it breaks a neighbour's window. Starting with the energy needed to stretch the rubber in the catapult, describe the energy changes that take place in this incident.

3 In most homes electric light bulbs are run from the mains supply. Identify the principal energy changes involved in lighting your house if you are in an area served by a coal-fired power station.

4 In most homes electric light bulbs are run from the mains supply. Identify the principal energy changes involved in lighting your house if you are in an area served by a hydroelectric power station.

Conservation of energy

It is an accepted scientific theory that there is a constant amount of energy in the universe. You may have heard it said that 'energy cannot be created or destroyed'. But you will also have been told not to 'waste energy', and the media are always telling us that 'the world is running out of energy', and we pay our fuel bills for the energy we have 'used'. If we try to build up an energy chain like the one in the previous section but working *forwards* rather than backwards and asking the question 'what happens next?' we soon grind to a halt.

There seems to be a contradiction between what the scientists are telling us and real life. To help us reconcile this conflict we need to look at 'useful' and 'not useful' energy.

Think about what happens when you cook dinner on a warm summer's day. You will soon realise that the energy does not just stay in the oven; it heats up the entire kitchen. There is no doubt that you are surrounded by energy, but it is of no use to you. Before you turned on the gas or electricity you had control over what the energy did. You could decide whether to release it or not, and how much, and where. But you have little or no control over the hot air in the kitchen. You can open the windows to spread the heat out a bit, but that is all it does. It doesn't disappear – it enters the atmosphere until it is so diluted that its effect is hardly noticeable.

This explains why our everyday experience of energy is of it 'disappearing' or being 'used up'. It is being transferred to a form that is less useful to us, and as it spreads out it becomes much harder to measure.

The law of conservation of energy is one of the classical laws of science, as energy has the tendency to spread out and as it does it becomes less useful. It underlies all the energy transfers that we have discussed – indeed, all the energy transfers that occur anywhere.

A useful analogy is once again money. Think of the lament 'Well, the money must have gone somewhere!' If you have drawn £100 from a bank, given that the money has not been burnt, it must be somewhere – possibly split up between shops, petrol station, children's pockets and even down the back of the sofa. So it is with energy.

The law of conservation of energy states that:

> **energy cannot be created or destroyed – it can only be transferred from one place to another.**

In order to help our thinking about what eventually happens to that energy we could add:

> **that it often spreads out when it moves from one place to another so ... in some of these places it is less useful.**

Using energy	Activity 5

How can this idea be used to explain why the world is 'running out of energy?'

Commentary

The world is running out of 'useful' energy, i.e., energy over which we have some control, particularly fossil fuels such as coal and oil that can store energy until we want to use it.

When fuels are burnt, the energy becomes less useful when it escapes into the atmosphere, and eventually into outer space. But that still does not mean that the world is losing its energy, because we are continually being bombarded by heat and light from the Sun. Plants have been trapping this energy for millions of years and putting it back into a form that we can control (food, wood, gas, oil, etc.). More recently, modern technology has produced the solar cell, which can convert solar energy into electricity, either for immediate use or for storing in rechargeable batteries.

Measuring energy

To complete this activity you will need:

▶ a selection of food packages showing nutritional information.

Find the line on each packet that shows the energy content of the food. (A typical example of the nutritional information on a can of soup is shown in Table 8.)

Table 8 Nutritional information

	Per 100g	Per ½ can serving
Energy	90 kJ/22 kcal	191 kJ/47 kcal
Protein	0.6 g	1.1 g
Carbohydrate (of which sugars)	3.9 g (1.5 g)	8.3 g (3.2 g)
Fat (of which saturates)	0.6 g (Trace)	1.3 g (Trace)
Dietary fibre	0.5 g	1.1 g
Sodium	0.3 g	0.6 g

How do food manufacturers make a fair comparison between the energy content of different foods?

What unit is the energy measured in?

By using the information given on one of the packages, you might like to try to work out how many kcals there are in I kJ. Check your answer by trying the same exercise on another packet. You should get the same answer!

Commentary

You should have discovered that although values are given 'per serving', there is always a value given 'per 100g', whatever the product. This allows you to make a fair comparison between different foods.

Energy is usually quoted using two measurements:

kJ (= kilojoules = 1000 joules)
kcal (= kilocalories = 1000 calories)

The Calorie, with a capital C, that is well known to weight-watchers, is in fact 1 kcal.

The standard unit of energy that is always used in science is the joule, but because people have been more familiar with the out-of-date British unit, the Calorie, usually both are quoted. They are just different ways of measuring the same thing, like metres and yards are both ways of measuring distance. 1 kcal = 4.1868 kJ (or about 4.2 kJ).

So energy is measured in joules, but what *is* a joule? Is it a big unit or a little one? What, in everyday terms, do you feel like if you do 100 J of work? In fact, 1 joule isn't much in human terms. You do 3 or 4 joules of work opening a tin of cat food; you would do 100 J of work putting your briefcase on the luggage rack in a train; and you may have to expend 3000 J to 6000 J to push-start a vehicle. The amount of energy in one person's food for a day is about 10 million J. At the other extreme, the amount of work done by a single beat of a fly's wing is about one-millionth of a joule.

Heat and temperature

Once again we come across some everyday words that we use quite happily in conversation, but which have very specific meanings in science.

These can be summarised as:

▶ If the temperature (i.e., level of hotness) of an object is increased, then energy has been transferred to it.

▶ If the temperature of an object falls then energy has been transferred out.

▶ Some objects need more energy than others to raise their temperatures by a certain amount. We say they have different 'heat capacities'.

▶ Where two objects are in thermal contact with each other (i.e., they are not insulated from each other), energy will always flow from where the temperature is higher to where the temperature is lower until the temperatures are level.

Explaining heat and temperature	Activity 7

Think about the following situations and try to explain them in terms of heat and temperature.

(a) Anyone who has been on a canal boat holiday or who has watched river locks in operation will be familiar with the way that locks fill and empty. As soon as the sluices are opened there is a gush of water and a rapid change in water level in the lock. But as the water levels get closer to each other it seems to take forever before the levels are the same and the lock gates can be opened. Try to predict and explain how quickly a hot cup of tea will lose heat to the cooler air around it, in comparison with a lukewarm cup of tea. You might like to devise an investigation to test your prediction.

(b) As a substance, water has a high 'heat capacity', i.e., it takes a lot of energy to raise its temperature. Think about why water is such a good substance to use in a hot water bottle.

(c) On fireworks night we are encouraged to have buckets of water around to douse any stray sparks from a bonfire or firework. The temperature of a spark may be several hundred degrees Celsius, whereas that of the bucket of water is only a few degrees Celsius. What happens to the amount of energy and the temperature of both the bucket of water and the spark?

Commentary

When something is heated or cooled, as in the cup of tea in (a), energy is transferred from one place to another and causes a change of temperature. Energy moves from hot to cold objects spontaneously, so that the temperature of the latter increases while that of the former decreases. If the energy that is transferred by heating is great enough, materials can be made to change from a solid to a liquid and then to a gas.

To explain why this happens we can use the particle model, which states that matter is made up of tiny particles, atoms and molecules, held together by forces. In the solid state, the particles are vibrating, but they are held in position quite firmly, and are usually arranged in some kind of regular pattern. If the amount of energy in the material is increased by heating, the movements become greater and the material changes from a solid to a liquid. Transferring more energy to the material through heating causes the movement of the particles to become so great they start to fly off into the space above the liquid – and the material changes to a gas. So, as the kinetic energy of the particles increases, they spread out more and more widely.

Temperature is a measure of how fast the particles are moving, but not of the total amount of energy in the substance. So a few particles with a lot of kinetic energy have a high temperature but little heat, a spark for example, while a lot of particles with relatively little kinetic energy have a low temperature but a lot of heat, a bucket of water for example.

Making connections

As we have already mentioned, many of the technical terms used in this topic are also used in everyday language, often interchangeably, and with a vague commonly understood meaning. For example, force and energy are often used to mean roughly the same thing in everyday speech. The same is true of force and **pressure**, and energy and **power**. Although we have not dealt with pressure and power so far they may have come up in your writing and discussions. However, scientists have very precise definitions of these words and one way of explaining them is to point out the differences and the connections.

Making the connection – forces and energy

In thinking about forces and energy it is perhaps more helpful to identify the distinctions between them rather than trying to make connections. Forces and energy are two different things, although we often associate them both with movement.

A force is something that has direction and is always the effect of one object on another. It can make objects speed up, slow dawn, change direction, stop, or change shape.

Energy has no direction and is about 'things happening'. It can be stored in an object or released from it and transferred to another object.

Making the connection – force and pressure

Pressure is a way of describing a 'concentration' of force. The classic example of this is the comparison between the damage that an elephant would do to a lino floor and the damage that someone in stiletto heels can do. The elephant's weight is spread over the wide pads of its feet, whereas the weight of the person is concentrated into the small area of the tip of the stiletto heel. The pressure through the heel is greater and so causes more damage.

You may have noticed when doing Activity 1, where you were asked to feel the force in lifting objects, that some objects weren't actually as heavy as you might have expected when compared with others. Two objects of identical weight but different size will *feel* as though they are of different weights because of the different pressures that they exert on your hand. (Try it!) Hence the importance of using some form of weighing device rather than relying on our own sense to make accurate measurements.

Pressure is the amount of force exerted on a particular area.

Force is usually measured in newtons (N), and area in square metres (m^2), so pressure is measured in newtons per square metre (N/m^2).

Making the connection – energy and power

We say that energy is produced in *power* stations, but up to now the term 'power' has not been used in this text, although you may well have used it in your discussions.

Going back to the idea that energy is transferred, we can say that power is a measure of how quickly energy is transferred.

Power is measured in watts (W) or kilowatts (kW = 1000 W).

For example, a 3 kW fan heater will transfer electrical energy into the air in the room much more quickly than a 1 kW heater. We say that it is more *powerful*, and that 1 watt is one Joule changing every second.

In this section we have seen that:

- Energy is needed to make things happen.
- Things only happen when energy is transferred from one form to another.
- Energy is the capacity to do work.
- Movement energy is called kinetic energy.
- There are different forms of energy such as chemical, heat, light and sound energy.
- Things can have energy because of their position. This is potential energy.
- Energy cannot be created or destroyed, it can only be moved from place to place – but some places are less useful.
- Energy is measured in Joules.
- When energy is transferred to an object it can result in a rise in temperature and vice versa – loss of energy can result in a drop in temperature.
- Power is a measure of how quickly energy is transferred and is measured in watts.

Part 2

This section of the book looks at specific science topic areas, building on the key ideas of science presented in Part 1.

In Chapter 5 the emphasis is on living things and how they carry out the necessary functions to live. It explores the characteristics of living things and how plants and animals carry out these functions to stay alive and what it means to be healthy.

Chapters 6 and 7 explore the large concepts of continuity and change by looking at the diversity of plants and animal life and how characteristics are passed from generation to generation. How these characteristics can change leads into the way animals and plants interact within their environment. Key concepts of ecology are briefly studied to build a broader picture of how living things interact.

The key or big ideas in Chapters 2, 3 and 4 underpin many of the activities and text in Part 2. If you are unsure of some aspects of these bigger ideas refer back to Part 1 as you work through these chapters. Very few resources are needed in this section and are listed with the relevant activity.

5 Living Things and Life Processes

Structure and function of living things

Look at the list below:

centipede	sheep's wool	mushroom	limestone	buttercup
oil	snail	apple	coal	cat
shell	cork	bean seed	yoghurt	granite
moss	cloud	milk	cut flower	

If it is difficult to think about these ideas without samples. Collect a selection of objects together.

Consider each in turn and try to list them under the headings **living** and **non-living**.

Commentary

Categorising objects into two closely defined categories is not easy as there are always those objects that fall between the two categories. Were there some that you found difficult to decide where to put? Why? Could you have used categories such as once lived or never lived that would have helped you sort more easily?

All living things can be distinguished from non-living things by the processes that they have to carry out in order to live. Living things can then be divided into smaller groups. It does not help us classify things into living and non-living when gas companies advertise their fires as 'living fires' or when food shops say 'no animals' but we still continue to go in and buy food but do not take in the dog. This general everyday use of scientific terms can confuse our scientific understanding. We need to be aware when we are using terms loosely or incorrectly in science. Many non-living things such as crystals can 'grow' but this is not the same concept as that of living things. Crystals do not carry out all the other processes inherent in being alive. All living things carry out all these processes in some way or other in order to live.

In the list above, centipede, snail and cat are animals. Apple, cork and flower are parts of a plant. The bean seed, a product of reproduction in a bean plant, is dormant but will grow in suitable conditions. Moss and buttercup are plants that belong to different groups. Mushroom belongs to the fungi and yoghurt contains bacteria.

Things such as cut flowers are still living because for a short time they are able to continue to carry out living processes. After that they will die.

Sheep's wool, limestone, coal and oil were living once or have remains of living material in them, e.g. fossils in limestone. Granite and limestone are rocks but limestone may also contain fossil material.

The two kingdoms most commonly known to most people are plants and animals but scientists now often include bacteria, protoctista, viruses and fungi as separate kingdoms. The kingdoms are the first steps in identifying and classifying living things into groups that share broadly similar observable features.

The seven characteristics of living things are:

- feeding/nutrition
- respiration
- excretion
- growth
- sensitivity
- movement
- reproduction.

Activity 2	Life processes

Write a statement about what you think each process above involves.

Different living things, depending on their complexity and structure, carry out these processes with varying degrees of sophistication and complexity, and we will look at some of this variety as we study communities and diversity. Listed below are definitions of the processes for you to compare with your initial ideas.

Commentary

- *Feeding/nutrition* – by the process of photosynthesis, green plants use the energy of sunlight to combine carbon dioxide and water to produce carbohydrates, which they use as their energy source for growth and to carry out the other processes of life; animals obtain their energy by feeding on plants or other animals.

- *Respiration* – is the process by which plants and animals release the energy from their food, using oxygen from the air or dissolved in water. Respiration takes place in all living cells.

- *Excretion* – plants and animals get rid of waste materials produced as a result of processes taking place in their cells.

- *Sensitivity* – is the ability to respond to stimuli and modify behaviour because of this.

- *Movement* – the leaves of plants turn towards the sun and their roots grow in the direction of water; most animals can move freely from place to place.

- *Growth* – is the increase in size and complexity of a living thing. Plants grow all their lives, animals grow to maturity and the growth of new cells is then diverted towards replacing old, dying cells.

- *Reproduction* – if an organism survives to reproductive age, it may then pass on its genetic material to a new generation of offspring. Reproduction is the means by which animals and plants replicate and provide new generations.

There are distinct differences between plants and animals and the way they carry out these processes. Table 9 lists the main areas of difference related to the processes of life.

Table 9 Areas of difference in processes of life between plants and animal

	Plants	Animals
Feeding (nutrition)	Food synthesised from inorganic molecules	Eat plants or other animals
Respiration	Energy stored as starch	Energy stored as glycogen
Elimination of waste	Oxygen and CO_2, leaf fall	CO_2, urine, defecation
Growth	Branching, continues to death	Compact, continues to maturity
Response to stimuli	Slow (growth), no obvious nervous system	Rapid, through nervous system and sense organs
Movement	Anchored, rigid cell walls	Mobile, skeleton and muscles
Reproduction	Frequently asexual, embryos as seeds	Infrequently asexual, embryos in eggs or live-born
Cellular structure	Rigid cellulose cell wall, chloroplasts present in green plants	Thin cell membrane

(*Source*: adapted from Farrow, 1996)

From this table we need to look in more detail at the building blocks of living things and how they fit together to carry out the processes of living things. All living things are made of cells, and both plant and animal cells have the following parts:

▶ the nucleus, which contains genetic material and controls what the cell does

▶ the cell membrane which controls movement of materials in and out of the cell

▶ the cytoplasm in which most chemical reactions take place.

Activity 3	Cellular differences

Figure 20 shows examples of a typical plant and animal cell. Look closely and try to list the main differences between each cell.

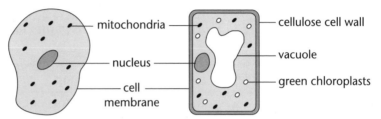

Figure 20 Typical plant and animal cells

Commentary

Plant cells have extra features compared with the animal cell. These include a cellulose cell wall, a fluid filled vacuole and chloroplasts, which give plants their green colour, play an important part in photosynthesis. The shape of cells, in both plants and animals, varies according to the functions the cells are to carry out. In other words the cells become specialised.

Groups of cells of similar structure and function are called tissues and examples include muscle tissue and blood in animals, and xylem and phloem tissue in plants. Different tissues working together form an organ such as the heart in animals and a leaf in plants. Organs can work together and form an organ system such as the digestive system, which includes, stomach, liver, pancreas, intestines and rectum. 'Organism' is another term for a living thing, not to be confused with organs. Figure 21 shows some specialised cells. You can still see the nucleus, cell membrane and cytoplasm but their shape and function have changed.

Let's now look at how these systems work. Taking each characteristic of living things in turn, we explore the key factors and how plants and animals carry these out but the main focus will be on how we as humans carry out the living processes.

(a) Rocothair cell

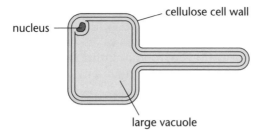

nucleus

cellulose cell wall

large vacuole

(b) White blood cell

Figure 21 Specialised cells

Nutrition

All living things have to feed and digest food in order to grow and reproduce. How different plants and animals carry out these processes is a huge topic. In this section we focus mainly on how green plants and humans function but refer to some other groups where relevant.

Plants

It is important to understand that all life depends on the ability of plants to make food from inorganic materials. Whatever animals feed on, whether they are herbivores or carnivores, can be traced back through a food chain to a plant, which through the process of photosynthesis makes sugars. During photosynthesis the energy from the sun helps to combine hydrogen, from the water taken up by the roots, with carbon dioxide that the plant has taken in from the atmosphere, to produce carbohydrates or sugars. The chlorophyll in the plants absorbs the energy from the Sun that is then used to to combine the water and carbon dioxide. These sugars are the food source and can be stored as starch within the plant – for instance in the leaves or the root.

The word equation for photosynthesis is given below alongside the chemical formula to summarise the process.

Water + carbon dioxide → Energy from Sun → glucose + oxygen
$6H_2O + 6CO_2$ → Energy → $C_6H_{12}O_6 + 6CO_2$

Photosynthesis is therefore the most important process taking place in plants and the rate is affected by the amount of light, carbon dioxide and temperature.

Animals

Feeding in animals involves taking in food, breaking the food down through physical and chemical processes into pieces small enough to be absorbed into the body. This process is called digestion. For some animals, catching or collecting food is an important part of their daily activity. For some animals, most of their daily life is spent grazing to gather enough food.

In animals, once the food is found or prepared it is ingested through a mouth of some description where it is then broken down by physical means such as chewing and churning in the stomach(s). As the food moves down the alimentary canal chemical processes come into action. Digestive juices are produced which lubricate the food to ease its movement along the alimentary canal and contained within these juices is a range of enzymes that act as biological catalysts in the digestion of foods. These enzymes are specific to particular foods. For instance, the enzyme amylase found in saliva begins the chemical breakdown of starch. Food that is chewed well has a bigger surface area for the enzymes to act upon and so speeds up digestion.

In humans (see Figure 22) food is swallowed and passes down the oesophagus into the stomach, which contains an acid medium. The stomach wall secretes gastric juices that contain hydrochloric acid and the enzyme pepsin to break down the proteins into peptides and then into amino acids, the building blocks of proteins. From the stomach the

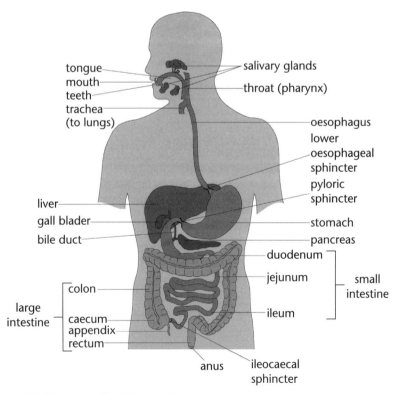

Figure 22 Human digestive system

food passes through the pyloric sphincter, a muscle that controls the flow of food from the stomach into the small intestine. In the small intestine, which is in fact longer than the large intestine, carbohydrase, protease and lipase enzymes are produced. They change carbohydrates to glucose, proteins to amino acids and fats to glycerol respectively. The liver produces bile, which is stored in the gall bladder and emulsifies fat (breaks into tiny globules) so that the lipase can break them down into fatty acids and glycerol. Bile, as it enters the small intestine, neutralises the acidic material that has come from the stomach to protect the intestinal wall.

As the food passes along the small intestine into the large intestine or colon the products of digestion are absorbed into the body through the villi which line the intestine. These are finger-like folds in the lining that greatly increase the surface area and assist absorption. In the colon excess water is reabsorbed from the remaining material which consists largely of fibre cellulose from plants and dead skin cells. The remaining material passes into the rectum where it is stored until ready to be passed out of the body.

Other animals digest food in similar ways, although the structures and systems in simpler animal groups are not as complex as humans.

Human digestion	Activity 4

Read the above carefully and then without referring to the text try to explain to yourself on paper or to a friend how digestion works in humans. Check your answer against the text and if necessary work through the ideas again.

Commentary

Key points about digestion are that food has to be broken down into small parts so that it can be absorbed through the lining of the intestine and used in respiration and in the creation of new substances. These new substances can be used to:

▶ build new tissues

▶ repair damaged tissues

▶ maintain body temperature

▶ enable movement.

As the food passes down the alimentary canal different enzymes within the system act as catalysts to speed up the breakdown of carbohydrates, proteins and fats. Any food material broken down by the physical processes of digestion and not taken into the body is eliminated from the body. This process is called defecation. Any waste materials from the chemical breakdown of the food is passed out of the body or excreted through the kidneys, liver and the lungs. The air you breathe out has more carbon dioxide in than the air you breathe in because it is a waste product of respiration. Respiration and excretion are two systems closely linked with nutrition, which we look at later in this chapter.

In this section we have seen that:

▶ All living things carry out respiration, nutrition, excretion, movement, sensitivity, reproduction and growth.

▶ Plant and animal cells are different.

▶ Plants feed by carrying out photosynthesis.

▶ Photosynthesis needs light from the Sun, water and carbon dioxide, and produces glucose and oxygen.

▶ Animals feed on other plants or animals and food has to be digested.

Respiration

All living things respire. Respiration consists of a sequence of chemical reactions that release energy from the food made or eaten. It can be either aerobic or anaerobic. The difference is dependent on the levels of oxygen available. The vast majority of living things carry out aerobic respiration, which is the release of energy from the breakdown of glucose by combining it with oxygen inside living cells.

Anaerobic respiration is the release of energy from the incomplete breakdown of glucose in the absence of oxygen. Fungi such as yeast respire anaerobically and it occurs in humans when the muscles are working hard and the body cannot deliver oxygen quickly enough for the cells. This results in the build-up of lactic acid and it is this that can give rise to cramp in the muscles because of an 'oxygen debt'. Deep breathing, after exercise, will provide that extra oxygen to oxidise the lactic acid to release carbon dioxide and water.

The energy produced within the cells is used to build molecules of substances needed in the body. It is also used to make muscles contract and to maintain temperature in warm-blooded animals. It also provides the energy to actively transport substances across the cell membranes.

In humans, when we breathe in, the oxygen enters the lungs and flows down through the trachea into the bronchus, to the bronchioles and into the alveoli where the oxygen dissolves into the moist lining of these air sacs. The air is drawn into the lungs when the intercostal muscles contract and pull the ribs up and out and the diaphragm contracts pulling down. These two simultaneous actions lower the air pressure within the chest and air is automatically drawn into the lungs to even the pressure on the inside with that on the outside of the chest. Figure 23 shows the process of breathing in and out but which is which?

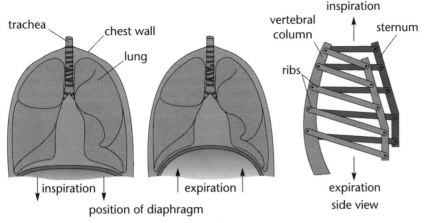

Figure 23 Breathing in, breathing out?

Look closely at the diagrams in Figure 23. Now place your hands firmly on your chest and breathe in slowly and deeply. Look in the mirror as you do this and you will see that your hands and arms move upwards and outwards. Which diagram represents this stage? What happens to your hands as you breathe out?

Commentary

Diagram (a) is breathing in and (b) is breathing out.

Once the air enters the lungs the oxygen dissolves in the moist lining of the **alveoli** and then diffuses through the wall of the lungs into the blood capillaries where it combines with the **haemoglobin** in the red blood cells to form **oxyhaemoglobin**. This is then transported around the body to the cells where the oxygen is needed for respiration. The waste product from this process, carbon dioxide, is taken back to the lungs dissolved in the plasma of the blood. The air breathed in has a higher proportion of oxygen in it than that breathed out and the air breathed out has more carbon dioxide than that breathed in.

The release of energy can be summarised by the word equation below.

Glucose + oxygen → Carbon dioxide + water + energy

Respiration takes place in plants all the time and not, as some people think, only in the dark. Plants carry out photosynthesis during the day because light from the Sun is the necessary energy source. Respiration takes place all the time but we are more aware of it at night because photosynthesis is not masking the small amount of oxygen used and carbon dioxide excreted.

Circulation

Another important system within the body must be mentioned here and that is the circulatory system which plays a vital role in respiration in transporting substances around the body to where they are needed. This transport system consists, in humans, of the blood, the arteries, veins and capillaries, and the pumping organ, the heart.

Activity 6	Circulation

Look carefully at the diagrams in Figure 24 of the structure of blood and the circulation system. When you have studied them carefully try to write in your own words how the blood circulates around the body.

Commentary

Which part of the blood carries what? Look carefully at the differences in structure between the arteries, veins and capillaries. These differences are related to their function. Can you match the lists below to the right vessel? (See also Figure 25.)

(a) Structure of the blood

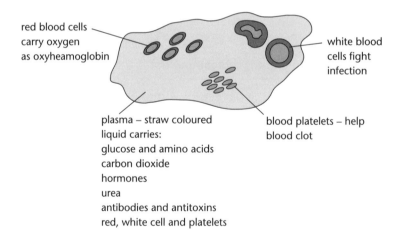

red blood cells carry oxygen as oxyheamoglobin

white blood cells fight infection

plasma – straw coloured liquid carries:
glucose and amino acids
carbon dioxide
hormones
urea
antibodies and antitoxins
red, white cell and platelets

blood platelets – help blood clot

(b) Cross sections of blood vessels

aorta   arteriole   capillary   venule   vena cava

Figure 24 The exchange of gases in (a) lungs, (b) cells

(a) In the lungs

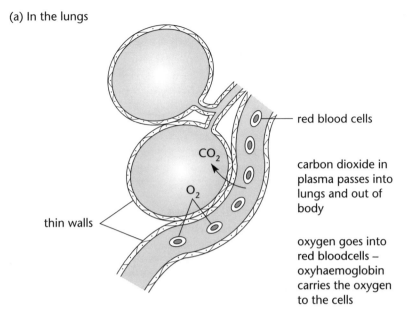

red blood cells

carbon dioxide in plasma passes into lungs and out of body

oxygen goes into red bloodcells – oxyhaemoglobin carries the oxygen to the cells

thin walls

(b) In the cells

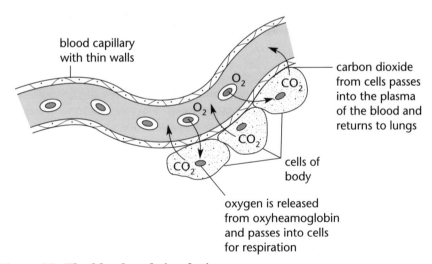

blood capillary with thin walls

carbon dioxide from cells passes into the plasma of the blood and returns to lungs

cells of body

oxygen is released from oxyheamoglobin and passes into cells for respiration

Figure 25 The blood and circulation

A

▶ one-cell thick, thin-walled vessel, narrow

▶ links vessels together

▶ microscopic

▶ exchange of substances between blood and cells takes place here.

B

- thick elastic walls
- narrow bore
- no valves
- carries blood away from heart.

C

- thinner, less elastic walls
- bigger bore to vessel
- valves to restrict flow-back
- carries blood to the heart.

The diagrams of the cross sections of the arteries, veins and capillaries show the difference in structures that relate to the function of each. Arteries (B) have thicker muscular walls that enable them to push oxygenated blood round the body under pressure. Veins (C) carry deoxygenated blood back to the heart from where it goes to the lungs to collect more oxygen. Capillaries (A) have very thin (one-cell thick) walls that allow the exchange of gases and other substances to happen in the lungs and in the cells of the body.

It is important that we understand the different effects that things like exercise and stress have on our bodies and particularly our hearts.

Activity 7	Take your pulse

For this exercise you need to find your pulse first and then to record it at rest and after exercise. To take your pulse you need to use the middle finger as your thumb has its own pulse. You can take your pulse in the side of your neck or on your wrist in line with your thumb.

What do you notice? Is it always the same? How long does it take for your pulse to return to normal? Try this exercise with a friend or colleague and compare results. Are there differences? Can you explain the results?

Look now at the diagram of the heart (Figure 26). Can you relate this to what you felt?

Commentary

The heart beats faster during and after exercise, and this increases the amount of blood and therefore oxygen that is transported to the tissues. This enables the rate of respiration to rise and increases the energy released to carry out the exercise or to recover from the exercise.

Deoxygenated blood from the body is carried to the right atrium and from there it is pushed into the right ventricle. This contracts and pushes the blood

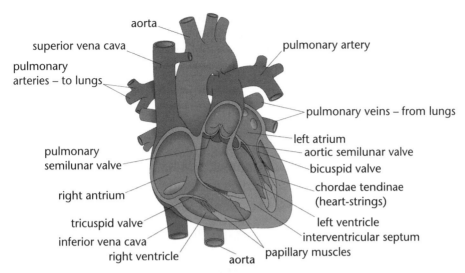

Figure 26 The heart and its circulation

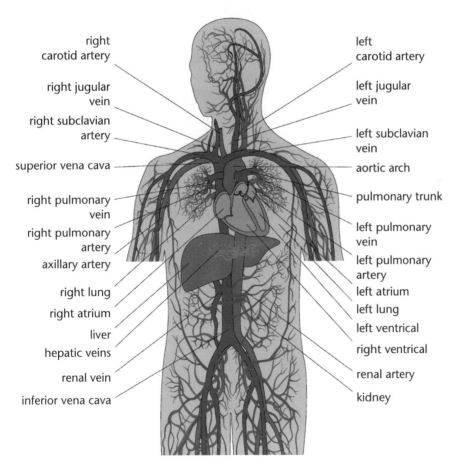

Figure 27 The circulatory system

along the pulmonary artery to the lungs where the red blood cells take up more oxygen and carbon dioxide is passed into the lungs. The oxygenated blood returns to the left atrium via the pulmonary vein and from there the blood passes to the left ventricle and on round the body (Figure 27).

The veins normally carry deoxygenated blood to the heart and arteries carry oxygenated blood away, except in the circulation to the lungs where it is reversed. The pulmonary vein carries oxygenated blood to the heart from the lungs to the heart and the pulmonary artery carries deoxygenated blood from the heart to the lungs.

Transport in plants

The surface membrane of a plant controls what moves in and out of a cell because it is semi-permeable. This means that it will let some particles through, such as water, but not other substances. A plant cell contains a lot of water and when full of water the cell is said to be turgid. If the cell loses water it is said to be flaccid. This can be seen with house plants which if they are not watered become limp and floppy. Watering plants will restore them to an upright form, if watered in time.

How is water drawn up the plant?

Water evaporates from the surface of leaves on a regular basis. The rate of evaporation will vary according to temperature, and other weather conditions. As the water evaporates more water is pulled up to take its place because water molecules have strong bonds that cause them to cling together in an unbroken stream from root to shoot tip. This process is called **transpiration** and the rate of transpiration pull varies according to conditions. On the surface of the leaf are small structures called stomata. These are smaller holes in the leaf surface controlled by two sausage-shaped cells, called guard cells. The guard cells can change shape by gaining or losing water and depending on the weather conditions this opening and closing of the pores controls gases in and out of the plant.

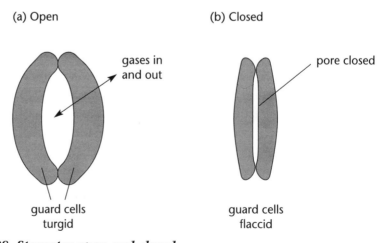

Figure 28 Stomata: open and closed

Figure 28 shows the two states of the guard cells and the stomata. When the stomata are open the transpiration pull is active and the plant is able to diffuse gases; photosynthesis and respiration take place. When a plant is well watered, all the cells will draw water into themselves by **osmosis** and become turgid. Osmosis is the movement of water molecules from high concentrations of water to lower concentrations across a semi-permeable membrane. The water in the cells presses on the cellulose cell walls and this makes the plant more rigid, providing support. This is very important as young non-woody plants grow taller. The water enters the plant by osmosis through the root hairs and travels on up through the xylem cells to the leaves.

Plants transport food, water, and minerals to all different parts of the plant through the **xylem** and **phloem** tubes. These two tube systems are situated close to each other but are separate. Phloem, which is made of living cells which have small pores in the interconnecting walls, carries food. The xylem, which is made of dead cells joined together with no interconnecting walls and **lignin** in the cells' walls, carries water and minerals around the plant. Plants need nitrates, phosphates and potassium for healthy growth. Lack of these minerals can lead to some of the following symptoms: stunted growth, yellow leaves, poor root growth and dead spots on leaves.

The different ways that particles and substances are moved around plants and animals is important in understanding how they function. These systems are closely linked with many of the other characteristics of living things and need to be seen as part of several organ systems.

Movement and support

Plants

The description above of turgidity in cells is the basis of support systems in plants, but as plants grow bigger and mature into shrubs and trees the cellulose cell walls are thickened with lignin. This provides mechanical support and does not involve using any energy once in place.

Plants do not move in the same way and sense that animals do. Plants move by growing towards or away from stimuli that they do or do not like. They can and do move in the wind because of the properties of their cellular structure but it is outside forces moving them.

Plants respond positively to light by growing towards light and are said to be **phototropic**. Light is important for photosynthesis. The roots of plants grow towards water and are said to be **hydrotropic**, i.e., they respond positively to water. You can show how plants respond to light by watching a houseplant over a period of time and see the leaves and stems turn towards the light. To keep a regular shape to your plant you need to turn plants around at regular intervals.

Animals

Animals have developed a variety of ways of supporting their body structure. These have developed as animals moved from water to land and as they became larger and more mobile. This adaptation to the environment the animal lives in is very important to survival.

Many animals without backbones have developed **exoskeletons**. An exoskeleton is a rigid outer case, made of a protein called chitin, that provides protection for the animal but it limits their growth. As a result of this some of these animals have developed ways of moulting or shedding their exoskeletons at intervals in their life cycle to allow for some growth. Insects and crustacea are two groups of animals that have many examples of animals with exoskeletons. Stick insect and locusts grow by shedding their exoskeleton fives times before reaching maturity. Molluscs have developed hard shells that protect their soft bodies.

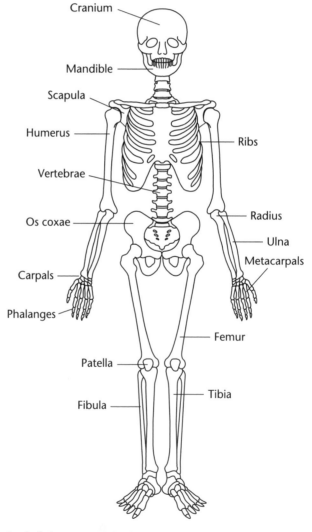

Figure 29 A skeleton

Vertebrate animals have all developed **endoskeletons**, that is, internal skeletons. These skeletons have common features that support the idea of evolution. The basic form includes a skull and backbone and within these a brain and spinal cord respectively. Vertebrates other than fish have limbs, which are based on a common pattern of one long upper bone connected to two long bones, and attached to this are feet or hands or adaptations, or modifications on this basic pattern can be found in some animal groups.

Figure 29 shows a human skeleton with the key bones and ways they are linked together to provide support and mobility Also important in the effective functioning of the skeleton is the structure of bone, cartilage, ligaments and the attachment of tendons and muscle to the bones.

Animals can move in many different ways such as swimming, running, walking and flying. When a bird flaps its wing or a horse runs or a person bends an arm similar patterns of events follow as happens when we move.

Bending and straightening	Activity 8

Look at the two diagrams in Figure 30 carefully before bending and stretching your arm slowly. Can you now annotate the diagrams to show the stages and changes that take place in your arm as you bend it and straighten it?

(a)   (b)

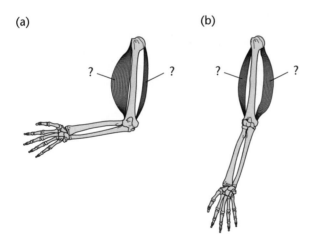

Figure 30 Bending your arm

Commentary

The arm is raised when the biceps muscle contracts, pulling up the radius and ulna bones towards the chest. The triceps muscle relaxes so that it can stretch around the elbow. To straighten the arm the muscles reverse their actions with the biceps relaxing and the triceps contracting and so the arm moves down. Many muscles work in pairs and in opposition to facilitate movement in two directions like the elbow and knee movements. These muscles are said to be antagonistic. The muscles are attached to the bones by tendons which are strong inelastic strips of tissue. Ligaments are strong elastic fibres that bind the bones together at joints and help to hold them in place. The joints are lubricated by synovial fluid which is contained in the synovial membrane that surrounds all joints. If a bone slips out of its normal position in the joint it is said to be dislocated. Another problem that can occur with joints, particularly when involved in very active sports, is the build up of fluids, which can give rise to problems such as tennis elbow, where there is painful swelling that hinders movement.

Within the body there are two types of joint, **fixed** and **movable**. Fixed joints are found in the skull where maximum protection is needed for the brain. Movable joints, which are found around the body, can be subdivided into three types.

▶ Sliding joints – such as those found at the ankle and wrist.

▶ Hinge joints – such as those found at the knee and elbow.

▶ Ball and socket joints – such as those found at the shoulder and hip, which allow for all-round movement.

The energy that the muscles need for moving comes from the food we eat and is brought to the cells in the muscle by the blood. This relates back to the sections on nutrition and energy.

Activity 9	Energy chain

It is possible to devise an energy chain for the bending of the arm similar to those you attempted earlier when we looked at energy flow generally. Start with the arm at rest and try to devise a flow diagram that shows the energy changes that happen as you lift up a heavy ball with your hand. If you find this idea difficult, try bending your arm so that you can feel some of the effects and relate these to the energy changes.

Commentary

Your chain will have some or all of the following parts to it, depending on how many stages and how much detail you put into the activity.

Solar energy (light) → food (chemical) → muscle energy (kinetic) → potential height energy → movement energy.

This supports the law of conservation of energy which states that energy can neither be created nor destroyed but can be changed. There is energy loss at each stage of this chain, e.g. in the refraction of light, heat energy, friction, etc. This idea of energy being lost or wasted is discussed in the section on energy, and is discussed further in the section on trophic levels.

In this section we have seen that:

- Respiration involves the exchange of gases and the 'burning' of food to give energy.
- The circulatory system carries food etc. to all parts of the body.
- The heart, veins, capillaries and arteries form the circulation network in humans.
- Exercise affects the rate the heart beats, and increases transport of materials to and from the cells.
- Plants and animals have support systems to help them move and grow.
- The skeletal system, with muscles, tendons and ligaments, works to help us move.

Sensitivity

For plants and animals to survive and breed it is important that they are sensitive to their surroundings so that they can respond appropriately to significant changes. This could involve immediate change, such as moving away from danger, e.g. deer moving away as they sense lions around. Longer-term changes such as the lack of food and changes in temperature at certain times of the year that force hedgehogs to hibernate during the winter.

Plants

Plants respond to stimuli by growing towards light or gravity and water. Changes in daylight at different times of the year also affect the life cycle and the way the plant functions, e.g. flowering and seed production.

Responses	Activity 10

The following words are the terms used to describe the response of plants to particular stimuli. After reading the above paragraph can you allocate the correct term to the stimuli?

   Photoperiodism, geotropism and phototropism

Commentary

Photoperiodism is the response to changes in periods of light. **Geotropism** is a response towards gravity. **Phototropism** is a response towards light.

In plants **auxins**, which are growth hormones, control the growth of the shoot and root-tips. These auxins are produced at the very tip of the root or shoot and are passed to the cells behind the tip which stimulate the cells to elongate, i.e., grow. If the tip is removed no auxins are produced and that part of the plant may stop growing. Gardeners remove growing tips to encourage side shoots to grow to give a bushier plant that produces more flowers.

Animals

Animals have specialised organs, or sensors, that allow them to sense and respond to the environment. This system of specialised cells and tissues together form the nervous system, and the level of complexity varies from animal group to animal group according to their place in the classification of animals. (See the section on variety of life.)

In humans these sense organs are linked to the muscles and glands by a network of nerve cells and form the **peripheral nervous system (PNS)**. The PNS is linked to the **central nervous system (CNS)**, which consists of the brain and spinal cord.

When a stimulus is received by the sensory cells in the body, e.g. in the eye, an impulse is triggered by the cells that passes along the sensory nerve fibres or neurones to the spinal cord and from there to the brain. Nerve cells do not actually join together. There is a space between each one known as a **synapse**. The impulse, which can travel up to 120 metres per second, stimulates the production of a chemical transmitter which allows the impulse to cross the gap. The next cell is stimulated and the process is repeated again until the impulse reaches the brain. The brain decodes and interprets the stimulus and from this a course of action is

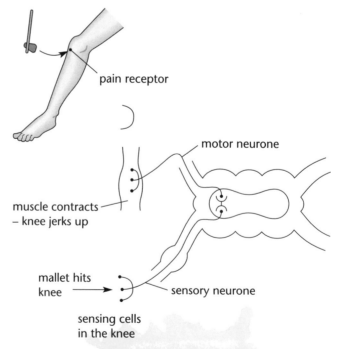

pain receptor

motor neurone

muscle contracts
– knee jerks up

mallet hits
knee

sensory neurone

sensing cells
in the knee

Figure 31 Knee-jerk reflex arc

decided. How the brain perceives and reacts to these stimuli is complex and still challenges scientists.

Not all sensory stimuli are transmitted to the brain. Reflex actions, which are mainly defence mechanisms, speed up response time by short-circuiting the brain. In a reflex action the spinal cord acts as the co-ordinator by means of a relay neurone which passes the impulse directly from a sensory neurone to a motor neurone. This brings about the required response quickly. The diagram in Figure 31 shows how the knee-jerk reflex occurs. The message bypasses the brain and so the knee flicks up very quickly after being tapped.

The senses

We have five basic senses that help us to respond to our environment. Taste and smell are very closely related senses. Our tongues respond to sweet, sour, salt and bitter tastes. Smells and our response to them are very individual. Many food smells enhance and complement our tasting of the food. The sense of smell is important in detecting unpleasant or dangerous foods and smells.

The third sense to mention here is touch. (Seeing and hearing are dealt with in the chapters on light and sound.) Our skins have sensory nerve endings in the dermis that respond to pressure and temperature. This enables us to move away from danger, respond to pain and control our body temperature. This regulation or maintenance of a constant body temperature is achieved because the sweat glands excrete sweat on the surface of the skin. As the water evaporates from the surface it takes heat from the skin, thus assisting in cooling the body. The blood capillaries in the skin, by dilating or contracting, can increase or decrease the cooling process.

Within the sweat or perspiration are salts and urea that are excreted from the body when we perspire – another way the body excretes the waste products of processes in the body.

Table 10 Hormones and their effects

Gland	Hormones	Effect
Pituitary gland at base of brain	Growth	Controls growth
	Thyroid stimulating hormone	Controls thyroid
	Prolactin	Controls mammary growth and milk production
Thyroid	Thyroxine	Controls energy release at all levels
Pancreas	Insulin	Controls blood sugar levels Lack of insulin causes diabetes
Adrenal	Adrenaline	'Fight or flight' hormone Raises blood sugar to help react

continued

Gland	Hormones	Effect
Testes or ovaries	Testosterone	Controls male sexual development
		Controls production of sperm
	Oestrogen	Controls female sexual development
		Controls menstrual cycle

(*Source*: adapted from Farrow, 1996)

Endocrine system

This system provides another way for the body to respond to stimuli both in the environment and within the body. It involves the production of chemical substances known as hormones that bring about the changes. They either work over a period of time, as in growth hormones, or immediately as in adrenalin, which is the flight or fright hormone that enables us to run away if scared. The hypothalamus, which is in the brain, controls the pituitary gland that produces hormones and controls the other endocrine glands. Other glands include the thyroid, the pancreas, the adrenal glands (kidney) and the testes and ovaries. Table 10 shows the hormones that are produced by the various glands and their effects.

Plants

Plants are sensitive to light, moisture and gravity, as we have already explained, but the responses to these stimuli are controlled by hormones. These are produced in the growing tips of shoots and roots and are transported to where they are needed. They can accumulate in some areas and cause irregular growth in different parts of the plant.

Reproduction

Reproduction is the process or processes by which individual living things increase their number. It can be **asexual** or **sexual**. In this section we first explore some terms before looking at how living things reproduce.

Asexual reproduction

Asexual reproduction is common in simple living things where a genetically identical copy or clone is made of themselves. This can happen in four different ways, namely:

▶ budding – e.g. yeast

▶ fission, splitting in two to form two identical individuals, e.g. bacteria

- spore formation – e.g. bacteria
- vegetative reproduction is when parts of a plant can develop into a new individual with the same genetic material but may look different – e.g. taller due to environmental factors. It becomes detached from the parent plant and grows independently. This is a very important way that gardeners are able to overwinter plants. Examples of plants that can reproduce in this way include strawberry runners, bulbs such as daffodils, crocuses and iris rhizomes.

Sexual reproduction

This involves the production of specialised cells known as **gametes** that contain genetic material from either a female or male individual. Each gamete may vary slightly from the next in the genetic material it contains, therefore it is impossible for two individuals resulting from sexual reproduction to be absolutely identical. These gametes, a male and a female, fuse together to form a **zygote** that grows to form a new individual. This individual has a different genetic make-up from the parents as half the information has come from the male and a different half from the female. This increases the diversity in the gene pool and does not have the limiting factors of asexual reproduction. This will be explored further in the section on diversity later in this chapter.

Plants

Most green plants produce flower buds inside which the flower develops. The flower is a series of modified leaves and a typical cross section of a flower looks like the one in Figure 32.

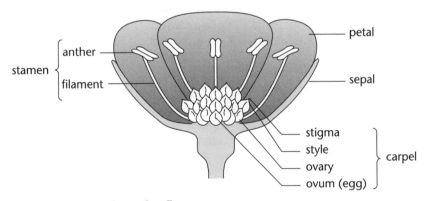

Figure 32 Cross section of a flower.

The ovaries produce the egg or female gamete and the pollen contains the male gamete. For the gametes to meet and fuse the pollen has to be dispersed. Many plants, to aid the cross-fertilisation of genetic material, produce pollen and ova at different times so that pollen from the same plant cannot fuse with ova on the same plant. The scattering of pollen or **pollination** is an important process by which pollen is transferred from the anther to the stigma of the female part of the plant. Cross-pollination allows the exchange of genetic material and therefore strengthens the genetic pool. Pollen can be carried by wind or by insects, and pollination occurs when it lands on the stigma of a similar flower and a pollen tube containing the male gamete grows from the grain towards the ovary (Figure 33).

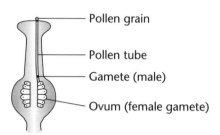

Figure 33 Growth of a pollen tube

When it reaches the ovary the tube penetrates the embryo sac. The nucleii from the ovum and pollen grain fuse together. This is called fertilisation. The resulting cell is called a zygote and this contains the genetic information for the new plant that will develop from the seed. Within the seed can be found one or two cotyledons or food stores, a shoot or plumule and a root or radicle. The seed has a coat or testa to protect the developing embryo. The ovary, containing the seeds, develops into a fruit. There are a variety of fruit types that offer one way of sorting plants.

The word 'fruit' as used in everyday living is not the same as that just described here. All plants produce fruits but in our everyday life we call some of these vegetables, e.g. marrow, courgettes, but they are technically fruits. Vegetables such as potatoes and carrots are a result of swellings of different parts of the plant to store food for the winter and are a vegetative or asexual means of reproduction. This further serves to confuse people about the scientific meaning of a fruit, whilst vegetable has no scientific meaning.

Seeds need scattering to find suitable ground to grow. If the seeds just fall where the flower grew, overcrowding could occur and thus many would not survive to maturity because of the competition for resources. Plants produce large amounts of seeds to ensure that at least some of the seeds will be dispersed to suitable surroundings and grow to maturity. Many seeds and fruits produced are food sources for animals.

Seed dispersal is carried out by the wind, animals, water and by dehiscing (splitting and shooting out seeds) and some examples can be seen in Figure 34. This process coupled with the cross-fertilisation of plants extends the genetic diversity and range within species. This helps to ensure the species continuity, strength and resistance to disease or catastrophe.

Wind dispersal

Sycamore fruits

Animal dispersal

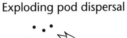

Strawberry

Dandelion

Exploding pod dispersal

Vetch

Figure 34 Seed dispersal

Animals

Sexual reproduction in animals involves internal or external fertilisation of the egg. In external reproduction a large number of eggs are produced and fertilised outside the female body by the male. Many will be eaten by predators or not survive because of environmental conditions and so large quantities of egg and sperm are normal. Most external fertilisation of ova takes place in water so is found within many of the invertebrate groups of animals and fishes and amphibians within the vertebrates. Usually the parents play little part in the development of the young after fertilisation.

As animals moved on to the land internal fertilisation became a crucial factor in survival. Amphibians have to return to the water to breed. The higher order vertebrates and many invertebrates, particularly the arthropods, have developed ways of internally fertilising eggs so that they do not need to return to water to breed. In looking at sexual reproduction in animals we focus particularly on humans but will briefly consider insects.

Insects as the largest group in the arthropods have a life cycle that normally has four very distinct changes or stages in it.

Eggs are fertilised internally and are either laid in a suitably protective place or carried round by one of the adults until they hatch.

Each stage involves distinct changes in the shape and form of the animals. A typical life cycle includes egg, larva, pupa and adult stages. This life cycle is said to show complete **metamorphosis** (meta means change and morphis shape), that is four stages of change of shape and form as shown in Figure 35.

Some insects, like locusts and cockroaches, do not change shape completely as they grow and develop to adulthood, but instead when the egg hatches they emerge as a small immature animal that looks like the adult. This nymph, as it is called, feeds and grows until its outer skeleton or exoskeleton will not let it grow any more. At this stage the nymph moults its skin and the new skin is softer and allows for more growth. The number of moults is usually five before the adult becomes sexually mature and ready to reproduce. This type of life cycle is called **incomplete metamorphosis**.

Other animals such as amphibians show different stages in their life cycle that reflect their adaptation to the environment that they live in.

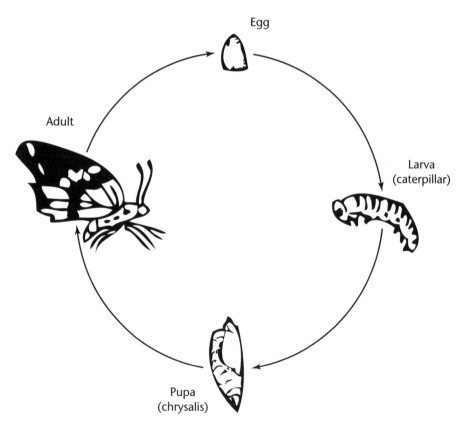

Figure 35 Life cycle of a butterfly (Complete metamorphosis)

Frogs and toads lay large quantities of eggs which are fertilised externally by the male. These eggs hatch in water and the tadpoles go through some very observable physical changes as they grow. They absorb the external gills and grow back legs first and then front legs. The tail is absorbed into the body as the frog reaches maturity and stages in this life cycle are shown in Figure 36.

Studying different animal forms and their life cycles is fascinating. This book only highlights a few examples to show the many varied ways animals live and reproduce.

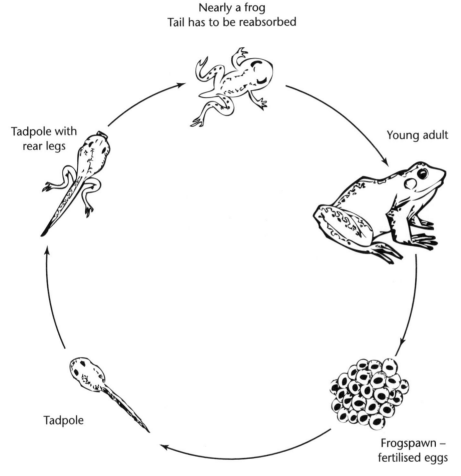

Figure 36 Life cycle of a frog

Humans

Reproduction in humans can only occur when males and females have reached sexual maturity.

Females are capable of becoming sexually active once they reach puberty and begin ovulating and menstruating. This process is controlled by sex hormones and brings about the development of secondary sexual characteristics such as breasts, body hair and a change of shape, especially the widening of the hips.

Puberty in males heralds the production of sperm in the testes and secondary sexual characteristics such as the voice breaking and the growth of body hair.

Human cells normally have 46 (or 23 pairs of) **chromosomes** in the nucleus. These chromosomes contain all the information about that person and how they will develop and grow. When the cells in the ovary or testis divide to form gametes (egg or sperm) the number of chromosomes is halved. This special cell division that halves the number of chromosomes in an egg or sperm is called **meiosis**. It is explained in more detail in Chapter 6. It is important to realise here that when fertilisation of the egg by the sperm happens a zygote is formed. This zygote has 46 chromosomes – 23 from the egg + 23 from the sperm. If this halving did not happen the zygote would have 92 chromosomes and would not be viable.

(a) Male

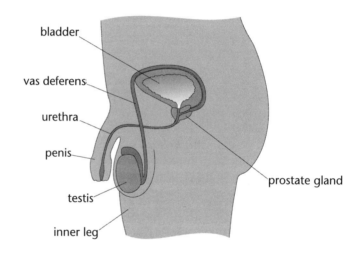

(b) Female

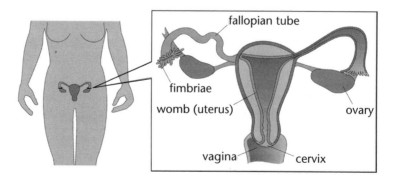

Figure 37 Male and female reproductive systems

Sexual intercourse takes place when the erect penis is inserted into the vagina. Ejaculation occurs and large numbers of sperm are released by reflex muscular spasms that occur during orgasm. The sperm swim towards the ovum that has been released into the fallopian tube. One sperm fuses with the egg and a zygote is formed. Fertilisation has taken place. The zygote begins to divide, replicating identical cells to start with. These then begin to differentiate as the zygote grows and tissues and organs begin to form. The zygote, now a ball of cells known as a blastocyst, moves down the fallopian tube to the uterus where it implants in the lining of the womb. This takes place about a week after fertilisation. Once implanted in the womb the placenta develops alongside the embryo and acts as the crucial link between the mother and the foetus. There is no direct link of blood supplies but food and waste materials are exchanged across the placenta by diffusion. The embryo develops in a fluid-filled sac, which is surrounded by a membrane, known as the amnion. This provides support and protection for the baby. From about two months onwards the embryo is recognisable as a human foetus with arms, legs and spinal cord developing. It takes nine months for the foetus to grow to the stage when it is ready to be born.

The birth of the baby happens when the wall of the uterus begins to contract at regular intervals, forcing the baby down the birth canal. The early stages of labour are concerned with the dilation of the cervix and widening of the birth canal. As the contractions increase in intensity and frequency the baby is ready to be pushed out through the birth canal. The amniotic sac often bursts at this stage and the fluid is released. This last part is hard work and involves the mother in pushing the baby out as the uterus contracts. Most babies are born head first and as they are born the umbilical cord which connected the baby to the placenta is cut. The afterbirth or the placenta is delivered a few minutes after the baby.

Human babies are helpless and very dependent on parental care for many years. Other mammals such as deer are often able to walk within minutes of being born so that they can move away from danger. Young animals are easy prey for predators.

Healthy lifestyles

How we behave and what we eat and drink can have very important effects on our health and emotional well-being. Developing a positive approach to life and maintaining our health and fitness needs us to consider many factors.

Making decisions about what and when we eat, what we wear, when and how we wash and what exercise we take needs to be informed by our understanding of how our body works and how to keep it healthy. It is important to be aware of how infections can be spread so that individual and collective decisions about actions and routines that we follow are successful.

Personal hygiene

Personal hygiene, as well as having a social dimension (e.g. body odour), is about preventing illness and infection. Washing oneself, washing clothes, handling and storing food safely, cleaning teeth and washing hair regularly are all part of the process of preventing illness.

Many factors such us diet, exercise, drugs, alcohol and tobacco can have positive and negative effects on our bodies and lifestyle.

Diet

It is important that we are aware of the need for a balanced diet over a period of time. It is not bad to eat foods such as hamburgers but it is probably not good to eat hamburgers at every meal for they do not provide all the nutrients that we need to maintain healthy bones, teeth and body. In a balanced diet it is important to eat carbohydrates for energy, proteins for growth and repair, and fats for insulation and energy.

Alongside these it is important to include minerals and vitamins in a diet. These are found in a range of foods and are needed in small quantities to ensure healthy tissues and organs. Variety in our food means that we are more likely to consume the necessary ingredients of a balanced diet and also it is more interesting to eat a range of foods.

Exercise

In order to maintain physical fitness regular exercise is needed. To be effective the exercise, whatever it is, needs to raise the heartbeat and so increase the flow of blood round the body. This increases the capillary network and keeps it trim and working more effectively. It also keeps the muscles and joints in working order as well as giving one a feeling of well-being. Many people say they work better if they undertake regular exercise.

It is as important not to do too much exercise as it is to do no exercise. Over-exercise can cause particular problems such as strain, broken bones and deformity, if carried to extreme. A balance between rest and exercise is therefore important. The body's main way of resting is through sleep. An average of eight hours' sleep per night is commonly advised for adults. Young children need more sleep as their metabolic rate is higher because of greater activity and growth and so more sleep is needed to recover.

Drugs

People often associate all drugs with bad effects but in fact many drugs are particularly useful in controlling or curing illness. It is the abuse or misuse of these medicinal drugs that can cause problems. Many medicinal drugs and solvents affect the nervous system. Many drugs give the taker a sense of feeling calm, or of stimulation, and can change their outlook or perception on events. Regular use of such drugs can develop a dependency or addiction. Also the more you use a drug the more you need to take to achieve the same effect. Analgesics suppress the awareness of pain, sedatives are used to slow the nervous system and hallucinogenics (e.g. cannabis and LSD) change perceptions.

Alcohol

In small amounts alcohol is said to be beneficial to health, e.g. it can contribute to the prevention of heart disease. A sedative drug, it can work in a similar way to drugs producing a sense of well-being and relax tension.

Drinking too much at one time can lead to loss of control, blurred vision and speech, poor co-ordination and inability to judge situations sensibly. Severe drinking bouts can be very dangerous, particularly in the young. They can lead to coma and even death.

Alcoholics are people who have become addicted to alcohol in the same way that drug addicts become dependent on a stimulant. The physical effects of regular heavy drinking can be life threatening. It can cause severe damage to the liver and destroy brain cells, as well as cause social problems such as loss of job, relationships and self-esteem.

Educating young people in a sensible approach to alcohol is an important preventative measure that society has a responsibility to take.

Tobacco

This is another form of addiction that has similar consequences to those listed above. Tobacco is a stimulant but is also addictive. The drug nicotine in cigarettes and tobacco is responsible for this.

Smoking affects various systems in the body. It attacks the lining of the lungs and trachea, stopping the cells lining them from taking in oxygen effectively. It can actually destroy the cells and reduce the area for gaseous exchange. The tar in tobacco is key in this reduction and is also a carcinogen, i.e., it causes cancer. Cancer is an uncontrolled growth of abnormal cells that can spread to other parts of the body attacking cells there. Smoking increases a person's chances of developing lung cancer.

The other main health anxiety about smoking is the effect it has on the heart. Smoke contains carbon monoxide and as it is inhaled into the lungs it passes into the blood. As it combines with the haemoglobin this reduces the efficiency of oxygenating the blood. In this way it reduces people's ability to do exercise, as the amount of oxygen in the blood is reduced. Carbon monoxide can also increase the amount of fat being deposited round the arteries which stops them being able to contract and relax as freely. This can lead to heart attacks.

There are also social aspects to smoking that are not always appreciated by some people. People who do not smoke, inhale smoke, whether or not they want to if people are able to smoke in a public place. Many places now provide specific rooms or spaces for smokers so that people can choose whether or not to be involved in secondary smoking. The smell from smoking also penetrates clothing and furnishings, and some people find this unpleasant.

In this section we have seen that:

- Plants and animals are sensitive to their surroundings.
- Plants and animals reproduce. This can be asexual or sexual.
- Seeds are dispersed in different ways.
- Sexual reproduction involves the fertilisation of an egg by a male gamete.
- Our health can be affected by exercise, diet, drugs, alcohol and tobacco.

6 Continuity and Change

In this chapter we explore the understandings that underlie the variety of life and how all the diverse forms of things alive today derived from those living in the past. Very few resources are needed and they are listed in the specific activities if necessary.

The key ideas included are:

- recognising the diversity of life
- thinking about how to group plants and animals using similarities and differences
- the need to classify living things into major biological groups understanding individual variation
- looking at how organisms have changed over time
- finding the evidence for evolution.

Diversity in living things | Activity 1

In one minute write a list of as many living things as you can. Look at the list – can you divide them into groups? What criteria did you use to group them?

Commentary

Most of us are able to group objects into plants and animals and may even have divided them into sub-groups under either of those headings, e.g. putting a fly into a group called insects. We may be able to sort some plants – but often we are not as knowledgeable about plants, unless a keen gardener. Sorting plants and animals and other living things into groups is known as classification.

For this we use similarities and differences in appearance or morphology to distinguish between types.

Living things can be divided into plants and animals but modern classifications include fungi, bacteria, protoctista and viruses as four extra kingdoms. Viruses operate differently because they can only reproduce by entering a cell of another organism and using the growth mechanisms in that cell.

Can you now regroup your lists or had you already taken account of these groups?

We do not always use scientific terms in the correct way in everyday conversation. For example, we are animals but in our everyday life we use the terms 'humans' or 'people' to refer to us, and use the term 'animal' to mean all other creatures (although birds are sometimes wrongly separated from animals).

The number of different living things is difficult to estimate because there are still many species that have not been found or identified yet. Also many scientists do not agree with each other about the grouping or classification of animals and particular plants.

When discussing diversity and classification we frequently use the term **species**. What is a species? In biological terms a species is a population of organisms that can interbreed with one another, but are reproductively isolated from other groups of organisms. Members of the same species can therefore exchange genetic information.

Activity 2	Classifying arthropods

Figure 38 shows nine different arthropods.

Write down two characteristics that they all share.

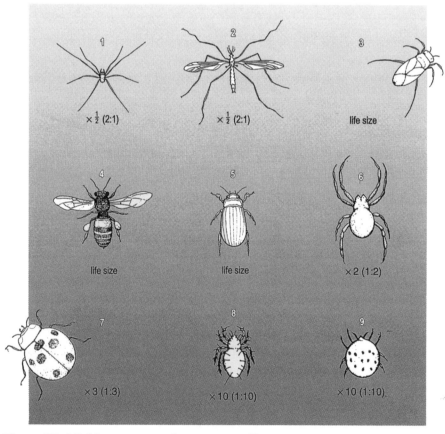

Figure 38 Making groups of creepy crawlies
(Source: *adapted from Adey et al., 1989*)

Now list at least *four* characteristics you can see that are not common to all the animals.

Next, use one of the characteristics that are not common to all animals to make two groups.

Now choose another and divide all the animals into two different groups.

Finally, use both characteristics together to make four groups of animals.

Design a way to display your responses to this activity, so that a friend could easily interpret your groups and reasons for the groups.

Commentary

You should have noticed similarities like jointed legs and antennae – did you spot any others?

How about differences? These could include presence/absence of wings, number of legs, number of body segments, patterns on the body and size. Notice that not all the animals are drawn to the same scale. This could be important in distinguishing between animals 6 and 8, but size alone is not an ideal characteristic to use when classifying, as organisms of the same species can be different sizes – they grow! Close observation and comparison are important skills when classifying animals and using **keys** – systems that have considered the characteristics that allow you to identify different species.

Some groups of organisms are more similar to each other than others, for example cat-like animals form a closely related group that is very different from the group containing insects. But both cats and insects are animals and they have more in common with each other than with flowering plants. The system of putting similar things together into groups and then into larger groups is termed the **taxonomic hierarchy**. The arrangement of millions of species in the taxonomic scheme of classification reflects the evolutionary relationships between the members of each group. Within each kingdom there are progressively smaller divisions, each nesting within another as shown in Table 11.

This system of classification, which groups species that are similar to one another in form into the next group, the genus (plural genera), similar

Table 11 The taxonomic hierarchy.

Kingdoms	The most inclusive category
Phyla	Within each kingdom
Classes	Within each phylum
Orders	Within each class
Families	Within each order
Genera	Within each family
Species	Within each genus

genera into the same family, and so on through order, class, phylum and kingdom, was first devised by the Swedish biologist Carl von Linné (1707–78), better known by the Latinised form of his name, Carolus Linnaeus.

Along with the system for classifying organisms, Linnaeus devised a system for naming them. Each species is given two Latin names. The first of these, the generic name, is the genus to which the organism belongs, and the second, specific, name indicates the species. In science the names are printed in italics (or underlined if writing by hand). The generic name comes first and has an initial capital letter; the specific name follows and begins with a lower-case letter. For example, the blackbird is *Turdus merula* and the song thrush is *Turdus philomelos*. The blackbird and song thrush have many similarities but are classified as separate species because they cannot interbreed and produce fertile offspring. When it is clear which genus is being referred to, it is common to abbreviate the generic name to its initial letter, followed by a full stop. For example, the fruit-fly *Drosophila melanogaster* could be abbreviated to *D. melanogaster*.

Figure 39 illustrates how the classification system works for one group of animals, the arthropods, which share the characteristics of a hard external skeleton, a segmented body and jointed limbs.

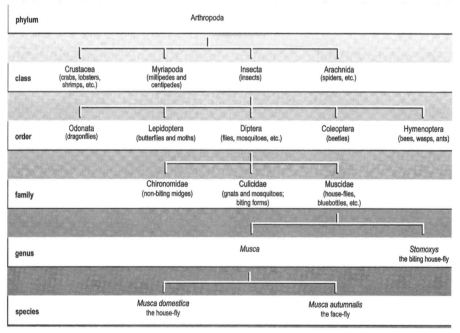

Figure 39 An example of the classification of a group of animals: the arthropods

You will notice that Figure 39 includes popular names as well as scientific ones. Why use scientific names at all? First, the scientific name is international while popular names vary from one country to another and often within a country. Second, the name gives an indication of how organisms are related. The lion is *Panther leo* and the leopard is *Panthera pardus*. Lions and leopards are closely related and their generic name reflects this. However, the cheetah is not closely related to either lions or leopards and has the quite different scientific name *Acinonyx jubatus*.

In such a scheme of natural classification the names describe evolutionary relationships as far as we know them. Figure 40 illustrates part of the animal kingdom classification to show where mammals and humans fit into the scheme.

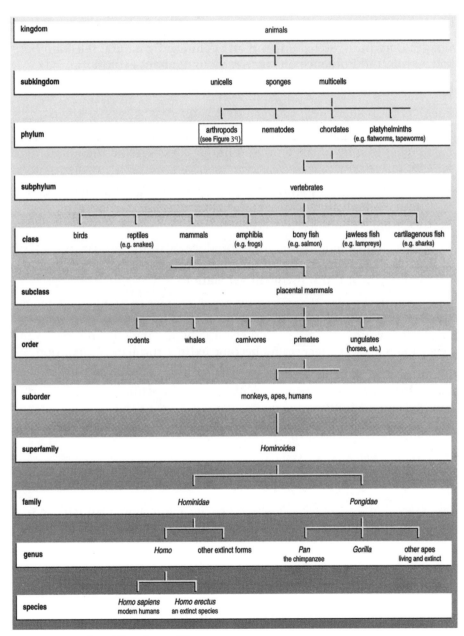

Figure 40 Classification of humans

What is evolution?

Here we look at the way in which scientific ideas have changed over the years. Before about 4,000 million years ago there was no life on Earth; now there are millions of kinds of different organisms. Since life began on our planet, whole groups of organisms have flourished and become extinct. For example, the dinosaurs were on Earth from about 200 million years ago until they died out 65 million years ago. Insects and flowering plants have been on Earth for about 130 million years and humans for only around 300,000 years. The processes by which changes in life forms have occurred over time are encompassed in the term **evolution**.

Charles Darwin's (1809–82) theory of evolution by natural selection has had a profound influence on current thought about evolution.

Darwin's theory has four basic premises:

1   More individuals are produced than can survive.

2   There is a struggle for existence because of the difference between the number of individuals produced in reproduction and the number that can survive.

3   Individuals show variation. No two individuals are exactly the same. Those with advantageous features have a greater chance of survival in this struggle (natural selection).

4   As selected varieties will tend to produce offspring similar to themselves (the principle of inheritance), these varieties will become more abundant in subsequent generations.

Selected varieties may therefore increase in frequency within a population, altering its character with time. Darwin went on to argue that such favoured varieties could eventually become separate species. As new species arose, others would become extinct through competition.

To understand these ideas you need to know something about the concepts of adaptation, fitness, inheritance, competition and selection, and their interactions.

Activity 3	Evolutionary terms

Take each term – adaptation, fitness, inheritance, mutation, selection – in turn and try to explain what you think it means. Look at Darwin's basic premises.

Adaptation

Organisms appear to be 'adapted' to their environment and there is a close relationship between the form or structure of an organism and its function – its form suits the particular type of environment in which it lives. Adaptation can take many different forms; one example is camouflage. A stick insect's legs and body are so twig-like in colour and shape that the insect is difficult to see in its natural surroundings. Animals that are well camouflaged often tend to behave in a way that makes them even less visible, such as remaining motionless near a predator. By contrast, other insects, such as bees and wasps, are brightly coloured and move about openly. In this case they have a defence mechanism – a sting – and their bright colouration may act as a warning to would-be predators.

Fitness

Fitness is the term used to define the relative ability of an organism to survive and produce offspring that can themselves survive to produce offspring.

H.B.D. Kettlewell in the 1950s studied the frequency of two different coloured forms of the peppered moth in different habitats, namely, a sooty piece of woodland and an unpolluted woodland. He looked at two out of the three forms of the peppered moth, the typical, which is pale and speckled, and the carbonaria form, which is sooty black. The moths are active at night and settle on the bark of trees during the day. They are normally hard to see with the naked eye because of their camouflage, however Kettlewell compared how the different types fared in each environment. Through various activities and patterns of release he was able to show that the longer an organism survived the more likely it was to produce offspring. He showed that the typical pepper moth, because it was more easily seen in the sooty woodland, was first to be eaten by predators, leaving more carbonaria to reach a reproductive stage.

Natural selection is the term used to describe the process whereby the nature of the environment determines the relative fitnesses of different inherited characteristics.

Inheritance

This is the process of passing genetic information from generation to generation. This process involves chromosomes that are found in the nucleus. A character is inherited and beneficial to organisms in a particular environment. Organisms with that character will increase at the expense of other forms. This is natural selection by 'survival of the fittest' and contributes to evolution. However, if a character is not inherited but is acquired during the organism's lifetime, it is not passed on to offspring, so the frequency of the character will not change (except randomly) from generation to generation.

Mutation

This occurs when an organism develops a new characteristic that has not been seen in an individual before. There are several ways that mutations occur and all affect the functioning of DNA (deoxyribonucleic acid). They usually happen when the DNA is replicating itself.

Mutations are common but an organism possessing a mutation is rare and less able to survive than other members of the population. However, in certain circumstances, for instance if the environment were to change, the mutant form might be better able to survive and produce offspring. Mutations are important because they are a source of new characteristics.

Mutant characters tend to occur as a well-defined proportion of a total population. In humans, cystic fibrosis has an incidence of 1 in 2,000 in Northern Europe. The disease of haemophilia, where blood clotting is impaired, is a result of a mutation and has an incidence of around 1 in 5,000 births. Most mutations are not advantageous, and many are lethal, so few or no offspring are produced and the mutations are not passed on to future generations. However, mutations are also responsible for different forms of characters, such as eye and hair colour, which do not appear to confer different biological fitnesses in humans – although some may be preferred by some individuals! The same sorts of differences in other animals could confer quite different fitnesses. Think how the coat colour of a small rodent could affect predation by owls in different coloured environments. Mutations may also be brought about by a wide range of environmental factors, including chemicals and radiation.

When considering inheritance we need to bear in mind that some characteristics are caused or influenced by environmental factors and are not inherited. Shape, size, behaviour and sometimes colour may all be affected by environmental factors. In some cases the effect is only slight, but in other cases the effect can be quite dramatic. For example. the colour of hydrangea flowers is determined by soil type: blue flowers occur only when the plant is growing in an acid soil; in other soils the flowers are either pink or white.

These basic definitions are important and will help us to explore a little more how characteristics are passed on from generation to generation and how they change over time.

How does inheritance work?

To understand the variation that we see between individuals of the same species we need to look at the mechanism by which characteristics are passed from parent to offspring. The study of the way features or characteristics are passed from one generation to another is called **genetics**. The foundations of modern genetics were laid by the monk Gregor Mendel, who experimented on the garden pea in the monastery garden at Brno in Czechoslovakia. His results were published in 1865 but his work was essentially ignored until 1900. Mendel used three procedures in his study of inheritance. First, he experimented, crossing plants that looked different, for example in flower colour. Second, he counted the number of offspring of each type. Third, he ensured that the original stocks from which his crosses were derived were pure breeding. His results were presented as statistics, which were obtained by counting many specimens and calculating averages. A strain of plants (or animals) is pure breeding for a character when all breeding within the strain leads to offspring with the same character, for example flowers with the same colour. Starting with pure-breeding strains of peas was a key factor in enabling Mendel to make sense of the ratios of different forms of offspring he obtained.

In Mendel's experiments with peas, he selected and cross-pollinated pure-breeding plants that had purple flowers with those that had white flowers. All of the offspring, known as the F_1 generation, had purple flowers. The white-flowered characteristic had apparently disappeared. He then crossed these purple-flowered F_1 plants and found that three-quarters of the offspring in the next generation (the F_2 generation) had purple flowers and one-quarter white flowers – the white characteristics had reappeared. This ratio of 3:1 in the F_2 generation was found for many pairs of characters investigated; examples are shown in Table 12.

Table 12 The numbers of F_2 offspring possessing particular characters in seven breeding experiments carried out by Mendel. The character in italics is the one that is found in all of the F_1 generation offspring

Experiment number	Character	Numbers	Ratio
1	Flower colour: *purple* or white	705 : 224	3.15 : 1
2	Seed shape: *round* or wrinkled	5,474 : 1,850	2.96 : 1
3	Seed colour: *yellow* or green	6,022 : 2,001	3.01 : 1
4	Pod shape: *inflated* or constricted	882 : 299	2.95 : 1
5	Pod colour: *green* or yellow	428 : 152	2.82 : 1
6	Flower position: *along stem* or at tip	651 : 207	3.14 : 1
7	Stem length: *long* or short	787 : 277	2.84 : 1

We now use the terms **dominant** for the character that masks the other in the F_1 generation and **recessive** for the character that is so masked and reappears in the F_2 generation. If some of the purple-flowered F_2 plants were self-pollinated they would produced only progeny with purple flowers. However, when other purple-flowered F_2 plants were self-pollinated they produce both purple- and white-flowered offspring in the ratio of 3 purple to 1 white. How can this be? Figure 41 indicates how the dominant and recessive characters combine to give the forms Mendel observed.

The colour of the pea flowers is shown to be inherited, so the genetic make-up of plants with purple flowers must be different from that of plants with white flowers. There is something in plants with purple flowers that gives the instructions for the synthesis of purple pigment and something in the white-flowered plants that give instructions that result in white flowers. This 'something' is what we call a **gene**. In this example with different flower colours, each plant has two genes

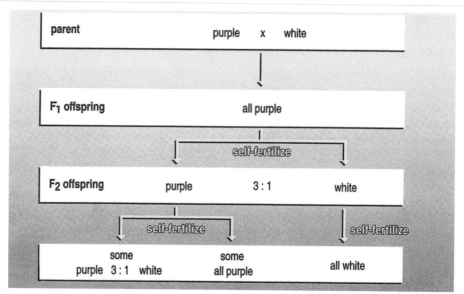

Figure 41 *The result of crossing pure-breeding purple- and white-flowered peas*

responsible for flower colour, and when the form of the gene (each form of a gene is known as an allele) determining the purple pigment is present, flowers are purple. When the reproductive cells (the **gametes**) of pollen and eggs are produced, one copy of the flower colour gene is passed to each gamete in each parent plant. When pollen and egg meet and fertilisation occurs, the plant that develops from the resultant **zygote** has two genes for flower colour again. The flower colour will depend on which forms of the genes have been inherited.

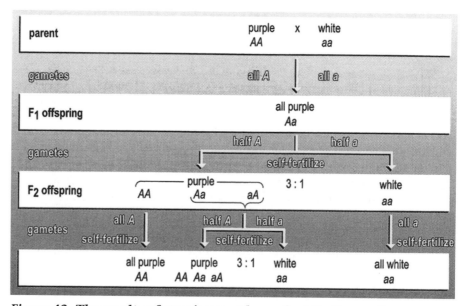

Figure 42 *The results of crossing purple- and white-flowered peas, with A representing the dominant purple form and a representing the recessive white form of the gene for flower colour*

We can use symbols to represent the genes. In scientific convention, **capital** letters are used to represent **dominant** forms and **lower-case** letters to represent **recessive** forms.

You will see from Figure 42 that purple-flowered plants can result from the combination of two *A* forms of gene or from an *A* with an *a*. The pair of genes making up the combination is known as the **genotype**. The expression of the combination of the genes, or what it looks like, in this case the colour, is known as the **phenotype** of the organism. Therefore, the purple-flowered phenotype can arise from two different genotypes, *AA* and *Aa*. The white-flowered phenotype has only one possible genotype, *aa*. When a plant with genotype *Aa* produces pollen, the number of grains with the *A* gene equals the number of grains with the *a* gene. In the same way, equal numbers of eggs with *A* and *a* genes will be produced from a plant with genotype *Aa*. You can show the combinations of offspring that result from a cross using a diagram known as a Punnett square, as in Figure 43.

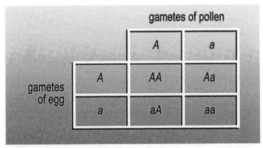

Figure 43 Punnett square to show the genotypes of the offspring of a cross between plants both with genotypes Aa

---

A Punnett square   Activity 4

Try to develop your own Punnett square. Let's use the simple variation of blue and brown eyes. Eye colour does not just work with these two forms of the gene but for our purposes it will do. Brown eyes (B) have the dominant gene and blue eyes have a recessive gene.

What are the possible genotypes for brown and blue eyes?

Make a Punnett square to show the combinations that can occur.

Commentary

The phenotype for brown eyes has two genotypes for brown and would be BB written like this (pure bred) or Bb. BB is known homozygous and Bb is known heterozygous. The genotypes for blue eyes is always bb.

Activity 5 — A blue-eyed child

If a brown-eyed person marries a blue-eyed person what is the chance of having a blue-eyed baby if the brown-eyed parent does not have pure bred brown eyes?

Commentary

If you put the parents at the top and then follow the exchange below you can see how the cross shows the possible offspring.

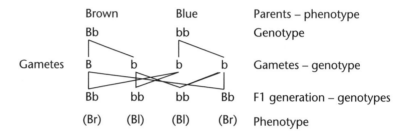

	Brown		Blue		Parents – phenotype
	Bb		bb		Genotype
Gametes	B	b	b	b	Gametes – genotype
	Bb	bb	bb	Bb	F1 generation – genotypes
	(Br)	(Bl)	(Bl)	(Br)	Phenotype

The parents have a 50:50 chance of having a blue-eyed child each time an egg is fertilised.

Activity 6 — A brown-eyed child

If two heterozygous brown-eyed parents (Bb) have offspring what is the chance of having blue-eyed children? Try the same kind of crosses as above.

Commentary

You should find they have a 3:1 chance for brown eyes and 1:3 for blue eyes. There is a greater chance of having a heterozygous brown-eyed child.

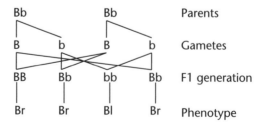

Bb		Bb		Parents
B	b	B	b	Gametes
BB	Bb	bb	Bb	F1 generation
Br	Br	Bl	Br	Phenotype

Passing on genetic information

Chromosomes are found in pairs and can be seen under the microscope most easily when cells are dividing. A chromosome looks like a rod or thread under the light microscope and consists of a single molecule of **DNA** packaged with proteins. The genes are made of DNA (deoxyribonucleic acid), which is found in structures inside the chromosomes.

Figure 44 shows the 46 chromosomes of a human male arranged in pairs. This arrangement to show the number of pairs of chromosomes is known as a **karyotype**. There are 22 matching pairs and two sex chromosomes, X and Y, that differ in size.

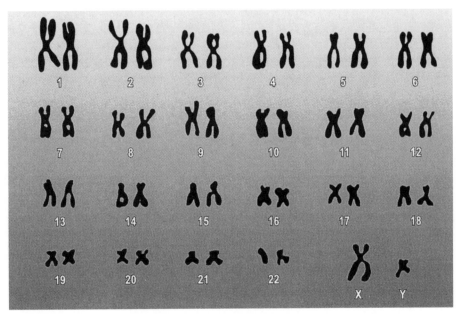

Figure 44 The karyotype of a human male

Sometimes extra chromosomes are found. For example, if a person has three copies of chromosome 21 there is a profound effect on the phenotype, resulting in Down's syndrome.

Fertilisation

At fertilisation, genetic material from the gametes of the two parents is joined together to form a new individual. In humans the male gamete is the sperm and female the egg. Once fertilisation has occurred, the resultant zygote (embryo cell) and the offspring that develops from it has a genotype that is a combination of genetic characteristics from both parents.

The number of chromosomes in the nucleus of the offspring's cells is the same as that in the nucleus of the parents' cells. So, before they combine at fertilisation, the gametes must have half the chromosome number of the parents. This is achieved by a special type of cell division, **meiosis,** which takes place when eggs and sperm are produced. Figure 45 summarises the processes of meiosis and fertilisation.

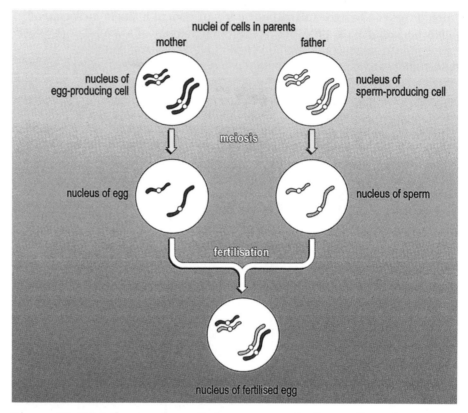

Figure 45 How the numbers of chromosomes in the nucleus change with gamete production and fertilisation. Only two pairs of chromosomes are shown for simplicity

The whole process of meiosis can take days, months or even years to complete, depending on the species of animal or plant involved.

During the process of meiosis there is some reciprocal exchange of genetic information between pairs of chromosomes. In addition, there is random assortment of each chromosome of a pair between the gametes. The more chromosomes an organism has, the more permutations are possible. The result is that very many different gene combinations can be produced in the gametes of any individual organism. If you try to imagine the variety of gene combinations possible when a zygote is formed after fertilisation, it is easy to appreciate that although inherited traits do run in families, no two children are identical unless they are identical twins formed from the same zygote. Therefore, populations that have more than one form of many different genes have a huge variety of genetic backgrounds on which natural selection can act.

Think back to the information about karyotypes and Down's syndrome. The incidence of having a child with Down's syndrome increases with maternal age. Why is this? In human females meiosis starts while the female-to-be is still an embryo inside her mother's womb and halts at an early stage of the process before the baby is born. Meiosis then starts up again at puberty, and one cell completes the cycle that gives an egg each time she undergoes a menstrual cycle. A cell that completes meiosis soon after puberty has been arrested at this early stage for 10–14 years, but a cell that completes meiosis late in a woman's reproductive life will have been arrested for around 50 years. Such very long durations of meiosis are accompanied by risks of genetic abnormalities. The usually precise divisions of meiosis may be disrupted, for example by the copies of chromosome 21 failing to separate. If the egg with two copies of chromosome 21 is fertilised, the resulting zygote will have three copies of chromosome 21. An egg with no copies of chromosome 21 never develops. A number of other genetic disorders are recognised in individuals with an extra chromosome, but in most cases the consequences of an extra or missing chromosome are so severe that no embryo develops.

How does one cell develop into a whole organism?

We have described how gametes are formed and how when two meet during fertilisation a zygote is produced. The new organism must develop from this single cell. This cell divides by the process known as **mitosis** to produce two new cells. These new cells then redivide until there are many new cells, all with the same genetic make-up as the zygote. Figure 46 shows the stages of mitosis. It is this process that allows an organism to grow and repair itself.

As an organism develops from the zygote, certain cells become specialised; in mammals, heart, nerve, liver, bone and blood cells appear. The formation of cells different from one another and from the original zygote is termed **differentiation**. During the early life of all organisms, growth, development and cellular differentiation must be highly ordered and controlled, with events occurring in the correct sequence and at the correct time. These sequential events are controlled by the DNA, where control genes switch other genes on and off at the appropriate time. What controls the control genes is still poorly understood and is the subject of much active research. Current work on how the cell cycle is controlled and on cancer cells (where the control of division and differentiation is defective) continues to provide further information about the processes that co-ordinate growth and development.

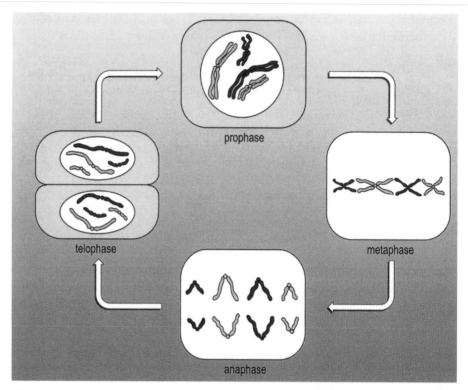

Figure 46 The successive stages of mitosis for an organism with four chromosomes. Cells divide and produce more cells with identical genetic make-up

How does DNA work?

A good way to think of DNA is as the chemical language of genes. Most genes are coded recipes for making proteins, and the code consists of the order in which four different chemical components are joined together in the length of DNA. These four components, or bases, are known as: **adenine** (A), **thymine** (T), **cytosine** (C), and **guanine** (G). Each gene has several thousand A, T, C and Gs joined together in a precise code that is different from any other gene.

Figure 47 show how A and T, and C and G pair up with one another, linking the two strands of a double helix of DNA like rungs on a ladder.

In 1953 Crick and Watson, along with others, discovered the double helix of DNA and enabled scientists to extend their understanding of inheritance.

Every second of every minute of every hour our cells use the gene recipes of DNA to make the proteins they need. When a particular protein is required, the part of the DNA that is the gene coding for that protein unwinds from its chromosome and a copy of the gene is made using one of the two strands as a template. This copy is not quite the same as the original DNA strand, as instead of T pairing with A, another chemical

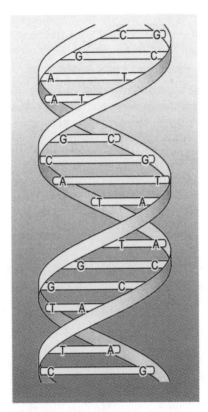

Figure 47 Model of the DNA double helix

component, **uracil**, is used. The chemical name of the 'copy' strand is **RNA** (ribonucleic acid). This particular type of RNA is known as messenger RNA (mRNA) as it takes the code for building a protein out of the nucleus of the cell to the cytoplasm where the rest of the machinery that is needed is located. Cellular components known as ribosomes and transfer RNAs (tRNAs) are involved in the processes that join **amino acids** together in the order dictated by the genetic code to synthesise proteins.

At the level of protein syntheses, a change in just one of the chemical components of DNA – A, T, C, or G – could result in a mutation. So, mutations can vary in size from a change in a single A, T, C or G component right up to a change in a whole DNA molecule, as in Down's syndrome. Remember that mutations may give rise to novel phenotypes and can form the basis for evolutionary change.

Genetic engineering

Genetic engineering can bring about changes in the genetic material within living cells by artificial means. Pieces of human DNA can be inserted into bacteria, where the bacteria's rapid rate of growth and division can be utilised to produce human proteins. Human insulin has been produced in this way to treat diabetes in place of insulin extracted from pig pancreas.

Genetic fingerprinting is a technique that exploits the variability of particular DNA base sequences between individuals. Genetic material, for example that found in blood from the scene of a crime, can be matched to specific individuals.

Discovering the characteristic sequences of bases in genes that give rise to genetic disorders enables carriers to be detected and permits pre-natal diagnosis of some genetic diseases. Gene therapy may be possible, whereby a 'normal' gene is inserted into the cells of an individual with a defective form of that gene.

Genetic engineering, genetic fingerprinting, identification of carriers of genetic disorders, pre-natal diagnosis of babies with genetic diseases and gene therapy all raise social and ethical questions. This text will not discuss these.

Natural selection can change gene frequences, but how can this lead to the evolution of new species?

Populations of living organisms are genetically very variable. We have seen examples where there are two alternative forms of a gene – there can be more alternatives, as in the A, B, O blood system and in some species of flowering plants, where there are many alternative forms of the genes responsible for preventing self-pollination. So, although an individual organism can have only two copies from those available for a character, there may be many possible combinations for some characters. This, coupled with the very many different characters in an organism, means that the permutations within a population may be vast. When we carry out investigations of relative fitness, we try to study the effects of changes in one character. However, natural selection does not act on only one character, but on the phenotype of the organism as a whole. Let us imagine that two populations of the same species become geographically separated from each other This could happen over thousands of years as a result, for example, of the climate gradually becoming drier so that the vegetation in lowland areas between two mountain ranges changes from woodland to scrub. Alternatively, it could happen in a matter of days as a result of lava flows from a volcano cutting off one area from another.

Populations that are separated so that individuals from the two groups can no longer meet to interbreed may diverge genetically from one another if different phenotypes are favoured in the different environments. If the populations are very small, each with a non-representative sample of the whole gene pool, there may be initial differences between the gene pools of the 'founder' populations. The effect of natural selection may be to further amplify these differences. If the two populations later come back into contact and have diverged in such a way that they cannot interbreed, **reproductive isolation** has occurred and they are now two separate species. Figure 48 illustrates this process of **geographical isolation** leading to speciation for butterflies.

If two geographically isolated populations rejoin and are not reproductively isolated then there is still only one species.

Reproductive isolation may also arise without geographical isolation. For example, small differences in the appearance or behaviour of individuals in two populations of a species may mean that they no longer recognise one another as breeding partners. **Behavioural isolation** may occur, for example, because members of the two populations develop different mating rituals, forage at different heights in a forest, feed at different

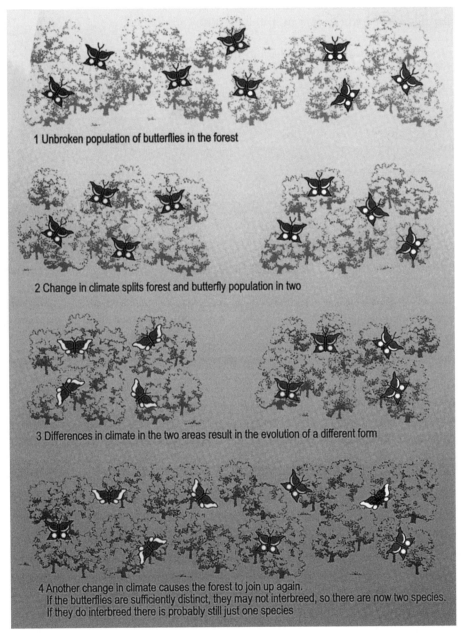

1 Unbroken population of butterflies in the forest

2 Change in climate splits forest and butterfly population in two

3 Differences in climate in the two areas result in the evolution of a different form

4 Another change in climate causes the forest to join up again.
 If the butterflies are sufficiently distinct, they may not interbreed, so there are now two species.
 If they do interbreed there is probably still just one species

Figure 48 A possible explanation of how populations diversify as a result of geographical isolation

times of day or flower at different times of the year. Once two populations have diverged in this way they may continue to develop in their own separate ways until they become reproductively isolated, and thus represent new species. A newly advantageous mutant gene in one species will not spread to the other species. A gene that is disadvantageous in one species but not in the other may disappear in the former but not in the latter. With time, newly formed species are likely to become still more distinct from one another. The formation of new species represents a crucial step in the evolutionary process. Darwin recognised this, and it is reflected in his major work on evolution entitled The *Origin of Species*, published in 1859.

7 Ecosystems

The aim of this chapter is to increase your scientific understanding of the ideas associated with the term **ecosystem**. You have probably come across words such as **species**, **habitat** and **community**, especially since they relate to environmental concerns that are so often the banner headline issues of the day. We start this chapter by defining terms and then exploring cycles and issues in the environment.

What do the words mean?	Activity 1

Jot down briefly what you understand by the terms species, habitat and community. Now use these ideas to explain what an ecosystem is.

Ecological terms

Species

Members of a species not only look similar (sexual differences apart) but they also freely interbreed. Sometimes members of two different species can interbreed, for example the ass (*Equus hemionus*) and the horse (*Equus caballus*), but the hybrid offspring (the mule) is usually sterile.

The genes of the individual within a species are part of a communal gene pool that doesn't leak out and isn't added to by the influence of the gene pools of other species.

Habitat

The habitat of an animal or plant is the space in which it lives. Different species often share the same habitat – think of a pond or a woodland. A small part of a habitat is called a microhabitat, for example the accumulated mud at the bottom of a pond. The individuals of the same species within a habitat or microhabitat represent a **population**.

Community

Different populations within a particular habitat are collectively termed a community. For example, a pond community would contain populations of snails, water boatmen and insect larvae (see Figure 49). These populations may be reproductively isolated, but in another sense communities are hotbeds of interaction – think of herbivorous animals (such as snails) feeding on plants, while other carnivorous animals (such as pike) feed on smaller animals.

Ecosystems

The term **ecosystem** means more than just the community of animals and plants that live in a particular habitat or group of habitats; it also includes the physical factors (the rainfall, the climate, the amount of light, the types of soil) that have an effect on organisms. The term reflects extensive *interaction* between living organisms and the physical world around them.

Life in a pond

Figure 49 shows a few (representative) animals and plants from a typical freshwater pond. Some are surface dwellers and are easily visible (e.g. water boatmen). Others, such as pond snails, live deeper in the water; to see them close to you would need to 'sweep' the pond using a strong aquarium net. You would need to use a very fine mesh net and microscope to capture and see some of the teeming invisible world of plants and animals that make up the microscopic **plankton**.

Figure 49 Cross section of a pond (phytoplankton are small, floating organisms that make their own food; water boatmen are predatory insects)

The plankton community is a rich mix of a huge range of different species; some move around, and are therefore likely to be animals, and others are coloured (usually green) and tend to stay put, and are therefore likely to be a particular type of plant called **algae**.

What plants do best	Activity 2

What is the significance of the green pigment in algae? Relate this to what you know about how plants make food.

Commentary

Photosynthesis is the process associated with the green pigment. It results in the formation of sugars, which are the major form of food for the plant. You'll appreciate that sugars are an important energy source, but algae are not so much 'making' or 'producing' energy as 'converting' the energy of sunlight into chemical energy in the form of sugars – a biochemical trick that no animal can perform. Plants, like algae, therefore store energy; they are termed **primary producers**.

The pond snail is an example of a **primary consumer**; some of the energy locked up in the plants on which it feeds is captured by its constant grazing. Mayfly larvae are also primary consumers. The mayfly's close relative, the dragonfly larva, is a fierce hunter, feeding on a variety of different primary consumers. It is a **secondary consumer**, as are sticklebacks and some other small fish. As you have probably guessed by now, the collective term given to animals such as herons that feed upon the animals that feed upon plants is a **tertiary consumer**. Animals often break these simple rules and can be included in two or three categories – for example, many owls are both secondary and tertiary consumers. Let's explore these ideas further in the woodland.

Woodlands

Trees are the most obvious organisms in deciduous woodland, but if you search the woodland floor you will find a host of worms, ants, spiders, beetles, woodlice, slugs and snails within the leaf litter. Their feeding activities help break down or decompose dead leaves. Smaller leaf fragments in turn become the raw material for microscopic decomposers (minute worms and small fungi).

Bacteria are present in huge numbers; a teaspoon's worth of woodland soil is likely to contain more than 4,000 million of them. They also get their nutrients by digesting dead remains and the waste products of others. The action of all these **decomposers** releases nutrients into the soil, helping to make the rich, brown, fertile soil that is characteristic of healthy woodland. These nutrients are in turn taken up by the roots of the growing trees and woodland plants on the forest floor.

Using the terms 'consumer' 'producer' 'primary' 'secondary' and 'tertiary' classify each of the following: bank voles; berries and seeds; grasses; weasels; tawny owls.

Commentary

Plants, such as grasses, are primary producers. Seeds and berries, which come from primary producers, contribute significantly to the diet of voles, which are therefore primary consumers. Because weasels feed on voles, they are secondary consumers. Like weasels, tawny owls sometimes feed on voles, so they are secondary consumers, but they also eat weasels, which means that they are tertiary consumers as well.

This is an example of a food chain; Figure 50 shows how another such chain can be represented.

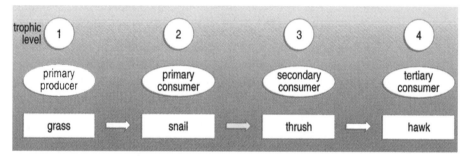

Figure 50 How food chains can be represented

In reality, in a complex ecosystem such as a woodland, primary producers are at the root of a number of chains (e.g. both mice and squirrels will feed on seeds) and a population of consumers (e.g. worms) will be a constituent of a number of different chains. This suggests a number of criss-crossing food chains – in other words it implies a food web of the type shown in Figure 51 for a temperate woodland habitat.

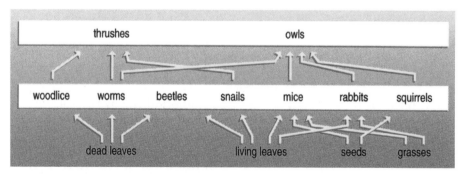

Figure 51 An example of a food web

Flow of energy through ecosystems

We now need to think about the movement of energy through ecosystems. Various layers are evident in the food chain in Figure 50 Each is called a **trophic level** – for example, primary producers belong to the lowest trophic level. You'll appreciate that a certain amount of the energy of sunlight will be 'trapped' by primary producers and 'stored' as the complex chemicals and structures that make up the plant tissue. When plants are eaten, some of the energy is transferred to the next layer as the plant tissue is digested. It is relatively easy to measure just how much energy (in terms of calories) is contained in plant (or animal) tissue by completely burning a sample of it in a piece of equipment called a bomb calorimeter – a name that neatly sums up the essence of the method. So, by estimating the total amount (i.e., the total mass) of tissue that is present in all the organisms within a particular trophic level, the total amount of stored energy in that level can be calculated. The total mass of organisms present per unit area of habitat is known as **biomass**. It can be expressed either in terms of mass (e.g. so many tonnes per square metre) or energy content (Joules per square metre).

The amount of energy 'lost' in moving from one level to the other will depend upon the availability of food to organisms and how well animals are able to digest and absorb the complex foodstuffs they take in. But even non-stop feeding and the most efficient digestion could not result in all the energy at one tropic level being passed on in its entirety. Animals do not just store the energy they obtain from their food, they use it – they need the energy to live and some energy is therefore 'lost' from their bodies. Remember energy cannot be lost; so what is meant here is that the energy is transferred from the animal to the environment, where it is less useful.

When the total energy content at each trophic level is presented graphically, the result is an energy pyramid (see Figure 52), because of energy 'loss' at each stage. In a woodland, the energy transfer is relatively inefficient, partly because so much of the plant material is woody and therefore unavailable to animals. So the pyramid is narrow at the top, as in Figure 52(b).

Energy pyramids reflect an ecological fact of life: predators are rarer than their prey. Think, for example, of the African savannah: antelopes and zebras are common, lions and leopards are less common. The biomass of the grassland is hundreds of times greater than the biomass of the zebras that feed upon it.

The difference in biomass at different trophic levels is even greater than it first appears, because the productivity of the grass is so great. Imagine what would happen if grazers such as zebras stopped their lawnmower action for some time. The effect would be akin to leaving your garden lawn untended during a fortnight's summer holiday. Before you went away, the biomass of the lawn may not have looked all that great. However, on your return, the productivity of the lawn is all too visible.

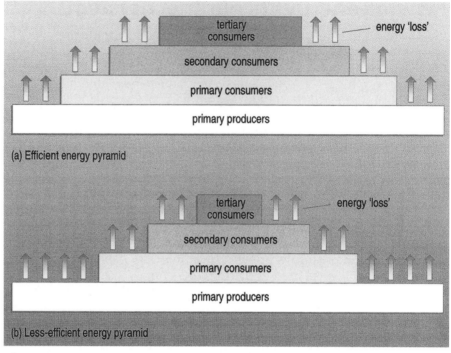

Figure 52 Energy pyramids

Consider the solar energy falling on the surface of green plants. In Figure 53, some is reflected or passes straight through (transmitted). You may know that light is a mix of components of differing wavelength.

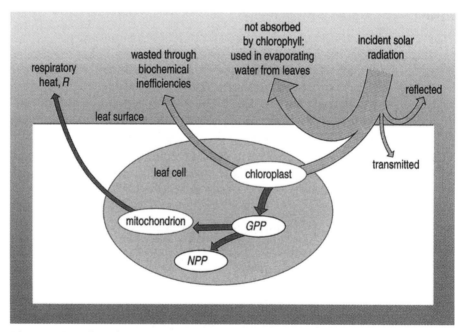

Figure 53 What happens to the incoming solar radiation (GPP and NPP are explained on page 135)

Photosynthesis can utilise light only of a certain wavelength, which means that some solar energy is 'wasted'. (In fact 'wasted' is not the right word – some of this energy helps to evaporate water from the surface of leaves.)

Evaporation of water requires a certain amount of energy to be transferred from the leaf. You need to know about the process of evaporation and what happens in terms of energy when evaporation occurs.

Some of the energy of the useful light (of the right wavelength) is captured by the chlorophyll molecules inside chloroplasts. During photosynthesis a complex series of chemical interactions takes place, each of which has a built-in inefficiency – in other words some of the energy of the sunlight is wasted rather than stored in a useful form. The result of all this is that only a tiny fraction – something between 1 and 5% – of the solar energy that reaches the leaf surface is actually converted into the chemical energy of newly synthesised organic compounds such as glucose.

Such captured energy is called the 'gross primary production' (*GPP*), see Figure 53. It can be measured as an amount of energy, expressed in so many kilojoules (kJ). The usual convention is to express *GPP* in terms of chemical energy (kJ) per unit area of ground (i.e., per square metre) per unit time (i.e., per year); it can also be expressed in terms of mass of product rather than amount of energy.

Not all the *GPP* contributes to plant growth, i.e., to an increase in the plant's biomass. Plants need energy simply to keep ticking over, and this comes from respiration (involving structures called mitochondria). This component can be measured, again in terms of kilojoules (or grams) per square metre per year and is usually termed *R* (for respiration), see Figure 53. So part of *GPP* is taken up by *R*; what we are left with is the 'net primary production' (*NPP*) – the amount of new material that can be used for plant growth or for storage as food reserves (e.g. as starch). This quite complex relationship can be expressed as an equation using just the abbreviations:

$$GPP = NPP + R$$

Try translating these abbreviations back into phrases and say this to yourself in words to help you appreciate its meaning.

Using some relatively simple measurements, estimates and calculations it is possible to enter figures into the equation to work out *NPP* in a variety of situations.

Work on energy budgets is part of the specialism of 'ecological energetics'. The approach is important because it allows us, for example, to rigorously quantify the productivity of different ecosystems. Table 13 shows just how much variation in mean *NPP* there is.

The low productivity of deserts is not surprising; the high NPP of rainforests is also well known and is likely to be one of the reasons why these are such species-rich environments.

Table 13 Mean NPP in different ecosystems

Ecosystem	NPP/grams per square metre per year
Desert	70
Open ocean	125
Coastal zones of ocean	500
Temperate grassland	600
Temperate deciduous forest	1,200
Estuaries	1,500
Tropical rainforest	2,200
Algal beds and reefs	2,500

In this section we have seen that:

- An ecosystem includes a variety of organisms and factors that interact producing particular conditions.

- Food pyramids show the flow of energy through an ecosystem.

- The gross primary production (*GPP*) is how much energy is captured by the leaf and used to synthesise organic compounds into glucose.

- The net primary production (*NPP*) varies considerably from ecosystem to ecosystem.

The cycling of nutrients – global cycles

Energy in the form of sunlight is available in a (virtually) inexhaustible supply. In contrast, the chemicals needed to support life on Earth – carbon, nitrogen and sodium, for example – are available in fixed amounts. This means that the basic chemicals needed to build and support plants and animals have to be used over and over again. The thought that an oxygen molecule you are currently breathing in may have been released by photosynthesis from an oak tree in a medieval forest a few hundred years ago is an intriguing one.

The carbon cycle

Chemicals such as carbon pass through a global cycle. At any one time, far more carbon is locked up (as inorganic carbon in rocks and organic carbon in fossil fuels) than is in circulation.

Carbon is taken up by plants, released by plants and animals after respiration and transferred through food chains.

Carbon also enters the atmosphere because of the action of decomposers. These are important on the deciduous woodland floor. Leaf litter is broken down by worms (and sometimes eaten by animals such as moles) and by bacteria and fungi; the material of the leaf is broken down into manageable portions and so becomes available to other decomposers. Eventually, the carbon contained in the leaf litter is recycled to the atmosphere, because of both respiration and death.

Figure 54 provides a picture of the carbon cycle. The breakdown, i.e., weathering, of rocks containing much calcium carbonate (mainly limestone and chalk) releases CO_2 and is held in the ocean when the gas dissolves to form compounds of carbonate and bicarbonate. Some of these return to the atmosphere – equilibrium is reached, with amounts of CO_2 going in roughly equal to amounts going out. A state of dynamic balance exists in all the compartments of the cycle – atmosphere, the oceans and the land (soil and rocks). The carbon cycle shown in Figure 54 is therefore balanced.

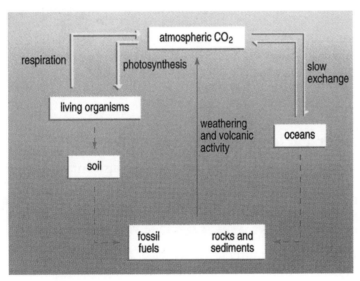

Figure 54 A model of the carbon cycle

Deforestation and burning fossil fuels both add to the amount of atmospheric CO_2 and could alter the natural balance. The burning of the cleared vegetation converts most of the biomass to CO_2. If the cleared area is subsequently ploughed, for agricultural use, CO_2 loss is much more substantial because the decomposition that ensues releases much of the carbon that was locked up in the soil. The amounts of carbon involved are staggeringly large: changes in how land is used in the tropics adds about 1,000 million tonnes per year; the total amount of carbon released by human activities is somewhere between 5,000 and 7,500 million tonnes per year.

What happens to all this extra carbon? Somewhere between one-half and two-thirds of it goes into the oceans, by the route shown in Figure 54 –

the oceans act as a storage receptacle, sometimes called a 'sink'. But so much CO_2 is currently being released into the atmosphere that the capacity of the oceans to mop up the excess has been exceeded – now the gas accumulates in the atmosphere.

Seasonal ups and downs are due to changes in primary productivity. In the summer, the greater amount of carbon fixed by plants decreases the concentration of CO_2 in the atmosphere. In the winter productivity is lower; this, together with continued release of CO_2 during respiration, leads to a higher concentration of atmospheric CO_2.

But what of the overall trend? A general upward trend has been confirmed at a number of monitoring stations around the world. In 1958, CO_2 concentration was about 315 parts of CO_2 per million parts of air by volume, i.e., 315 parts per million (ppm); now the concentration is rising. You may know that atmospheric CO_2 contributes significantly to the greenhouse effect, which accounts for warming of the Earth's surface. This effect certainly exists; were it not for CO_2 (and other greenhouse gases that trap heat) the Earth would be 33 °C cooler than it actually is. What is less certain is whether the increasing CO_2 levels have resulted in extra warming of the Earth's surface – so-called global warming. There is a strong consensus among scientists that, despite a number of uncertainties about the pace of likely temperature changes ahead, global warming is a reality and will be an environmental threat of increasing severity to future generations.

The water cycle

Life is based on water; typical plants and animals contain more than 70% water. With very few exceptions, all the reactions that together make up living processes within organisms occur in a watery 'soup'. Plants obtain most of their water from the soil through their roots and root hairs.

On Earth, water is constantly being recycled. One of the most important events on Earth is the regular rainfall, which brings plants and animals the constant supply of water they need to survive. But where does the rain come from and where does it go once it has fallen to the ground? The answers to these questions lie in an understanding of the water cycle.

Activity 4	The water cycle

The water cycle can be described simply as follows. The Sun's heat causes transpiration and the evaporation of water from the surface of oceans and lakes. Cooling and condensation of the resulting water vapour creates clouds. When clouds become saturated with water, the result is precipitation. Much of this percolates through the soil into underground water deposits, which seep through to the seas and oceans. Part of it runs off into rivers; part replenishes the water content of soils, to be absorbed by plants' roots and then to be lost again to the atmosphere by transpiration.

Design a chart or diagram to explain to colleagues how this cycle works to recycle water.

Your diagram should include the main features shown in Figure 55. Water is recycled around the system as it changes state. These changes are influenced by our orbit round the Sun and by changes in temperature.

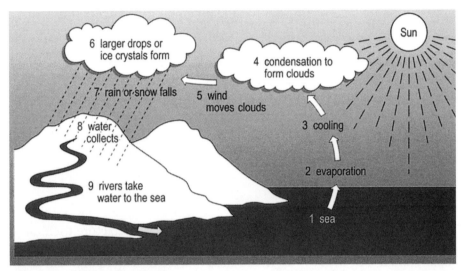

Figure 55 The water cycle

Because so many chemicals dissolve in or react with water (it is an *excellent* solvent), many threatening chemicals can enter the water cycle, e.g. DDT. This process of concentration or 'bioaccumulation' of toxic chemicals can be seen throughout the food chain, so that DDT levels in the fish-eating birds at the top of the chain can be as high as 25 ppm, which is high enough to poison them. Modern pesticides are more highly degradable and so do not persist in the environment.

Acid rain is another environmental problem. When fossil fuels are burnt, the by-products formed include the oxides of nitrogen (such as nitric oxide) and sulphur dioxide. When these pollutants react with water in the atmosphere, they form (very weak) solutions of nitric and sulphuric acid, respectively, which have the effect of increasing the acidity of rainfall at locations that may be hundreds of miles away from the source of the pollutants. Very acid conditions are known to adversely affect the growth of trees and to threaten plants and animals in lakes.

Acid rain	Activity 5

Lakes in areas where rocks have very low levels of limestone (calcium carbonate) are often particularly badly affected by acid rain. Why might this be so?

Commentary

Lime (an alkaline component) tends to reduce the effects of acidic components – an effect called buffering. So the impact of acid rain is reduced in the presence of limestone. If there are low levels of limestone then the effect of acid rain is much greater.

Acid rain therefore undoubtedly has the potential to cause environmental damage. But it can be difficult to link a particular observed effect (such as the death of fish in a lake) to a particular cause (the production of excessive amounts of oxides of nitrogen and sulphur).

Such issues are the stuff of present-day controversy, with environmental groups and industrial interests locked in dispute. In the case of acid rain, 'technical fixes' that restrict the emission of these pollutants from power stations are available but they are expensive; so there has to be a strong 'case for the prosecution' and the guilty party must be clearly identified before government advice or legislation comes into effect.

Nitrogen cycle

Plants need nitrogen to flourish and especially to manufacture their all-important proteins and DNA. Nitrogen is a very abundant element – it makes up 78% of the atmosphere, which represents a store of about a thousand million million tonnes. But only when the element nitrogen is combined with others to form compounds does it become accessible to plants in the form of nitrates, which are taken up through their roots (Figure 56). Inside the plants, nitrates are combined with the products of photosynthesis to form a variety of complex chemicals. Animals then use plants as their nitrogen source. If plants remove nitrates from the soil, how is the supply replenished?

First, naturally occurring bacteria in the soil can make nitrates out of atmospheric nitrogen. These 'nitrogen-fixing' bacteria do this by turning N2 first into ammonia and then into nitrates, much of which can be absorbed by plants. Some nitrogen-fixing bacteria are 'free-living' in the soil; others grow within root nodules associated with plants such as peas, beans and clover (such plants are called legumes).

Figure 56 also shows that other bacteria (the names need not concern you, but these are nitrifying and nitrobacter bacteria) transform the nitrogen contained within the proteins that are part of the dead and waste material of animals. These unseen recyclers are hard at work on cowpats, for example, breaking down protein to nitrates; the lush grass often visible around a cowpat is testimony to their effectiveness.

Some of these types of bacteria are present in such numbers that as much as 175 million tonnes of nitrogen is fixed in these ways per year. This adds four times as much nitrate to the world's soils as does the second, artificial, method – the application of fertiliser. Certainly artificially added fertilisers have the desired effects of increasing the yield of crops –

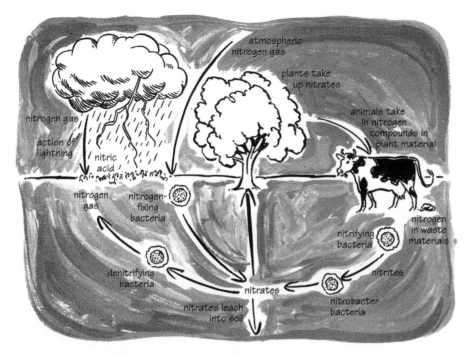

Figure 56 The nitrogen cycle

provided that no other limiting factor (such as lack of water) is holding back the plant. But too much nitrate overloads the system. More nitrate is added than can be used by plants and much of the surplus is washed out of the soil by rain (this is called 'leaching out') and carried into streams and rivers and into groundwater. In some parts of the UK, for example East Anglia, the nitrate level in drinking water exceeds 200 grams per cubic metre of water.

Excessive levels of nitrate are a health risk for humans – 'blue baby' disease is a result of the effect of very high nitrate intake on the blood. But if high levels pose a serious threat, do low levels necessarily pose a more modest threat? This might be the common sense response, but is it right?

Nearly all chemicals are damaging if given in large enough amounts – even oxygen – so perhaps there is a threat to health only if a certain threshold concentration is reached. It is impossible to get rid of all nitrates from drinking water (it doesn't just originate from fertilisers), so governments usually give an upper limit that is acceptable – the European Health Standard for nitrates in drinking water is currently 45 grams of nitrates for every cubic metre of water. The possible effects of high nitrates in ecosystems can cause damage, and environmentalists work and campaign to identify safe levels and ways of working. The hope is that below this threshold, nitrate is present in a safe amount, although, as you can appreciate, proving that such levels are safe – in that they offer zero risk – is very difficult.

In this section we have seen that:

▷ Carbon passes through a global cycle and is reused.

▷ The water cycle is vital to all living things in their communities.

▷ The nitrogen cycle is an important cycle that is crucial to all living things.

Ecology

Much of ecology is concerned with identifying factors that influence population size – especially factors that influence birth and death rates. In the example shown in Figure 57, the major influence was availability of food supply.

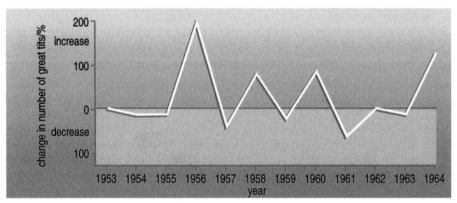

Figure 57 Numbers of great tits breeding at a particular site in Sweden

In Sweden, great tits feed on beech seeds. During the winter, a proportion of juvenile birds die, but far fewer are stricken if extra food is available because of bumper crops of beech seeds. When numbers increase, population density increases – in other words, the numbers of great tits per unit area of habitat increases. This means that in good years, mortality rates would be low and large numbers of great tits would therefore emigrate to new habitats.

Sizes of populations are also influenced by the numbers of predators (Figure 58) at a higher trophic level and by the availability of food at a lower trophic level. The abundance of parasites and pests can also have an effect. Because resources are limited, the extent of competition from fellow individuals will have an important influence, especially when population density is high. These are examples of biological factors that influence population size. Figure 59 shows this link between resources and populations.

Physical factors are likely to influence numbers of individual plants and animals too and include temperature – and for plants, light.

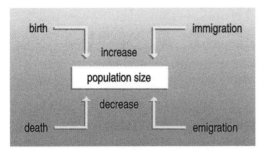

Figure 58 Factors that influence population size

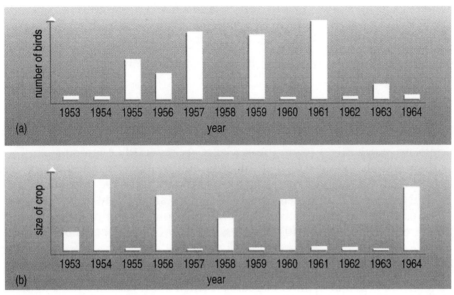

Figure 59 (a) Variations in bird population in Sweden; (b) size of beech crop in southern Sweden

---

Factors that influence population size   Activity 6

Figure 60 summarises the range of physical and biological factors that can influence numbers. Think of some animal and plant species with which you are familiar and try to identify the factors that are most significant in (i) increasing and (ii) decreasing population size.

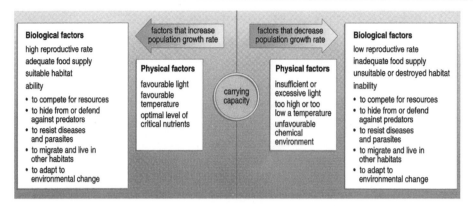

Figure 60 A range of physical and biological factors that can influence population numbers. (The carrying capacity represents the optimum number that can be supported in a given situation)

A case study of rabbits and vegetation

Important principles relating to animal and plan communities are evident.

Virgin ground, devoid of all plant and animal life is a rare sight. Left alone, with time, this land begins to be colonised with simple organisms such as lichens. Gradually plant species gain a foothold as seeds and fruits are brought in – leguminous plants are especially adept at such early invasions, because of their nitrogen-fixing abilities. Biomass increases and as organic matter accumulates and rocks are gradually weathered, a soil base develops, which in turn allows new plant species to be established. The changes in plant (and animal) communities over time from a standing start is a process called **primary succession**.

Secondary succession begins on soil cleared of original vegetation. Again the mix of species present changes over time in a predictable sequence. Immediately after clearance, which comes about from fire or physical removal of vegetation, a few short-lived (i.e., annual) plants become established, completing their life cycle from seed to flowering plant in a single year. Later a variety of species of grass become established. Then small trees and shrubs (hawthorn, for example) come to dominate the landscape. At least in the early stages of secondary succession, the number of different species present (i.e., the diversity of species) increases. Your garden lawn would provide a good example of these processes, if you were willing and able to abandon its care and watch nature reclaim it over a period of 50 or so years.

If left undisturbed over many years, succession continues until a woodland containing mature trees develops to the point where few new plant (or animal) species appear – the rate of primary production may slow down as the community 'settles'. This end-point of secondary succession is called a **climax community**, which in Britain is represented by oak woodland. A climax community is not inevitable – sometimes factors such as accidental fires or severe climatic conditions may delay or prevent its onset.

Conservation and species loss

Loss of species is now so familiar that it may no longer have the power to shock. It is a problem not just of large 'game' animals but is found here in the UK.

Below are three examples of mammals in the UK in difficulty:

▶ There are probably no more than 4,000 greater horseshoe bats in the country, which means the species can properly be described as 'on the brink of extinction'.

▶ The number of water voles has declined very sharply; it is currently estimated that there are 1.16 million. This may seem a lot but compare this with the number of rabbits, where the population is more like 38 million.

▶ Weasels and stoats are declining with the population of each at about half a million.

The picture is not entirely a catalogue of woe; the number of otters is increasing after the banning of hunting and the abandonment of harmful persistent pesticides. But there are many more reasons for concern than for complacency.

Those who currently claim that our modern age is witnessing a mass extinction of species are not wild alarmists – many published studies on the subject are reasoned and sober scientific arguments. Why is there so much argument and dispute? There are two questions to address, the first of which is not exclusively scientific.

Why does conservation matter?	Activity 7

What are your thoughts on this?

Commentary

Environmentalists are fond of pointing out that humans are custodians of the Earth rather than its masters. The sentiment may be overstated, but there is an undeniable arrogance in a world philosophy that always puts human interests before all others. The diversity of the world's animals and plants is a precious heritage. It represents the stock that will form the basis of future evolutionary change. Conservation matters too because cash is at stake. For example, living organisms are extraordinarily diverse 'chemical factories' that manufacture chemicals for pharmaceutical use. From the relatively small number of plants 'screened' so far several important pharmaceuticals have been identified for the treatment of diseases such as cancer. Many more chemicals of potential benefit as yet undiscovered will be lost for ever with the loss of plant species. In economic terms, the 'forgone' benefit (i.e., the potential, but never realised, value) of these lost drugs is estimated at more than £1 billion.

How many species are being lost?

The short answer is, we don't know. Remarkably, we don't even know how many species there are on Earth. There are about 1.4 million named species, but estimates of the numbers yet to be discovered range from 10 million to 100 million. New species are 'discovered' with impressive regularity. Towards the end of 1994, the Wollemi pine turned up. This tree, a distant cousin of the monkey-puzzle, is a remnant of a vegetation dominant about 130 million years ago. Yet this is hardly a species easily overlooked – it is more than 100 feet high and was discovered within 150 miles of Sydney, Australia. In the same year, two new species of bird were discovered in South America, plus a new tree kangaroo from New Guinea. If large organisms like these suddenly spring into the headlines, what of the less obvious? It has been estimated that there may be 30 million arthropod species (insects, beetles, centipedes and related organisms) living in tropical rainforests; at present only 875,000 species have been given a scientific name. If you consider little-explored environments such as the depths of the oceans and the tree canopies of the tropical rainforests, and the major groups or organisms (such as bacteria) of which we know very little, then you gain an impression of the vastness and richness of uncharted life.

Unfortunately, there is every evidence that the contribution of humans is more one of speeding the demise of this rich resource than of cataloguing it. The rate of species loss can only be estimated using 'best guesses'. Take birds for example. First, no bird species will last for ever, any more than the human species will. But this 'background extinction' is all too often used as an excuse to ignore present species extinction – 'after all, the fossil record is littered with species from the past'. The average life of a bird species is between 1 million and 10 million years. Suppose we accept the 'best guess' of the number of present-day species of birds as 10,000. This implies that we would expect one 'natural' extinction every 100 to 1,000 years. Yet if we consider the birds of one particular location – the Pacific Islands – the evidence suggests that there is one extinction per year (and this is a conservative estimate).

This implies that species loss is 100 to 1,000 times the natural 'background' rate. This is not an atypical example. There are many other well-researched examples – amphibians, for instance. There are about 4,000 different amphibian species, and between the nineteenth century and the 1960s only five were thought to have become extinct. In the past 25 years, populations have declined precipitously; there are currently 89 species of amphibians at risk of extinction. The sad tale is repeated with many animals and plants from freshwater fish to Australian mammals.

Pollution and overgrazing of food and other resources such as the cod fishing in the North Sea can have far-reaching effects not only on the species concerned but on the stability of the entire ecosystem within which it operates. The changes caused by such actions as the heavy felling of hardwoods in a tropical rainforest can affect the availability and even destroy the food supply and habitats for a wide range of species previously protected by the environment. Land, in this example, is then exposed to the effects of the weather in ways that may result in changes in climate and soil erosion thus limiting the recovery of the forests and the survival of interrelated flora and fauna. Fauna will flee the area causing overcrowding in other habitats and the subsequent pressure that brings to another area.

Pollution caused by mismanagement of resources and accidents such as oil tankers being washed up on the shore can have similar devastating effects on species that even with rapid response by environmental agencies has little chance of recovering its previous levels for many years if at all. The demands of a consumer society are using up resources at rapid rates and also producing quantities of waste that it is becoming more and more difficult to dispose of without harming the environment. The recent demands to recycle more and more of our waste material can only be a good thing.

The loss of species indicated above imply that we are not acting quickly enough or living with due care and attention for all living creatures, and the loss will be ours.

The unhappy implication of this is that the success of the human population has been achieved at the expense of our fellow creatures. Time and time again, when human and animal or plant populations come into conflict, species devastation is all too apparent. In North America, 12,000 years ago the land was rich with horses, long-horned bison, camels, various antelopes and mammoths. Some 70% of the large mammal types that existed then are now extinct. Human interference was probably not the only explanation (there were changes in climate too) but it was almost certainly the most significant.

Deliberate hunting and destruction is less prevalent; today's enemies are ignorance and indifference. Species loss occurs mainly because of the degradation or destruction of habitat, and sometimes alien species are introduced (intentionally or accidentally) and cause havoc with the local communities. Pollution and changes in land use also have unwelcome effects. But the problems are compounded by other changes, only indirectly of human origin. The advent of global warming has had some effect. When a combination of threatening factors are at work, the omens for the future do not look promising.

Awareness of the situation and a willingness and capability to respond are the first steps. Fortunately, a wide variety of conservation projects are under way globally. Habitats are protected and managed to ensure that species loss is minimised. The essential ingredient for an optimistic future is an informed and responsible attitude. Our success and our economic advancement must no longer be achieved at the expense of the rest of creation but must be thought of in terms of sustainable development. For this reason, raising awareness in old and young people is a task of utmost importance.

In this section we have seen that:

▶ Ecology is concerned with factors that influence communities and populations.

▶ Populations vary because of biological and physical factors acting upon them.

▶ Primary succession is the changes in communities over time from a standing start.

▶ Secondary succession takes place on soil cleared of original vegetation.

▶ Many species are in danger.

▶ Conservation is a serious concern for all.

8 Electricity and Magnetism

Introduction

Electricity has had a tremendous impact on people's daily lives throughout the last century, but how does it work? The aim of this section is to help you develop your own knowledge and understanding of electricity, with an emphasis on gaining confidence in practical work with electric circuits, both making them work and understanding what is happening.

Resources

To obtain the most out of this section you need to have access to some basic electrical equipment. This includes the following:

▶ 1.5 V (cell) batteries

▶ 1.5 V bulbs, or 2.5 V if using two cells

▶ wire – if plastic-coated make sure the coating is stripped off the ends; cut into short lengths

▶ bulb holder

▶ magnets

▶ ammeter

▶ variable resistor

▶ compass

▶ iron filings

▶ battery holders

▶ crocodile clips

▶ small screwdriver

▶ string.

Working with electricity has safety issues related to it. These have already been dealt with in Chapter 1. However, it does not hurt to reiterate here that you do not use mains electricity (230 volts) for any experimental work unless you use a transformer.

In general it is safe to handle an electricity supply of a few volts without taking any special precautions. For example, you can touch any part of any ordinary 1.5 volt torch battery or 9 volt radio battery (these are known as 'dry batteries') without feeling even the smallest electric shock. Car batteries are an exception to the 'low voltage means safe' rule – a car battery can produce much more of a shock than a 'dry' battery of the same voltage. Also, a car battery is filled with strong acid that would corrode and burn if spilt.

| Activity 1 | Lighting a bulb |

For this you need one piece of wire at least 10 cm long, a 1.25 V bulb and a 1.5 V battery (cell really – several cells constitute a battery).

Can you light the bulb? Try as many different ways as you can.

Once you have succeeded in lighting the bulb, i.e., completed the circuit so electricity can flow, see if you can change your circuit around and still light the bulb.

Take careful note of where you put the wires to make contact. Where are the two connections to the bulb? When you have lit the bulb using only one wire, try again with two wires. Is it easier to use two wires? What happens if you use three or four wires?

| Activity 2 | Drawing a bulb |

Look carefully at your bulb and other bulbs if you have some around and try to draw what you think is inside.

Commentary

Figure 61 shows what the inside of the bulb looks like. You can see why you need to connect the wire to the two specific points A and B marked on the diagram if you are to make the bulb light. These contact zones complete the circuit.

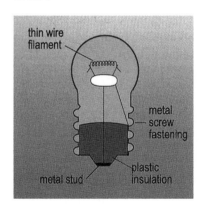
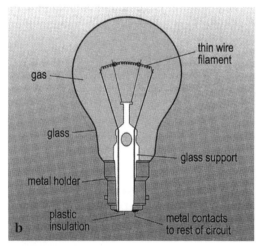

Figure 61 Inside a bulb (a) Cross-section through a torch bulb (b) Cross-section through a light bulb

In order to light a bulb, or make a buzzer work, there must be a flow of electricity, called an electric **current**. Materials that allow electricity to flow within them are called electrical **conductors**, and those that do not are called electrical **insulators**. Metals are good conductors. For the bulb to light, there must be a continuous conducting pathway, called a complete **electric circuit**, between the two connection points (called **terminals**) of a power supply such as a cell or battery and through the bulb.

For the time being, we will talk rather loosely of 'the electricity'. Later in this book, we will return to the question of what is actually flowing.

In order for the bulb to light in Activity 1 you need to connect up the circuit as shown in Figure 62.

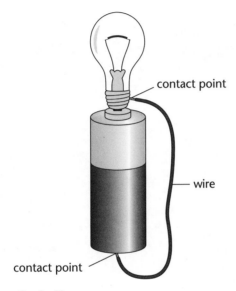

Figure 62 Lighting the bulb

This shows that you have a complete circuit. There is a complete conducting (normally metal) pathway that allows the current to flow.

Trying to light a bulb using just your fingers and hands to hold all the connections is difficult and that is why we have bulb holders and battery holders. In each case there are two contact points (terminals) that connect with the side and base of the bulb in the holder and the positive and negative terminals in the case of the battery holder. These contacts allow a complete circuit to form and so the bulb lights or buzzer sounds as the current is able to flow. Using more wires in the current reduces the brightness of the bulb.

Look at the circuits drawn in Figure 63. These all use bulb and battery holders. Can you say which will work just by looking? If not, try to set them up and see if they work. Give reasons why they do not work.

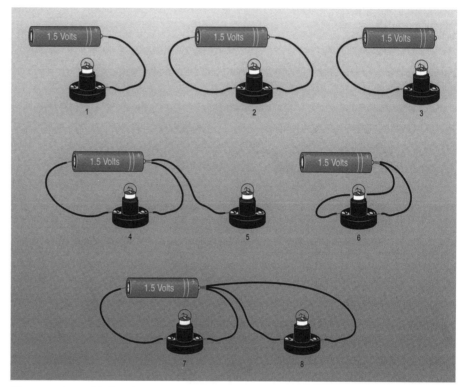

Figure 63 Which of these circuits will work?

Commentary

Numbers 2, 4 and 7 will work and the rest will not. If you had trouble making the bulbs light in 2, 4 or 7, you may want to check connections and apparatus – one thing at a time.

Air, rust and grease are insulators, and even a narrow gap or a thin layer of dirt between metal contacts is enough to interrupt a circuit and stop it working. Loose or dirty connections are therefore the most common faults in circuits. If you are sure that you have connected up a circuit correctly but it fails to work, *first* check that all the connections are clean and firm. If the circuit still does not work, the battery or bulb may be faulty. Try substituting these, one at a time, to check they are working. If you are using plastic-coated wires, the plastic may be hiding a break in the metal, so try swapping each wire, one at a time.

You can see the pathway through the above circuits and determine if they will work but in some pieces of electrical equipment it is not so easy to see the complete circuit.

Collect together some or all of the following and see if you can trace the circuit:

◗ torch with plastic case

◗ torch with metal case

◗ bulb holder from a circuit kit

◗ bicycle dynamo

◗ mains light bulb

◗ desk lamp

◗ piece of flex used for mains lighting.

Be careful not to have the mains equipment connected and switched on when examining them. The inside of the desk lamp and a torch bulb in Figure 64 show the contact points for the bulbs.

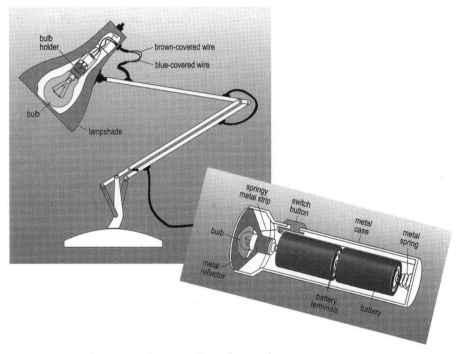

Figure 64 *Where are the metal pathways?*

Most direct current (DC) power supplies such as batteries, dynamos or low voltage transformers, have two terminals labelled positive (+) and negative (–). Most alternating current (AC) supplies such as mains sockets have three terminals: live (brown) earth (green and yellow) and neutral (blue).

When working with electricity it is time-consuming to do the drawings and, so, to make this easier and quicker we use symbols to represent the various parts of a circuit.

The main symbols you need are in Figure 65 and they are used in Figure 66 to show you what a basic simple circuit would look like in picture and diagram form.

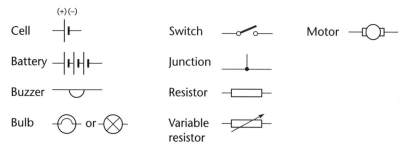

Figure 65 *Shorthand symbols used in electrical diagrams*

(a) A simple circuit

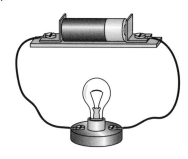

(b) A simple circuit diagram

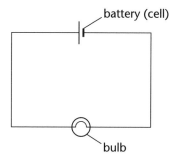

Figure 66 *Simple circuit drawings*

Activity 5   Drawing circuits

Set up your own circuits and try to draw them using only the symbols shown in Figure 65.

What happens inside a circuit

To explain the behaviour of an electric circuit, it is useful to use a model to help us understand.

Figure 67 shows us a continuous one-way model of electricity flowing from positive to the negative terminal. It is the conventional model of electric current and useful for us to begin to understand the ideas. The flow is commonly called a **current**.

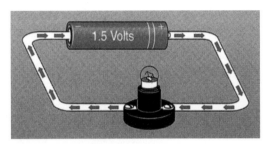

Figure 67 A continuous model of circuit

What is electric current?

An electric current consists of a flow of tiny particles called electrons that have an electric **charge**. You will have experienced electric charge if you have ever taken off a jumper quickly and produced a crackling sound, or rubbed a balloon against your sleeve and then made it stick to the wall. In these situations you have given the jumper or the balloon an electric charge. It turns out that there are just two types of electric charge, which have been named 'positive' and 'negative'. An uncharged object has equal amounts of each type, but if you can arrange to move electrons which have a negative charge from one object to another (as you do when you rub a balloon) then the object gets an overall positive or negative charge – it is the charge on the balloon that makes it stick to a wall.

When you rub a balloon on your sleeve, you are in fact transferring some tiny particles between your sleeve and the balloon. The individual particles are too small to see (they are millions of times smaller than the cells that make up living tissue) but each carries an electric charge. Transferring a large number of tiny charged particles produces the overall charge that sticks the balloon to the wall. It is actually quite difficult to deduce the direction in which charge is being transferred. Transferring particles with a negative charge of electrons from, say, sleeve to balloon will give the balloon a negative charge and leave a net positive charge on the sleeve – but transferring electrons from balloon to sleeve will have the same effect of making them stick together.

In an electric current there is a continuous flow of electrons from the negative battery terminal to the positive, rather than a one-off transfer of particles from one object to another. This is easy to confuse with the conventional representation of current flowing from positive to negative since a movement of positive charge in one direction has exactly the same effect as a movement of negative charge in the opposite direction.

When models of electric current were first being developed (in the nineteenth century) it became conventional to describe the direction of current as being the apparent direction of flow of positive charge. In a battery circuit, this flow is from the positive terminal to the negative around the circuit.

We now know that, in a circuit made up of metal, the current consists of a continuous flow of tiny particles, called **electrons**. Electrons are far too small to see, and each one weighs about 0.000 000 000 000 000 000 000 000 000 001 kg! Electrons have a *negative* charge. We first met electrons in the chapter about particles.

Activity 6	Current and electrons

Look at the circuit in Figure 68. Which arrow shows the conventional direction of current and which shows the actual movement of electrons?

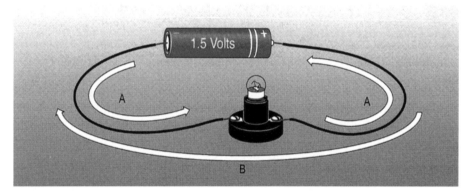

Figure 68 Which way is the current?

Commentary

Arrow B (from the positive terminal to the negative) shows the conventional direction of the current. Arrow A shows the direction of electron flow – since electrons have negative charge, a flow of electrons is equivalent to a flow of positive charge in the opposite direction.

You may be finding this discussion of direction confusing, and wonder why everyone doesn't simply adopt a new convention and say that the direction of the current is the same as the flow of the electrons. If so, you are not alone! However, the convention has become so well established that it would cause even more confusion to change it now. Also, in some circuits, where current consists of charge flowing within a gas or a liquid, there is some movement of positively charged particles.

In fact, for many circuits – including all those you will meet in this book – the actual direction of current is unimportant. *What matters is that there is a continuous flow of charge around a circuit.* However, it is often convenient to draw arrows to indicate current and it is best to adopt the same convention as you will see in other books, so we will draw arrows showing current going from positive to negative (and we won't worry about the fact that the electrons are actually going the other way).

It is tempting to think that it is charge that is lost from a battery when it goes flat – indeed, we talk of 'recharging' a car battery. However, that idea contradicts some things we have already established about circuits. We have established that there must be a continuous flow of charge all around the circuit, so any charge that flows out through one terminal of the battery is replaced by charge flowing into the other terminal. Unlike a rubbed balloon, a 'charged' battery does not stick to things – it has no *overall* electric charge. In a 'charged' battery, charge is pushed between terminals so that the positive terminal has a positive charge and the negative terminal has a negative charge (giving zero charge overall). As the battery is used, the flow of charge around the circuit moves positive charge away from the positive terminal and feeds it into the negative, but there is no overall loss of charge from the battery.

In order for the bulb to light (or a buzzer to buzz) there must be a continuous transfer of **energy** from battery to bulb (or buzzer). It is quite difficult to define what energy is, since it is not a physical substance (see Chapter 4) – but let's remind ourselves of key ideas. Energy is needed to make things happen. Change in movement, heat transfer, light and sound all involve a transfer of energy. (An object continuing to move with no overall force acting on it involves no transfer of energy to or from an object.) For example, you can move and keep warm only if you have a supply of energy from the food you eat; a car can move only if it has a supply of fuel to provide energy. 'Recharging' a battery involves supplying energy to enable it to push the charge from one terminal to the other.

We must therefore extend our model of an electric circuit. As well as the continuous circulation of charge all around the circuit, there is a net transfer of energy from battery to bulb.

A good analogy of a circuit can be seen if you consider a fleet of lorries driving continuously around a circular route. They represent the moving charge. As they pass through the depot (the 'battery') they pick up some gravel ('energy') which they deliver to the building site ('the bulb'). This analogy represents the continuous circulation of charge and the transfer of energy from the battery. But be careful not to take the analogy too literally – unlike gravel, energy is not 'stuff' as we said in Part 1. Also, in the real circuit, the current actually consists of vast numbers of electrons, each moving at only a small fraction of a metre per second.

In this section we have seen that:

▶ An electric current is a continuous flow of charged particles around a circuit.

▶ An electric current can only flow if there is a complete circuit.

▶ Materials that allow electricity to flow within them are electrical conductors.

▶ Materials that do not allow electricity to flow through are electrical insulators.

▶ Diagrams of circuits can be drawn using symbols.

More complicated circuits

Most electric circuits are slightly more complicated than just a battery and a bulb. We need to think about how the circuits' behaviour might be explained in terms of charge flow and energy transfer.

Activity 7   *Lighting more than one bulb*

(a)   Using one battery and two bulbs and wire(s) light the bulbs as shown in the diagrams in Figure 69.

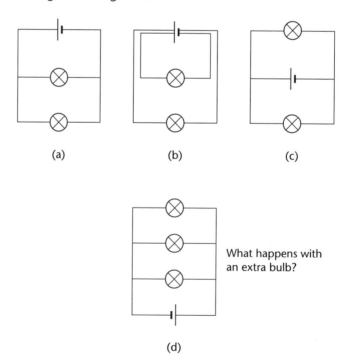

(a)   (b)   (c)

What happens with an extra bulb?

(d)

Figure 69 Lighting more than one bulb

(b)   Now try three bulbs and wires.

Commentary

Activity 7 illustrates two important points. First, the circuits look different but, as far as the bulbs are concerned, they behave in the same way. Second, there is a complete circuit through each bulb, independent of the other bulb, and connecting or disconnecting one bulb makes virtually no difference to the other that is sharing the same battery. Bulbs connected like this are said to be in parallel with each other. When you added three bulbs as in (d) the bulbs should light just the same.

There are now several routes between battery terminals, and charge circulates around each loop independently of the others transferring energy from the battery. In Figure 69 the circuits share the wires connected to the battery, but the current splits, so that some charge flows through one bulb and some through the other. If the bulbs are identical, the split will be equal.

Connecting in parallel	Activity 8

If you had a large number of bulbs connected in parallel to a battery, what effect might that have on the battery? Would it last as long as a battery that was lighting just one bulb?

Commentary

The battery supplies energy to each bulb. If there are a lot of bulbs, then the battery will supply energy at a greater rate than to just one bulb alone, and it will go flat more quickly.

Identifying equivalent circuits	Activity 9

Figure 70 shows three pairs of circuits that are equivalent to each other, and two odd ones out. Identify the pairs.

Commentary

The pairs are (a) and (g), (d) and (h), and (b) and (c); (e) and (f) are not equivalent. When designing a circuit to do a particular job, it is generally best to work it out on paper first, rather than using trial and error. A circuit diagram is a quick and easy way to record your design. Once you have drawn a diagram, it is sometimes helpful to check your design by tracing any complete circuits with a pencil.

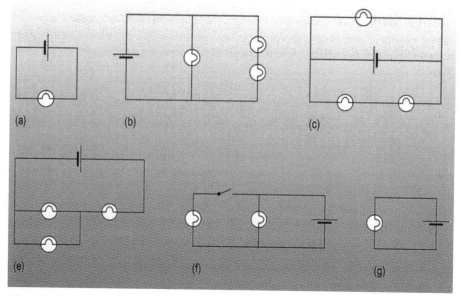

Figure 70 Find the pairs of equivalent circuits

How else can we light more than one bulb with one battery?

So far in this section we have built circuits with bulbs in parallel. But you have already seen that there are other ways to connect more than one bulb to a battery – they can be all in a row, so that there is just one complete circuit between the battery terminals, going through all the bulbs. Bulbs joined like this are said to be connected in **series** to form a series circuit.

Taking out a bulb

What happens if you take a bulb out of a series circuit as in Figure 71? Does it matter which bulb you take out?

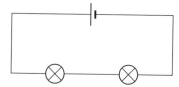

Figure 71 A series circuit

Commentary

A break anywhere in the circuit stops the flow of electricity. Opening a switch or taking out the bulb anywhere in a circuit breaks the conducting path.

There is no complete circuit, so there is no flow of charge and the bulbs do not light.

Build each of the circuits shown in Figure 72 to explore the behaviour of bulbs in series. In particular, look at the brightness of the bulbs. What can you say about the brightness of two or more identical bulbs joined in series? What happens to the brightness as you increase the number of bulbs in series?

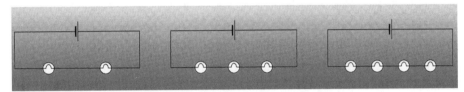

Figure 72 A collection of circuits

Commentary

What happens is that each electron still gets the same amount of energy from the battery, but shares it between all the bulbs throughout the circuit (if the bulbs are identical, they all receive equal shares). Also, adding more bulbs makes the charge circulate more slowly so energy is delivered at a reduced rate overall. You can try to relate this to the analogy of the lorry. If you picture the gravel lorries, you can more or less 'explain' the slowing down – the lorries take longer to make the journey if they make more deliveries – but if you say the electrons are behaving like the lorries you start wondering how the electrons 'know' there are several bulbs in the circuit, and why they don't give all their energy to the first one they reach. We will consider this later.

We will end as we began – with practical considerations of real circuits. This is an opportunity to apply and consolidate what you have learned.

Some of the circuits you have been using in this section are a small-scale, low-voltage equivalent of house lighting circuits. In a house circuit, are the lamps connected in series or in parallel? How can you tell?

Commentary

The lights in a house are connected in parallel, to allow you to turn each one on and off without affecting the others connected to the same power supply. If they were in series, a switch anywhere in the circuit would turn all the lamps on or off together.

Developing ideas of circuits and current

Our descriptions of electric circuits can be made more precise by introducing some measurements.

We have seen that an electric current is a flow of charged particles. The unit for measuring electric charge is the **coulomb**, abbreviated to C. A single electron has a charge of 0.000 000 000 000 000 167 coulombs – or, to put it another way, 1 C is the total charge on about 6 million million million electrons. The coulomb is named after the French scientist Charles Augustin de Coulomb, 1736–1806.

Current is a flow of charge. The current at any point in a circuit is defined as the number of coulombs moving past that point in one second. The unit of current is the **ampere** (abbreviated to A or amp). A current of 1 amp means that charge is flowing at a rate of 1 coulomb per second. To help you understand this, think of a heating system, where, for example, you could define the current as the amount of water flowing past a point in a given time – you could measure water current in gallons per minute, perhaps, or litres per second. The ampere commemorates another French scientist, André Marie Ampère, 1775–1836.

Even though we cannot see the charge flowing within a circuit, we can measure electric current fairly easily by inserting a meter, called an **ammeter** (derived from amp-meter) in the circuit. The charge must flow through the ammeter, so it must be in series with the rest of the circuit. Figure 73 shows an ammeter measuring the current in two different circuits. Notice the circuit symbol for an ammeter – A.

Activity 13	Measuring current

Will the current be different in different parts of the circuit? If you have access to an ammeter try the circuits in Figure 73.

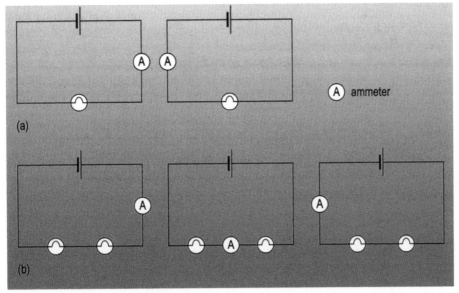

Figure 73 Measuring current in series circuits

Current in series circuits   Activity 14

Use an ammeter to measure the current in a bulb-plus-battery circuit at each of the positions shown in Figure 73(a). What do you notice about the two meter readings? Do they fit in with our model of continuous charge circulation?

Now set up one of the arrangements in Figure 73(b). Measure the current and then predict what you will find in the other two arrangements. Test your prediction.

Commentary

The current is the same at all points around a series circuit, and the current is less when there are two bulbs in the circuit. If you place even more bulbs in the circuit then you will have even less current. The bulbs will be dimmer the more you add.

Current in a parallel circuit   Activity 15

What do you think you will find when you measure the current at various points in a parallel circuit as in Figure 74?

Make the circuits shown in Figure 74 and measure the current at each of the places indicated.

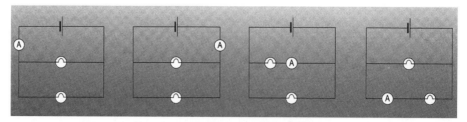

Figure 74 Measuring current in a parallel circuit

Commentary

In a parallel circuit there is a different effect on the current. The current is not the same in all parts of the circuit. Figure 74 shows how the current flows round the circuit and you can see that it splits to go round each separate circuit. If all the bulbs are identical the divide will be equal. The amount of current leaving the battery at the positive terminal is the same as the current arriving at the negative terminal.

What are volts and watts?

The labels on many pieces of electrical equipment include information about voltage or volts (abbreviated to V). For example, a mains light bulb might be labelled 230 V, 60 W; a torch bulb might be labelled 3.5 V, 2.5 W. What do these labels mean?

Volts and watts are both related to the energy transfers in an electric circuit. Energy is measured in joules (J), regardless of whether it has anything to do with electricity. For example, we have seen many foods labelled with energy values in J or kJ (kilojoules), which indicate how much energy the food will contribute to the total energy required by your body for such processes as keeping warm and moving. James Prescott Joule, 1818–89, was an English scientist.

The voltage of a power supply is a measure of the energy it gives to the charge moving around a circuit. One volt (1 V) means an energy of 1 J for every coulomb – so a 1.5 V battery supplies 1.5. J to each coulomb that passes through. The voltage of a battery is more or less fixed (it depends, on what is inside the battery), so a battery can be labelled with its voltage (1.5 V for a torch battery, for example). The current, on the other hand, depends on what is connected in the circuit – you saw this in Activities 14 and 15 – so you don't find batteries labelled in amps. The volt is named after Count Alessandro Giuseppe Antonio Anastasio Volta, 1745–1827, an Italian scientist.

The voltage label on a bulb (or other device, such as a buzzer) tells us what power supply the bulb is designed for. For example, a bulb labelled '60 W, 230 V' is designed to run from the 230 V mains.

The '60 W' part of the label refers to the **power** of the bulb. The power of a bulb (or other device) is a measure of how quickly it transfers energy. A power of 1 W means a transfer of 1 J per second – so a 60 W bulb means a transfer of 60 J in each second (the energy is given out as heat and light). The power label tells us what the actual power will be *provided* the bulb is connected (either on its own or in parallel with other devices) to a supply with that voltage.

Thinking about volts, watts and their relationships　　　　　　　　　**Activity 16**

1　What do you think would happen if you connect a bulb labelled 240 V, 60 W to the UK mains, which is now 230 V?

2　What do you think would happen if you connected a torch bulb labelled 2.5 W, 3.5 V to a 1.5 V battery?

3　What do you think would happen if you tried to run a mains bulb from a torch battery?

4　Suppose you have a hairdryer designed for use in the UK where the mains voltage is 230 V. What would happen if you tried to use it somewhere (the USA for example) where the mains voltage is 110 V?

Commentary

1　The actual mains voltage is lower than the bulb's 'design' voltage, but not very much lower. The bulb will still glow, though slightly less brightly than when the mains was 240 V. (You probably didn't notice any change in brightness when the voltage changed on 1 January 1995. In fact the mains voltage varies slightly anyway from day to day and from hour to hour, by anything up to about 10 V – it is not necessarily exactly the value that the electricity companies claim!)

2　The bulb would probably still glow, but it would look faint and reddish rather than bright white.

3　The energy transferred to the lamp is much less than it was designed for, so it will not glow at all. (Try this if you wish.)

If you used a voltage that was much too high for the bulb, you would get far too great a rate of energy transfer for the particular bulb, and the filament would get very hot, melt and break. You would 'blow' the bulb. If the supply voltage is only slightly too low or too high, then it doesn't matter much. For example, if a torch battery is going flat (i.e., its voltage is dropping) the bulb still lights, but it looks yellow and feeble. If you use a battery with a voltage that is a bit too high, the bulb glows very bright white (and will not last as long as it should because the filament becomes damaged).

As a rough rule of thumb, you can run a torch bulb off a battery that is anywhere between about half and twice the bulb's design voltage. Labels on bulbs and other devices are very useful when it comes to selecting suitable items to use with a given power supply.

4   The motor would move more slowly, and the air would be heated less than in the UK – it would take a long time to dry your hair. (In practice, you might be able to use a transformer to raise the voltage from 110 V to 230 V.)

How can we control the current in a circuit?

In this section we take a look at the two factors that influence the current in a circuit.

So far, you have been using just one battery, most likely either 1.5 V or 9 V. Using a different battery voltage alters the current in a circuit. You can make a battery of a different voltage by joining two or more batteries in series. You would join the positive terminal of one battery to the negative terminal of the next to make a chain of batteries that are all driving current in the same direction. If you put four 1.5 V torch batteries (cells) together you will form a battery of 6 V.

Changing the voltage	Activity 17

Make a circuit using a 1.5 V cell, a bulb and an ammeter connected in series. Record the current. Now replace the single cell with, in turn, two, three and four 1.5 V cells connected in series to make batteries of different voltage. Record the current for each different voltage. Can you identify a pattern?

Note that before you make these circuits you will need to consider what voltage bulb would be most appropriate.

Commentary

You have now seen that increasing the voltage increases the current. How does this relate to what we have already said about voltage and to our model of an electric circuit?

Increasing the battery voltage does two things: it increases the energy supplied to each coulomb of charge, *and* it drives the charge around the circuit at a greater rate. How might you picture this? In terms of the lorry analogy, each lorry takes a bigger load *and* more lorries go through the depot in a given time. If you think of the heating system, the water heater produces hotter water *and* pumps it round the system faster.

How else can we alter the current in a circuit?

The other factor that affects current in a circuit depends on what is connected to the battery.

When you connect two bulbs to a battery in series, the current is less than when there is just one bulb on its own. Having a bulb in the circuit makes it more difficult for the charge to circulate. We say that a bulb 'resists' the current, or that a bulb has electrical **resistance**. In fact, it is their resistance that makes the bulbs 'light'. Resistance is a measure of the difficulty of the flow of electrons in a material. Resistance is measured in ohms.

The wire filament in a bulb is still an electrical conductor (it forms part of the complete circuit between the battery terminals) but charge moves less easily through the filament than within the connecting wires. When charge is flowing through wire that resists its movement, it transfers energy to the wire. This energy heats the wire and, in a light bulb, makes it so hot that it glows.

There are two reasons why a filament has much more resistance than the connecting wires. First, connecting wires are usually made of copper, a metal that allows charge to move very easily within itself, whereas bulb filaments are made from a different metal, tungsten, which does not allow charge to move so freely. Second, if you look carefully at a bulb filament you will see that it is a long thin strand of wire (in a mains bulb filament you can see that the strand is coiled up to make it more compact), whereas the connecting wires are much fatter. Having a long, thin section of wire in a circuit reduces the current (rather like a single-lane section on a motorway reduces the rate of flow of traffic); the longer and thinner the wire, the greater the resistance. Good conductors of electricity have a low resistance and materials that act as insulators have high resistance.

A **variable resistor** (also known as a dimmer switch), which is designed to control the current in a circuit, consists of a coiled long thin wire (made from a metal that is a less good conductor than copper). Twisting the knob moves a sliding contact along the coil and so varies the length of wire that is part of the circuit. (You may at some time come across fixed resistors; these are also designed to resist current but they cannot be adjusted. You can see fixed resistors if you take the back off a radio – they are the small cylinders with coloured bands.) Figure 75 shows a circuit with a variable resistor in series with a bulb and an ammeter.

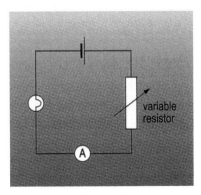

Figure 75 A circuit with a variable resistor

Notice the symbol for a variable resistor: a rectangle on its own is the symbol for a fixed resistor, and the diagonal arrow indicates that you can adjust it.

When a longer length of thin wire is connected into the circuit the resistance increases.

Activity 18	Changing resistance with a variable resistor

Set up the circuit shown in Figure 75 and explore what happens as you twist the knob. What happens to the current? What happens to the brightness of the bulb? Replace the bulb with a buzzer and repeat the activity. What happens to the buzzer? What is the current when the bulb or buzzer is not working? Is it zero, or just very small.

Activity 19	Increasing the resistance in a circuit

Explore what happens to bulbs and/or buzzers when you connect several of them in series to a battery. Include an ammeter in your circuit. How might you explain the fact that sometimes a buzzer doesn't work when you connect it in series with other components?

Commentary

These activities together with the discussion before them illustrate some important points:

▷ increasing the resistance in a circuit reduces the current

▷ the longer and thinner a piece of wire, the greater its resistance

▷ joining bulbs and buzzers in series increases the overall resistance in a circuit

▷ a buzzer or bulb may appear not to be working if there is only a small current. (Buzzers only work one way round so if the circuit doesn't work turn the buzzer round and if it still doesn't work then the current may be too low.)

So the *two* ways in which you can reduce the current in a circuit are:

▷ Reduce the battery voltage (replace the battery by one with a lower voltage).

▷ Increase the overall resistance (add more bulbs or buzzers in series, and/or use a variable resistor).

We will end this section with a special example relating to resistance that is important enough to be discussed on its own.

Short circuits and why you should avoid them

A **short circuit** is a path of very low resistance that either connects one terminal of the battery straight to the other, or is connected in parallel with a component (such as a bulb). A piece of connecting wire can make a short circuit. An ammeter is designed to have very low resistance (so as not to affect the current it is meant to measure), so it too can make a short circuit.

You have probably once or twice made a short circuit without meaning to – they are quite a common reason for circuits not working as intended. So what happens when you make a short circuit?

If the resistance is very low, the current is very large. Charge is circulating rapidly. Each coulomb carries energy from the battery, so if the current is large then energy is transferred very rapidly.

The rapid transfer of energy causes the wire to become quite hot, and the battery quickly goes flat. If a short circuit between battery terminals involves an ammeter, then the heating may damage the meter.

Also, for subtle reasons to do with characteristics of 'dry' batteries, a short circuit between the battery terminals causes the battery voltage temporarily to drop while the wire is connected.

If the battery voltage drops well below the design voltage for the bulbs and so on in the circuit, then they won't work.

If you connect a short-circuiting wire in parallel with just one component, such as a bulb, it effectively joins the two terminals of the bulb together and it won't light (like bulb 8 in Figure 63).

Looking for short circuits	Activity 20

In each circuit in Figure 76, use a coloured pencil to mark the wire that is making a short circuit and should therefore be removed.

Figure 77 shows various short circuits involving an ammeter. Which of those circuits could damage the ammeter? (Hint: look for circuits where the ammeter is connected directly to both battery terminals.)

Commentary

The ammeter in Figure 77(a) is the one that is short circuiting. There is a direct circuit through the ammeter in parallel to the ones with the bulbs.

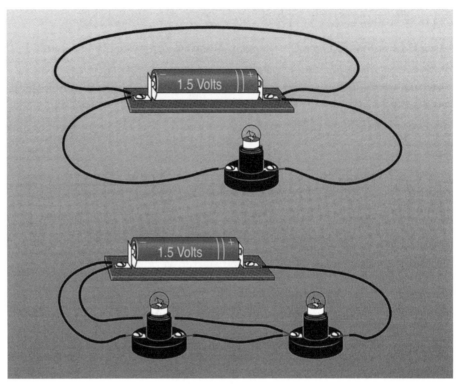

Figure 76 Where are the short circuits?

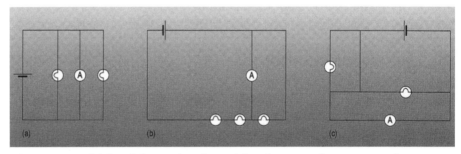

Figure 77 Which of these circuits might damage the ammeter?

In this section we have learned that:

◗ Increasing voltage increases current.

◗ Increasing the resistance in a circuit reduces the current.

◗ Resistance is the increase in difficulty of flow.

◗ Current is not the same in all parts of a parallel circuit.

◗ A short circuit is a path of low resistance that either connects one terminal of the battery to the other or is connected in parallel with a component.

◗ Power is measured in watts.

Magnetism

Magnets, such as fridge or horseshoe magnets, fascinate most people. Many people only have experience of magnets of this kind and do not realise that magnetism is more closely related to electrical current. The force that one feels when you place two bar magnets close to each other is evidence that a force field exists around any magnet.

Some materials have the property to attract iron, nickel and cobalt and we call this property **magnetism**. Lodestone is a natural substance that has magnetic properties. Not all magnetic materials are magnets themselves, even though they are attracted to magnets when placed next to one. Magnetic materials have domains or areas that act as 'mini-magnets' within the object but these domains point in all directions as in Figure 78. This cancels out any magnetic effect. In a magnet these domains are all in line as in Figure 79.

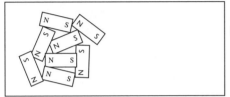

(a) Mini magnets point in all directions and therefore magnetic effect cancelled out

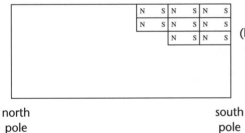

(b) Mini magnets all point in same direction and therefore north and south poles are formed

north pole   south pole

Figure 78 Mini magnets or domains

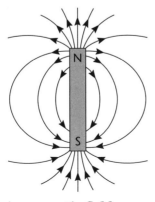

Figure 79 Lines of force in magnetic field

Magnets are made by rearranging the domains in magnetic material so that they lie in line as in Figure 79. The material the magnet is made of will affect its properties. Iron domains can be moved and aligned easily but are also more likely to become disorganised. Steel is the opposite – it is harder to magnetise but once done the domains are not easy to disorganise. Steel makes magnets which are more permanent. Dropping, hitting or heating a magnet can destroy it as it disorganises the domains, but let us investigate magnets a little further.

Activity 21	Magnetic fields

1   Place a piece of paper over one of your magnets and lightly dust some iron filings onto the paper over where the magnet is and see what happens.

2   Hold two magnets close together. What happens as you move them nearer? What happens if you change one of the magnets round? Can you feel the attraction or repulsion (pushing away)?

Commentary

1   The dusting of iron filings on the paper shows the magnet's force field clearly. The arrows on the line of force are shown. This indicates which direction another north pole would be pushed by the magnetic field.

2   As you place the two magnets close to each other you should feel a push or pull depending on which poles are facing each other. Like poles repel and unlike poles attract each other. This means that a pull occurs when the two poles facing each other are opposites (north facing south) and if they are the same they repel or push each other apart (say north north). This is shown in Figure 80 where the lines of force are shown with the two different arrangements of the magnet ends. What would happen if

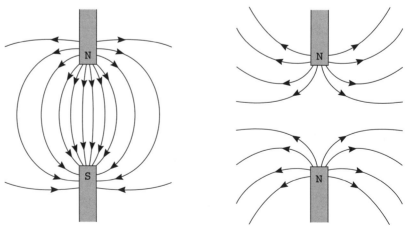

Figure 80 Lines of force when unlike and like poles are opposite each other (a) Unlike poles attract each other, (b) Like poles repel each other

you broke a magnet in half? Would there be a south pole on its own? The answer is that you get two new but smaller magnets each with a north and south pole.

Tie a piece of string around one of your magnets and hang it so that it can swing freely. Set a small plotting compass to north, not too near the magnet. What do you notice about the way your suspended magnet lies?

Commentary

Your magnet should be lying in line north to south. The Earth has its own magnetic field because it has an iron core. The magnetic South Pole is close to the geographical North Pole and vice versa for the South Pole. So your magnet has its north pole pointing towards the magnetic South Pole which is at the North Pole! The pole of the magnet facing north is a north-seeking pole.

Making a magnet – 1

Using a strong bar magnet and an iron nail you can make your own magnet by stroking the nail in the same direction several times as shown in Figure 81.

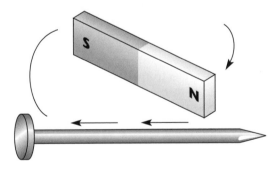

Stroke the nail many times with the magnet. Always go in the same direction and use the north pole end of the magnet. Which end of your magnet will be the South Pole? Which the North Pole?

Figure 81 Diagram of stroking a magnet

Making a magnet – 2

The other way to make a magnet is by induction. For this you need a battery (cell), some wire and a pencil as well as your iron nail. First wind your piece of wire around your pencil and connect the two ends of the wire to the two battery (cell) terminals. (Look at Figure 82 to see how to wind your wire. Place magnetic materials near the wire.) Can you feel/see any pull on the material? What happens if you increase the number of coils of wire? What happens if you replace the pencil with the iron nail?

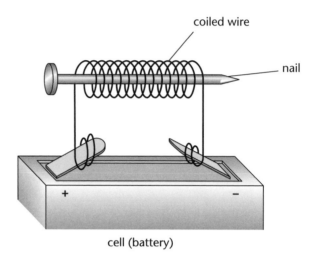

Figure 82 Making a magnet by induction

Commentary

1   Both these methods will make a temporary magnet. In the first method the magnetic force will depend on how many times you stroke the object being magnetised with the magnet and on the strength of that magnet.

2   This method produces an electromagnet. These are very simple, consisting of a solenoid or turn of wire wrapped around a nail or iron core. The current flowing through the wire creates a magnetic field. The effect of the iron in the centre of the solenoid is to increase the strength of the magnetic field when the current is switched on. The iron becomes magnetic but when the current is switched off the iron core is no longer a magnet. With a steel core you may find that the nail stays magnetised. This is because, as we said earlier, the domains or 'mini-magnets' are harder to rearrange. Increasing the number of turns in the solenoid increases the magnetic effect as does increasing the size of the current.

To make a permanent magnet you need to use steel instead of iron as the core in the above methods.

Using electromagnets

When an electric current flows through a conductor such as a wire or nail it produces a magnetic field. This effect is called **electromagnetism**. The field is circular and can be plotted with a small compass. The direction of the field around the wire depends on the direction the current is flowing through the wire. The direction can be worked out by using the right-hand grip rule. Hold up your right hand and make sure the thumb is facing in the same direction as the wire. The thumb points along the wire in the direction of the current and the clenched fist shows the direction of the field. If the current is passed through a wire around a nail as in a solenoid then the magnetic field produced is like that of a bar magnet. The strength of the magnet can be made stronger by increasing the number of coils in the solenoid around the nail.

Electromagnets are very useful as they can be switched on and off. Have you ever wondered how they manage to stack cars so high in a scrapyard? The answer is they use electromagnets. An electromagnet is switched on and picks up a used car, that may or may not have been crushed first, and carries it to the required place. The car is released when the current is switched off.

In this section we have seen that:

▶ A magnet has a force field around it as lines of force flow from north to south.

▶ Magnets have a north-seeking pole and a south-seeking pole.

▶ A magnet can be made by stroking an iron nail.

▶ When there is an electric current in a wire a magnetic field is created around it.

▶ If an iron or steel material is put inside a coil with a magnetic field, it becomes a magnet.

Simple motors

Magnetism and electricity together can bring about movement. We have found that when a current passes through a coil of wire, the coil behaves like a magnet.

Making movement   Activity 24

Set up a coil and battery as you did in Figure 82 but use a pencil instead of the nail. Connect up the current and place a compass alongside the pencil. What do you notice about the direction of the compass? Is it the same all along the pencil? Swap over the two wires to the opposite terminals and repeat the experiment. What do you notice this time about the compass direction?

Commentary

You should have found that with the current connected one way the compass needle faced one direction. When you reversed the terminals it should have faced the other way. What has happened is that as the current has changed so has the direction of the magnetic field.

Anything carrying a current has a magnetic field around it and when in a magnetic field it will experience a force. If the wire carrying the current is placed at right angles in a magnetic field there will be a force that is at right angles to both the current and magnetic field. You can predict the direction of that force by using Fleming's left-hand rule which is an easy mnemonic for working out the direction of the force (Figure 83).

thumb – motion – direction of force

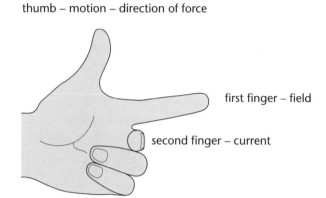

first finger – field

second finger – current

Figure 83 Fleming's left hand rule

Using your left hand point your first finger (field) straight out and point your second finger (current) at right angles to this and your thumb upwards. The thumb will show you the direction of the force of motion. Now you can work out the direction of the movement by aligning your first and second fingers with the current and magnetic field.

Figure 84 shows the direction of the force produced if you place a coil of wire between two magnets. A half-turn rotating movement is produced in the directions shown. To keep the coil turning it is necessary to change the direction of the current. This is done using a split ring commutator incorporated into the circuit. This commutator connects and disconnects with the brushes in turn, reversing the current and causing the coil to continue rotating in the same direction. This is a simple motor and can be used to drive small machines, e.g. using motors in children's construction kits and toys to lift objects.

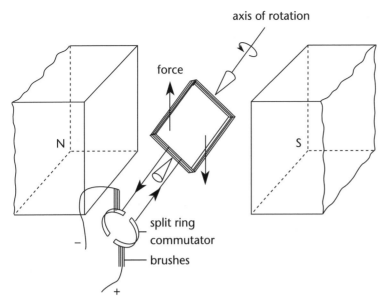

Figure 84 A simple motor

In this section we have seen that:

▶ Reversing the current in a coil of wire causes a reverse in the direction of the magnetic field around it.

▶ Motors use electricity and magnetism to produce movement.

▶ When a magnet is moved inside a coil a current is produced.

9 Waves and Light

Waves

Waves are an important concept that you need to understand to be able to develop your understanding of areas of science such as sound and light. This section explores briefly the nature of waves and their properties, and the detail of how they relate to sound and light follows.

For this section you may need the assistance of a friend and the following equipment:

- a rope
- a slinky (preferably metal) – you may need to borrow this from a child
- a notebook and pencil.

What are waves?

We wave to our friends and relations as we arrive or depart from a gathering but the kind of waves we are talking about here are different. We talk in everyday life about sound waves but do we really know what this means? How do they work?

Waves are regular patterns of disturbance, which transfer energy from one point to another without transferring any matter. The following activity shows the two basic kinds of wave.

Activity 1	Kinds of waves

(a) A simple way to explore waves is to attach a rope to a wall and then move away from the wall, and taking the other end gently shake the rope up and down. Draw the type of wave you get from this. What happens if you shake it up and down a little more vigorously, but not hard enough to pull the rope off the wall!

(b) Take one end of a slinky and ask a friend to hold the other end. Stretch it and then send an impulse down the slinky. What do you notice about the shape and form of the slinky as you do this? What happens if you push the slinky more vigorously? Warn your friend that you are going to do this so they do not let go of the slinky suddenly.

Commentary

The kind of wave produced with the rope is called a **transverse wave** (Figure 85) because the pattern of disturbance is at right angles to the direction of the movement of the wave. Light and waves in water are examples of

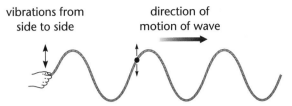

Figure 85 Transverse wave

transverse waves. The kind of wave produced in the slinky in Activity 1(b) is a **longitudinal wave** and is called this because the pattern of disturbance is in the same direction as the movement of the wave. This is shown in Figure 86.

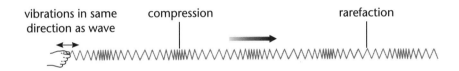

Figure 86 Longitudinal Wave

As the person pushes the slinky forward and back you can see the wave travel down the slinky. As the wave travels along the rings close up (compress) and spread out (rarefaction) as you can see in Figure 86.

Sound is an example of a longitudinal wave. It is possible, using a slinky, to produce both a transverse and a longitudinal wave depending on how you shake and move the slinky.

Waves have certain features regardless of their type and these have a significant role in how the wave behaves. First there is **amplitude** which is the distance that the wave reaches from the normal. **Frequency** is the number of waves that pass a particular point in one second and the unit of measure is hertz (Hz). The third feature, illustrated in Figure 87, is wavelength. This measures the distance between corresponding points on two successive waves, and both wavelength and amplitude are measured in centimetres or metres.

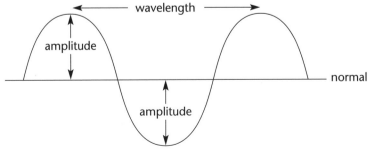

Figure 87 A typical wave

Waves move out in all directions from the source and all waves can be reflected, refracted or diffracted. How this happens and the difference between these three phenomena is important.

Reflection

A wave is reflected when there is an object or barrier in the path of the wave and the wave direction is changed and reflected away from the barrier. The angle of reflection equals the angle of incidence as shown in Figure 88.

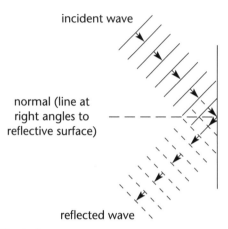

Figure 88 A reflected wave

Refraction

A wave is refracted, that is it changes direction, when there is a change in the speed of the wave. This change in speed happens when waves cross from one medium to another and it is the change in density of the two media that causes the change in speed. Figure 89 shows the effect of refraction. In water the change happens when waves pass from deeper to shallower water.

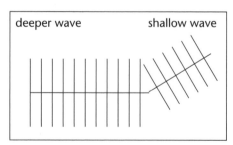

There is change in speed + wavelength
but not in frequency

Figure 89 A refracted wave (in water)

Diffraction

Diffraction is really just the spreading out of waves and is brought about when waves pass through a gap or by an object. This is how sounds can be heard around a corner because the sound waves spread out or diffract. The longer the wavelength the more it will diffract. This is shown in Figure 90. Sound waves diffract more because the waves tend to be longer.

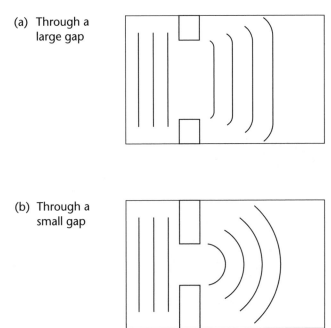

(a) Through a large gap

(b) Through a small gap

Figure 90 Diffraction of waves

In this section we have found out that waves:

▶ Are formed by something oscillating and they move out in all directions away from the source.

▶ Can be transverse or longitudinal and carry energy without transferring matter.

▶ Are mostly transverse, that means the vibrations are at right angles to the direction of travel of the wave.

▶ Can be longitudinal, that means that the vibrations pass along the same direction as the wave is travelling, e.g. sound can be refracted, reflected or diffracted.

Light

Visible light is one part of the electromagnetic spectrum. Within this spectrum there are seven connecting bands of electromagnetic waves.

Their properties change as the frequency or wavelength changes. The different kinds of electromagnetic waves merge into each other to form this continuous band. All the waves in the spectrum are transverse waves made up of oscillating electric and magnetic fields and carry energy from one place to another. All the waves travel at approximately 3,000,000 kms/sec in a vacuum. The electromagnetic spectrum and the types of waves are shown in Figure 91.

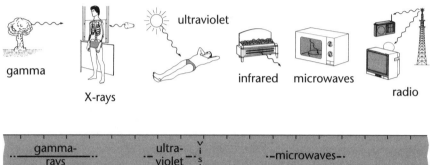

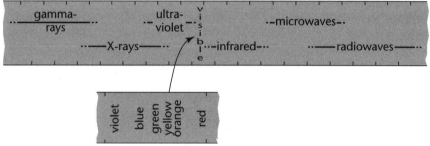

Figure 91 The elctromagnetic spectrum

This section deals with visible light, a very small section in the electromagnetic spectrum.

To work through this section you will need

▶ a torch

▶ a candle

▶ a mirror

▶ a ruler

▶ three pieces of card and, if possible, a mirror and a lens or prism.

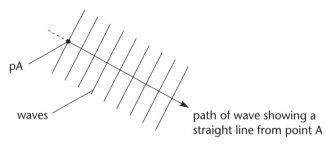

Figure 92 Light wave moving along

Light can be thought of as a kind of transverse wave. In order to be classified as such it must behave as described at the beginning of this chapter. We need to be clear that we are happy about the idea of waves being compatible with the notion of rays. If a beam of light were a wave first moving forward, as shown in Figure 92 and you marked a spot on one of the waves and followed that spot through as the wave moved, you would describe a straight line or ray.

How does light travel?	Activity 1

For this activity you need three pieces of card each with a hole pierced at the same height, a torch and supports for each piece of card.

Switch on the torch in a darkened room and align each card until you can see the light through the hole. You will have to adjust the cards.

Commentary

In Figure 93 you can see that the beam (some people talk of this as a ray although it really is a narrow beam) passes through the hole in a straight line. Rays are straight lines that we draw to represent the travelling light.

This activity shows clearly the idea of straight lines. Light will continue travelling in a straight line until it is absorbed or until it is reflected or refracted. Remember that reflection and refraction are properties of all waves.

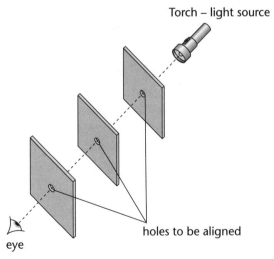

Torch – light source

holes to be aligned

eye

Figure 93 Light travels in straight lines

Looking through materials

Materials can be grouped according to whether or not they let light through. Translucent materials allow some light to pass through and opaque materials allow no light to pass. Let's look at some materials and see what we can see.

| Activity 2 | Can you see through it? |

Collect a range of household materials such as greaseproof paper, kitchen paper towel, foil and cling film. Which can you see through best? Which can you not see through?

Commentary

It is fairly easy to predict which materials do not allow light to pass through, but with translucent and transparent materials it is interesting to note how the amount of light passing through varies according to the clearness and thickness of the material.

| Activity 3 | What happens if light is blocked? |

For this activity you need a torch and a freestanding object. Switch on the torch and set up the apparatus as in Figure 94. The torch needs to be a reasonable distance away but not so far that the shadow does not fall onto the table or surface. Can you explain how the shadow is formed?

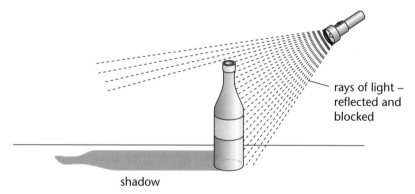

rays of light – reflected and blocked

shadow

Figure 94 What happens if light is blocked

Commentary

This shows clearly that light does not travel through all materials. The shadow formed has a definite shape that you can recognise as the outline of the object. The size of the shadow depends on where the light source is situated. The angle at which the light strikes the object affects the formation of the shadow. Shadows at midday, when the sun is higher in the sky, are shorter than those in the early morning or late evening when the sun is lower in the sky. Shadows are also affected by seasonal differences in the Sun's apparent movement across the sky. The midday Sun in winter does not rise as high as the midday Sun in the summer. You could try using some transparent, translucent and opaque materials to see which make the best shadows.

How is light reflected?

Light travels in straight lines from a variety of resources until it meets an object and then it is either absorbed, scattered or reflected. This means that the light bounces off the surface and travels on until it meets another surface and is reflected again. All objects reflect light but the nature of the surface of the objects affects how the light is reflected. If the surface is very smooth like a mirror then the reflection is even and regular, as shown in Figure 95(a), but if there is a rough surface then the reflection is irregular or diffuse as in Figure 95(b), and the light is scattered.

(a) Reflection on a smooth surface   (b) Reflection on a rough surface

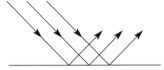

Figure 95 Reflection of light

Many materials have very reflective surfaces and one can see an image of oneself in the material. How does this work?

To show light being reflected	Activity 4

You will need the same equipment setup as in Activity 1 plus a mirror. In a darkened room shine the beam of light on to the mirror. Notice the reflected light beam. Can you change the direction of the reflected ray? How?

Commentary

The mirror is acting as reflective surface and the light is reflected. The light is bounced off at the same angle as it hits the surface. The angle of incidence is equal to the angle of reflection. This is shown in Figure 96. If you change the direction the ray hits the mirror you can see that the reflected ray travels out at the same angle as the ray going in. You could actually mark these on your white paper and measure the angle from the normal for both rays. The normal is a line at right angles to the surface, as shown in Figure 96.

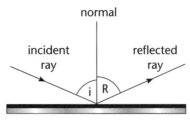

Figure 96 Reflection of light

However mirrors, because of their structure, add another dimension to reflection. This next activity explores what we see in the mirror.

Activity 5	How do we see an image in the mirror?

For this activity you will need a mirror that you can make stand up, a ruler, a pencil, some Blu-tak™ and a few pins.

Stand the mirror up on a plain piece of paper using some of the Blu-tak. Draw a line along the edge of the mirror. To one side of the mirror, about 3 cms away from the surface, fix a pin with a little Blu-Tak.

Look at the reflection of the pin in the mirror and then, using your ruler this time, look along it to the image you can see of the pin in the mirror. Draw a line along the ruler to the mirror. Repeat this several times looking from different positions at the image in the mirror. You should then have a diagram a little like Figure 97(a). If you drew lines from the mirror to the pin that meet with your lines you should have a diagram like 97(b).

Next extend the lines to go behind the mirror until they meet the line drawn from the object at right angles to the mirror. If you measure the distances x and y what do you find?

Commentary

We see an object in a certain place because light has bounced off the object and spread out from it in all directions (see Figure 97). You see the image in the mirror because your brain is 'fooled' into thinking that the light has not been reflected. The image appears at the point where the imaginary non-reflected rays would have started. In other words x and y are the same length. The image in the mirror is called a virtual image because the image appears at the point from which the rays appear to start. It is not real in the way that an image from a slide projector is 'real'.

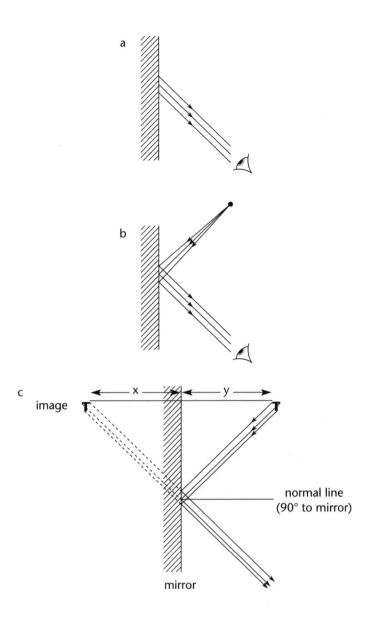

Figure 97 Reflection in a mirror

(a) Collect together a cup, a coin and some water in another container. Put the cup on the table and place the coin in it. Sit down and lower your head until you can just no longer see the coin. Keeping your head still, slowly pour the water into the cup and watch what happens.

(b) Fill a glass full of water and put a pencil or some other straight object into the glass and look through the side of the glass at the object. What do you see?

Commentary

(a) As you slowly poured the water you should have seen the coin appear to move up so that you could see it (Figure 98). This happened because as light passes from one transparent medium to another it is refracted, i.e., it changes direction. It has changed direction because it has changed speed as it passes between the water and the air.

(a) (b)

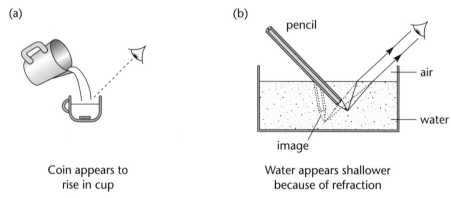

| Coin appears to rise in cup | Water appears shallower because of refraction |

Figure 98 Examples of refraction

(b) The pencil or other object in the glass appears to be bent. The light from the pencil or other object has changed direction as it left the water and passed to your eye. The angle at which the light strikes the surface affects how much the rays are bent. This can be shown by looking at light rays passing through different glass blocks and is the principle by which lenses work. The diagram in Figure 99 shows how the shape of the glass affects how the light meets the air at different angles as it passes through the glass to the air. Light rays at right angles to the surface do not change direction but when the angle is less than 90 degrees when the ray enters, it is bent as it passes out.

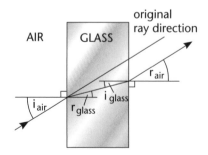

Figure 99 Refraction in glass

How lenses work

A lens is really like a series of different shaped glass blocks joined together. In Figure 100 you can see a simple diagram showing how this works. Different lenses of different thickness and shape will change what is seen as you look through them. A convex lens is a piece of glass that bulges on one or both sides. The lens drawn in Figure 95(c) shows a simple convex lens with a focal point on the optical axis. Different shaped lenses have different focal lengths – flatter lenses bend the light less and so the focal point is further way from the lens than if it was a rounder lens. The lens focuses the light to one point – the focus.

(a)

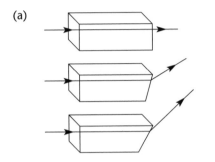

(b)

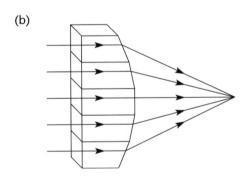

(c)

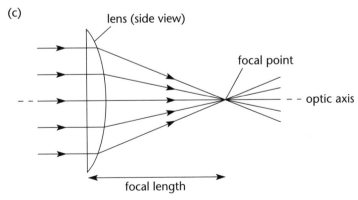

Figure 100 Light bending through different glass blocks

a) If you can, collect together some different magnifying glasses (different thicknesses) or lenses from old spectacles. Otherwise look carefully at the diagrams in the commentary to help you understand theoretically how lenses work.

   Look at a variety of objects through the magnifying glass. Experiment with where to hold the lens. Are they clearer if you hold the lens close to the eye or closer to the object?

b) Hold the lens close to the object and adjust the position until you get a clear image of the object. Now move the lens out slowly away from the object and watch the image. What do you notice about the image?

c) This time hold the lens near a sheet of paper and a few feet from a window. Move the lens forward and backwards until you get a clear image of the window on the paper. What do you notice about the image? Can you explain why this has happened?

Commentary

The convex lens decreases the angle the rays of light make when they pass through the glass, i.e., they make the rays of light 'converge'. The diagram in Figure 101(a) shows the rays being bent to form an image.

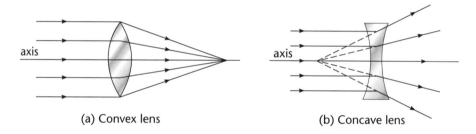

(a) Convex lens   (b) Concave lens

Figure 101 Lenses

A concave lens diverges or spreads the light out as it passes through. These two properties of lenses are important in making spectacles.

How our eyes work

If you look at your eyes in the mirror you can see some of the outer features and structures, and the individual variations that identify you as yourself, e.g. colour, shape and size. So how do these structures help us to see and what is inside the eye to aid our seeing?

In a bright room look at your eyes and then move into a darker part of the room and watch what happens to your pupil. Can you make up a rule about what happens to the pupil when the light intensity changes?

Commentary

As you increase the light the pupil will get smaller thus limiting the amount of light that enters the eye. The reverse is also true that the pupil enlarges as the light intensity decreases. We will now look at why this happens and see what part it plays in how we see the world.

Looking at a cross section of the eye sideways (Figure 102) will help us to see the process more clearly.

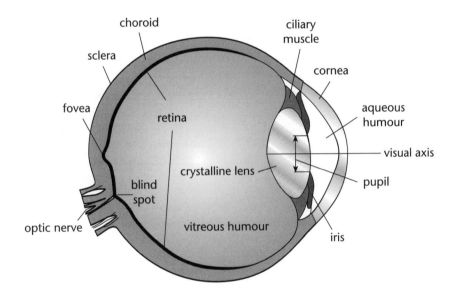

Figure 102 Cross section of the eye

When we look at something like a child playing on a swing, light from the sun is reflected off the surfaces of the swing and child and some of it reaches our eyes. It enters our eye through the cornea and passes through to the aqueous humour which is the fluid-filled cavity in front of the iris.

There is some bending of the light as it passes through the cornea because of the change in materials. Remember earlier in the chapter we saw that waves are refracted (bent) as they pass from one medium to another. The amount of light entering through to the chamber behind the eye is controlled by changes in the size of the pupil which is brought about by two sets of muscles. As the light passes through to the vitreous humour and onto the retina it has to pass through the lens of the eye. The shape of the lens can be changed and this is controlled by the ciliary muscles. The changes are important as this bends the light from near or far objects and focuses it onto the retina. On the retina there are sense cells, rods and cones that, having been stimulated, pass messages to the brain. The image on the retina is upside down. This is not because of the lens, since a pinhole camera (with no lens) will also invert the image, but because the rays of light from the object must cross at the opening (hole). Where the light enters the eye the same crossing over of light happens as it passes through the lens and is refracted. It is the brain that turns the image around for us so that we don't see an upside down world and it is the brain that interprets what we see.

So why do some people need to wear spectacles or contact lenses to be able to see clearly? The answer is that to see clearly the image needs to be focused exactly onto the retina. But for many people the lens and its muscles are not able to achieve this. The light from the object is either focused short of the retina (short sight) or beyond the retina (long sight).

Opticians can correct this by using very precisely shaped lenses that bend the light back onto the retina. Figure 103 shows the different ways this is done for short and long sight. A convex lens is used to correct long sight by converging the light to focus on the retina and short sight needs a concave lens that diverges (bends out) the light to help lengthen the focal length for the eye.

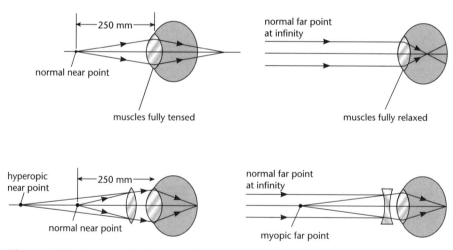

Figure 103 Long and short sight

But how do we see colours? Why are things different colours? The last part of this section tries to answer these questions.

Why are things different colours?

All visible objects give off light but they are either a light source or they reflect some or all of the light falling on to them.

It is important to understand first that light travels at a constant speed. It travels fastest in a vacuum but the difference between the speed of light in air and a vacuum is so small we can take this measure of 300,000 ku/second as the fastest speed of light. Light changes speed when it passes from one medium to another and as it does it is refracted.

Visible light as we know it is actually part of a bigger range of waves known as the electromagnetic spectrum. This spectrum is continuous with visible light in the middle – because scientists have described it that way.

Why are things different colours?	Activity 9

For this activity you will need a prism (glass or perspex), light source (torch) in its box with a hole, two sheets of white A4 paper and access to a darkened room as this makes it easier to see the effects.

Place the paper on the table and stand the box with the torch along one side of the paper so that the beam (ray) shines across the paper. Place the prism into the line of light and slowly twist until the light ray shows a range of colours. You may have to play around with this until you achieve the best angle for splitting the light into its constituent parts. (See Figure 104.)

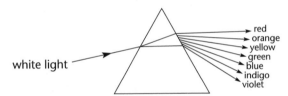

Figure 104 Splitting of white light through a prism

Commentary

This is the spectrum of visible light and is made up of the colours of the rainbow. The mnemonic 'Richard of York gains battles in vain' is one of many that you may have heard to help you remember the order of the colours. The colours, in order from longest to shortest wavelength, are red, orange, yellow, green, blue, indigo and violet and this also reflects the increasing frequency of the waves from red through to violet.

The light at the violet end of the spectrum moves more slowly in glass and so is bent more than light at the red end of the spectrum, which is how the rainbow effect is formed. Visible light or white light is made up of these rainbow colours. Darkness is the absence of visible light.

So why are things different colours? We need to look at a dress or flower with a particular colour. Why is it that colour? Where is the colour? Is it in the flower or the light? Can you begin to explain what happens when we see colour from what we have discussed so far? Try the next activity and see if this helps you to answer the question.

You will need a book with a plain coloured cover, a torch and a piece of white paper.

Lay the book on the table and shine the torch onto the surface of the book. As you do this hold the paper at right angles to the cover so that the reflected light from the cover falls on the white paper. What do you notice about the colour of the paper? Can you suggest why this is so?

Commentary

The colour you should have seen on the paper should have been the same as that of the book. The reason for this involves three different factors. The first of these is that when light hits a surface that is a particular colour then all the light in the spectrum except the light that is the same colour as the book is absorbed and the coloured light is scattered or reflected. Figure 105 shows the different amounts of light that are reflected if you look at white, red and black surfaces respectively.

Secondly, in Figure 105(b) the red light at the end of the spectrum has longer wavelengths, and the nature of the pigment that gives the colour to the book affects how much light is absorbed and how much is reflected. Remember all visual things give off light, but they do it in two ways. Some objects are actually light sources, i.e., they produce light, the rest reflect light that has hit them. The light that hits the object may be white or coloured light and the pigments, dyes etc. used to colour the object will affect what light is absorbed and what is reflected. Dyes, paints and pigments give objects their colour because they absorb particular frequencies of light. The other parts of the spectrum are reflected off the surface. However, the light falling on the book can affect the colour of an object of a particular colour. If a blue book is seen in blue light or white light it will still appear blue because all the light is absorbed except the blue which is reflected. However, if you shone an orange light on the blue book you would see the book as a dark grey colour. This is because the book has absorbed all the colours including most of the orange but not the blue. It is very difficult to decide what colour the book cover is in coloured light. You could try to think what might happen to a green car if you saw it in a sodium light (orange). What colour do you think it might be?

What colour would you see if you shone a red light and green light onto the same spot on a wall? The answer is yellow and not reddish-green or greenish-red as you might expect. You may wish to try this with two torches and some red and green coloured cellophane taped on each torch. If you add a third torch with blue cellophane then the colour on the wall is white. Isaac Newton showed how to split light into the colours of the spectrum. The activity above shows how you can add colours to make white light. You do not need all the colours of the spectrum to combine to make white light. Red, green and blue light will give you white light. These colours are called the 'additive primary

(a) White light reflected from a white surface

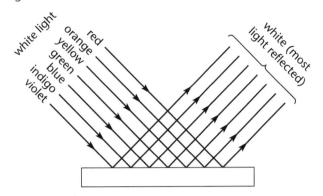

(b) White light falling on a red surface

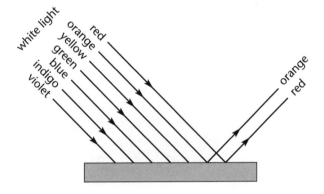

(c) White light falling on black surface

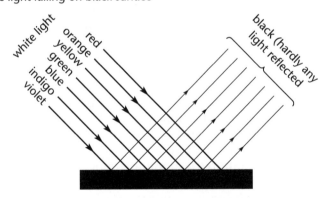

Figure 105 Reflecting white light on different surfaces

colours', i.e., you add them together to make white light. In Figure 106 the primary additive colours are shown and around the side are the secondary colours that are achieved when two primary colours overlap.

The three secondary colours here are: cyan (blue and green), yellow (red and green) and magenta (red and blue).

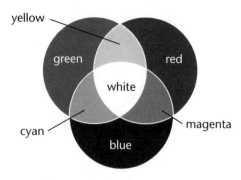

Figure 106 Primary additive colours

Pigments, dyes, paints and fabrics etc. make our world more colourful by not making colour but taking it away. The pigments absorb some of the colours of the spectrum, i.e., take it away, and reflect the rest. If an object absorbs all the light then it is black, if it reflects all light it is white (Figure 107).

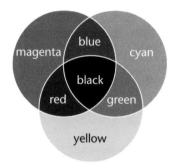

Figure 107 Colours by subtraction (pigments)

The final idea to explain about colours is to look at the sense cells in the eye. Light, which falls on the back of the retina, stimulates the rods and cones (mentioned earlier when looking at how the eye works) – light-sensitive cells. It is the cones that sense colour. Different cones respond to different colours (wavelengths). The rods respond to low levels of light and are responsible for our night vision. The message is sent to the brain as an electrical impulse along the optic nerve. The brain interprets these impulses into the colours that we see. The process for sending messages and their interpretation are complex and need not be part of this discussion.

In this section we have seen that light:

- Is part of the wider electromagnetic spectrum.

- Travels in straight lines.

- Can be reflected, refracted and diffracted.

- When it is white, is made up of the colours of the rainbow.

- Can be split into the colours of the rainbow.

- Is important for us to see and the eye is the sense organ that detects light through its rods and cones.

- Can be bent by the use of lenses and these are used to correct focal lengths of our eyes.

10 Sound

Introduction

In this section we investigate some basic principles and features of sound. We pick up and develop the ideas explored in the section on waves looking at how sound as a particular kind of wave can be transmitted and how we hear. For this work you will need the following equipment:

- collection of musical instruments – make sure you have some that you pluck, beat, blow and scrape
- collection of objects for making sounds
- pencil and notebook
- tuning fork
- cling film
- stopwatch
- tape measure.

Ninety-five per cent of the information we take in through our senses comes via our ears and eyes. Most of us are able to hear a wide range of sounds and we use this information to determine the kind of action we may take. If you are asked a question you will respond and if you hear a ringing at regular intervals you know to answer the telephone, even if you can't yet see it. For those with less effective hearing other ways are available for us to know that the phone is ringing, such as using a flashing light or making the mobile phone vibrate in your pocket. Our developing understanding of sound and how we hear has helped to provide many different ways of supporting blind and partially sighted people to live independent lives. So what exactly happens when we hear sound, and how are sounds made? The first section will explore how sounds are made and the second how we hear.

Activity 1	How quiet is it?

Close your eyes and just sit and listen for a minute or two to the sounds you can hear. When you stop write down all the sounds you heard and could recognise and then describe the other sounds that you heard but could not identify.

Why can you recognise some sounds and not others? What can you say about the different sounds? Do they give clues as to how they are made? Can you say how they are made?

(a) Collect together a range of objects or musical instruments to make a noise and spend a few minutes making sounds. As you do this look at the ways the sounds are made. What did you have to do to make the sound?

(b) Stretch some cling film across a container and put a few grains of sand or rice on the surface. Try hitting the surface and watch what happens to the rice or sand as it makes a noise.

(c) If you have access to a tuning fork collect this and a bowl of water. Hit the tuning fork against the table and then place it immediately in the water. What happens to the fork and water?

Commentary

Sound is made when an object is made to vibrate backwards and forwards. Blowing, plucking, hitting or rubbing can do this. The sounds produced will only be heard if they are within the frequencies we as humans can normally hear. The vibration causes particles to move towards and then away from each other, creating alternate areas of higher and lower pressure, which transmits the sound through the air. The jostling of air particles is carried outwards from the sound source through the air until it disturbs the particles next to your eardrum, causing it to vibrate so that you can hear the sound. This is the sound wave and it travels at a constant speed depending on what it is travelling through. Sound travels faster through denser media. In a denser medium there are more rigid bands between the molecules and so it is easier for particles to vibrate. Sound cannot travel through a vacuum because there are no particles/molecules to vibrate in a vacuum. With both the cling film activity and the tuning fork you can see the vibrations that arise as a result of the hitting the cling film.

Use the same equipment as in Activity 1 and play around trying to alter the pitch of the sounds. What do you have to do to change the sounds?

What kind of sound can you produce?

Commentary

The pitch of a sound can be high or low. Change in a sound is caused by increasing or decreasing the frequency of the wave. A high frequency, i.e., more waves passing a fixed point, gives a high pitch and a lower sound is the other way round.

The higher the frequency the higher the pitch of the sound and the shorter its wavelength. The upper limit for humans to hear is about

20,000 hertz and lower limit is 20 hertz (1 hertz equals 1 vibration per second). Sounds above that level are said to be ultrasonic and can be used in medicine for pre-natal scanning and in industry for cleaning. Sounds below 20 hertz are subsonic. Many animals have wider hearing ranges than humans, extending to both ultrasonic (e.g. dogs) and subsonic (e.g. whales) frequencies.

Middle C frequency is 256 Hz and the compressions that form the waves are 1.3 metres apart in air. The note an octave above middle C is produced by an object vibrating at 512 Hz, double the frequency.

In a wind instrument the pitch is determined by the length of the column of air – it is the turbulent air moving in the tube that vibrates and resonates giving off the sound. When playing a recorder it is possible to change the length of the tube by opening and closing the holes.

How does sound travel?

As sound travels the air oscillates back and forth along the length of the wave. This is called **longitudinal wave motion** as in waves in water. No substance moves from the source to the hearer as many people think, but energy is transferred from the source to the hearer. Sound travels at 332 metres per second in air at sea level. It travels faster in liquid – 1,461 metres a second in water and still faster in solids, e.g. granite is 6,000 metres per second. Sound travels better and faster when molecules are close together. Most objects vibrate at several frequencies at once rather than in a simple way. If frequencies have mathematically simple ratios then sounds are pleasant but if not then it sounds to us like noise.

What are amplitude and loudness?

Loud sounds are produced when the amplitude of the vibrations is larger. This is shown in Figure 108.

The extent of any movement of a molecule from its midpoint is called the **amplitude** of the wave. The distance is actually quite tiny. We can hear sounds that move a molecule a thousand millionth of a centimetre. Sound that moves molecules a hundredth of a metre, i.e., 1 cm, will damage the ear! If amplitude is doubled the loudness increases four times (squared).

Loudness is measured in decibels (dB). It is important to realise that decibel scales are not linear either – every increase of 10 dB represents a doubling of volume. Figure 109 shows the range of loudness and the effects on the listener.

Sound loses its energy as it travels away from its source and so the decibel rating depends on both the actual energy produced by the source and how far away the listener is. As sound spreads out in all directions only a tiny amount of energy reaches the listener.

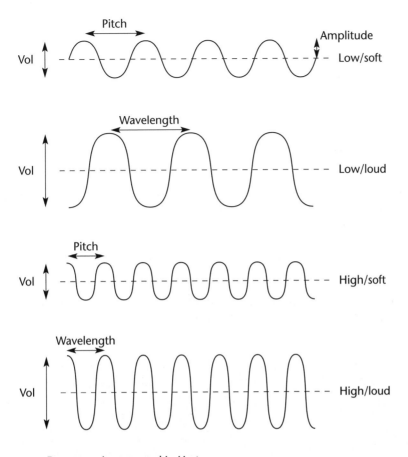

Frequency is measured in Hertz
Noise is measured in decibels.

Figure 108 Loud and soft, high and low sounds

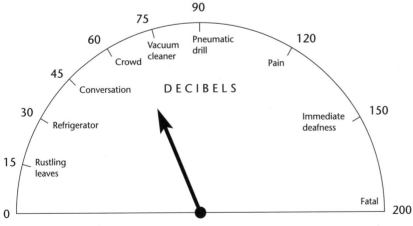

Figure 109 Decibel ratings

How can we show sound travels?

Sound can travel through any substance (e.g. sounds can be heard through a central heating system). If sound travels better through solids you would think shutting a window or door would not decrease the sound passing through – but actually because sound can be reflected from the surface as well not all sound passes through. Less sound passes through hard surfaces because they are better at reflecting sound back towards the source.

Have you ever noticed that when you look into the sky to see an aeroplane, if you look when you hear the plane it is not in the sky where you expected it to be but is ahead of the sound? As a child I am sure you counted the delay between seeing the lightning and hearing the thunder to determine how far away the storm was. An interval of three seconds from lightning to thunder means it is 1 ku away. This shows the difference in the speed that light and sound travel.

How fast does sound travel?

Activity 4	Measuring sound

To measure how fast sound travels you need a stopwatch, a drum and a trundle wheel. Measure with the trundle wheel or pace out about 660 metres and ask a friend to stand at one end. You stand at the other end and ask your friend to hit the drum as hard as possible. As soon as you see the drumstick strike the drum start the stopwatch and stop it as soon as you hear the sound.

If you divide the distance between you and your colleague by the time it took for the sound to reach you, you will have a fairly accurate measure of the speed of sound. The sound from the drum should have taken about two seconds to reach you.

Commentary

Sound travels at 330 metres per second in air. Your answer should be somewhere around this mark. It is necessary to repeat this exercise several times to obtain a better average. But do not worry about the exactness at this time, what is important is to experience the actual delay between sound being made and its arrival at your ear.

Some objects such as supersonic planes like Concorde travelled faster than the speed of sound. The plane accelerated until it reached the speed of sound and as it did it caught up with the sound waves travelling in front of it and pushed them against each other. This forms a barrier of compressed or squashed air in front of the plane. At the speed of sound the plane overtakes the compressed air. This air then spreads out rapidly behind the plane in a loud shock wave. On the ground you would hear a loud noise not dissimilar to thunder as this happens. This is called a **sonic boom**. This is shown in Figure 110.

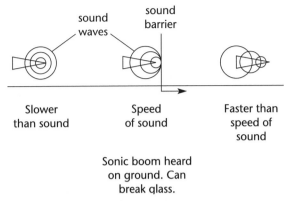

Figure 110 Sonic boom

What happens when sound hits an object?

An echo	Activity 5

As you walk under bridges and through tunnels or stand in empty rooms try to make your voice echo. What do you have to do to make this happen?

Commentary

Sound is reflected and it is reflected more off harder, smoother surfaces than soft or irregular ones, which diffuse the sound. When you visit the theatre or concert hall the acoustics of the room are very important in enabling you to hear a clear and rounded performance. The nature of the surfaces and the shape of the walls and room affect the sound and how well it is transmitted. Ear trumpets or the bell of a musical trumpet use reflected sound, and gather it up and direct it towards the ear or out of the trumpet.

Bats and dolphins use the reflection of the high-pitched sounds that they make to help them move about. How do we hear? The next section explores this.

How do we hear?

Activity 6   **How the eardrum works**

For this activity you need a cardboard tube, a balloon and rubber band. Stretch the balloon over one end of the tube with the rubber band and speak into the open end of the tube, whilst touching the balloon end. What can you feel?

Commentary

You should feel the vibrations as the sound reaches the balloon which is acting as the eardrum in this case.

In Figure 111 you can see where the eardrum or tympanic membrane is situated.

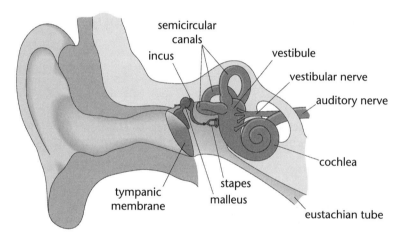

Figure 111 How sound reaches the ear

As the vibrations move towards the ear the sound is funnelled down the outer ear to the eardrum, or tympanic membrane, which vibrates when the sound hits it. From here the vibrations are amplified as they pass through a series of loosely connected bones known as the malleus (hammer), incus (anvil) and stapes (stirrup) to the inner ear. The coiled structure called the cochlea, which means snail, in the inner ear contains hair-like nerve cells – each one sensitive to a particular pitch. The vibrations pass into this fluid-filled structure where the movement of the liquid stimulates the cells and signals are passed along the auditory nerve to the brain. It is the brain that interprets these messages into the sounds that we recognise.

Animals have a variety of different shapes of ear that are adapted to the lifestyle that they lead. You only have to watch a dog out in the park to see how they twitch and move their ears to respond to sounds. They do it even when we cannot hear anything as they can hear a much higher pitch of sound than we can. Humans can hear frequencies from 20 Hz to 20,000 Hz whereas many animals can hear frequencies much higher. For example dog whistles are high pitched but some young children may be able to hear them. Deer have very sensitive hearing and can move their ears to maximise the sound that reaches them and determine the direction of the sound. Sounds above 20, 000 Hz are called ultrasounds. This astute hearing linked with their strong sense of smell enables deer to judge whether the stimuli are from a friend or foe and so can respond appropriately.

In this section we have seen that:

- Sound waves are produced by vibrations.
- They travel through different media at different speeds.
- Sound waves have different frequencies and amplitude.
- Sound is passed to the ear through the incus, malleus and stapes to the cochlea.
- Sound can be reflected, refracted and diffracted.
- Sound travels at 332 metres/second in air.

11 Earth and Space

This chapter explores some basic ideas about day and night, seasons and phases of the Moon. These are related to our own experiences, and explore, briefly, the use of models to help us explain phenomena that are not possible to show by direct experiment. The second part of this chapter goes wider and looks briefly at our place in the universe.

Resources

For the activities in this section you will need:

- some different sized balls
- notepad and pencil
- sticky labels.

Building a model of the Earth, Sun and Moon

Modelling is an important part of doing science, since it enables us to simulate how a system works. It allows us to compare the results of an experiment with a prediction generated using an idealised model. A model can be formulated either after or before collecting data, but it must be based on some experience of the phenomenon being modelled. Models usually concentrate on certain properties or effects while ignoring others. For example, a group of children acting out planetary motion to find out more about how day and night occur would be creating a model. The model would isolate and display certain properties of the real situation in order to explain something about the motion of the Earth, but it would not include such properties as the size of the Earth, its distance from the Sun, and so on. Thus, this model would have certain limitations, and it is important to recognise these. In theory, the simplest and most reliable answer to the question of how the Earth relates to the Sun and the Moon would be found by travelling sufficiently far away from all three of them and having a look from the outside. Alas, this is not yet possible for all human beings. Nevertheless, we should still be able to develop an understanding of this relationship, even within the limitations of our Earth-bound observations. What we must do is to analyse our observations carefully, and use the information that we glean to build a picture of the relative positions and motions of all three bodies.

Think about what you know about the Earth, the Sun and the Moon from everyday experience and observations. For example, you may say you know the Earth is a sphere, that it spins on its axis and orbits the Sun. For every statement you make, ask yourself 'How do I know this?, and include any evidence you can to justify your statement.

Day and night

Activity 2

This activity builds on the work you have just completed. Write down everything you know about day and night. What evidence do you have to support your statements?

Commentary

The regular sequence of day and night is one of the most common experiences shared by all people, and indeed by all living creatures on the Earth. It is taken so much for granted that it represents an ideal of certainty, permanence and regularity. Yet a closer look soon reveals that this sequence does not have a perfectly rigid pattern. To begin with, it is not the same over the whole Earth. In addition, an observer who stays in one place will experience variations in the relative length of daylight and darkness. These variations are related to the position of the Sun in the sky.

Approximately halfway through the daylight period, which we know as noon, the Sun reaches its highest point above the horizon. This is known as the **culmination point**. This culmination point is not the same all the time, and it is common knowledge that days are long when the Sun culminates high above the horizon, and short when the culmination point is low. The relationship between the height of culmination and the length of daylight connects the day–night cycle closely with the cycle of seasons.

Although there are local as well as seasonal variations in the relative lengths of days and nights, the time interval between two consecutive culminations of the Sun is constant. It is the same for all observers everywhere on the Earth and is the same throughout the year, except for the polar regions, where the Sun does not appear above the horizon for a long time during polar winters. The interval between two consecutive culminations of the Sun became one of the first natural units for measuring time, and is known as a **solar day**.

Use a south-facing window, and using small sticky labels and from the same spot in the room, plot the apparent movement of the Sun across the sky/window at regular intervals, e.g. every hour. Do this once or twice over two–three weeks if you can. Do you notice any difference in the pattern?

Commentary

Your results for Activity 3 should give you an arc across the window. The height of the arc may have changed a little over a period of two to three weeks – either up or down depending on the season. This activity shows that the Sun appears to move across the sky but it is important to realise that it is not the Sun that is actually moving but you on the Earth who is moving as the Earth spins on its axis – once every 24 hours.

The four seasons

When the relative durations of daylight and darkness within each solar day are systematically measured and recorded over several years, a clear pattern emerges that repeats itself regularly. This pattern is reflected in seasonal climatic changes, and there is an obvious relationship between the length of the day, the height of the culmination of the Sun, and the amount of light and heat received ftom the Sun at the place where the observations are being made. Table 14 summarises these observations for locations in the Northern Hemisphere, starting from summer.

Table 14 The seasonal cycle in the Northern Hemisphere

Relative lengths of daylight and darkness	Culmination point of the Sun	Name of day [date]	Climatic observation	Name of season that begins on this day
Longest day and shortest night	Highest	Summer solstice (21 June)	Hot	Summer
Day and night of equal length	Average	Autumnal equinox (21 September)	Mild	Autumn
Shortest day and longest night	Lowest	Winter solstice (21 December)	Cold	Winter
Day and night of equal length	Average	Vernal) equinox (21 March)	Mild	Spring

As you are aware, different parts of the Earth do not have the same season at the same time. When Britain enjoys its summer, Australia has to endure its winter. In fact, the whole pattern is reversed for the parts of the Earth to the north and south of the Equator (the Northern and Southern Hemispheres, respectively). Furthermore, the intensity of seasonal changes varies with location. Around the Equator, seasonal changes are hardly noticeable, but in the Arctic regions they are so great

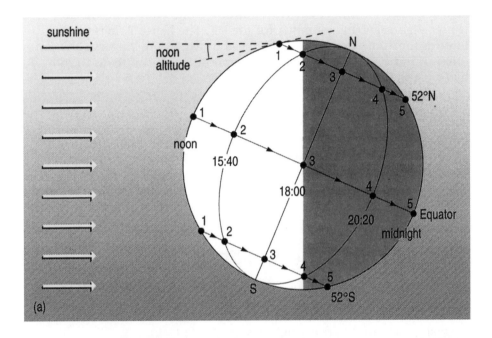

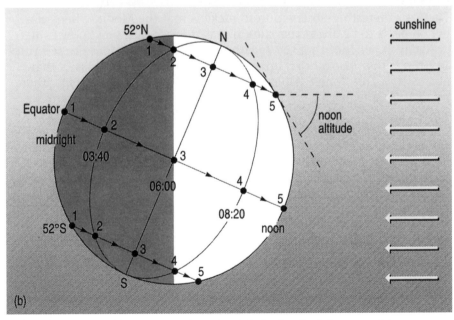

Figure 112 Variation of day length with latitude (a) around 21 December, (b) around 21 June

that even the day–night cycle is different. There is a time (which amounts to several months at the poles) during which an Arctic observer always sees the Sun moving about the horizon and never setting below (polar day in the Arctic summer) and a similar period during the Arctic winter when the Sun never emerges above the horizon (polar night). Figure 112 shows the variation in day/night that occurs with latitude for around December 21 and June 21. You can see that in 112(a), we, on latitude 52 °N, have longer nights and shorter days. This must therefore be winter, i.e., December 21. The North Pole tilts away from the Sun in winter. Figure 112(b) is summer for the UK. The North Pole is tilting towards the Sun. The shadows produced in winter are longer as the sun is lower in the sky at noon and in summer they are shorter as the Sun is higher in the sky.

From this point all detail will relate to the UK or places of similar latitude within the Northern Hemisphere.

In spite of all the local variations, there is one common feature. For any place on Earth, the time interval between two identical observations is the same (for example, between two consecutive summer solstices, see Table 14). There is some underlying regularity reflected in the constant length of one complete seasonal cycle, whatever its local details.

The Sun and the Moon

The Sun and the Moon appear to be the two largest natural objects visible in the sky, and are the *only* two objects that appear to the unaided eye as large circular discs. All other celestial bodies visible at night appear as small points of differing brightness.

The first interesting observation to make is that the Moon, when seen full, appears to be about the same size as the Sun. But you know from everyday experience that the *apparent size* of an object does not tell you anything about its *real size*, unless you also know the distance of that object from you. A matchstick held at arm's length appears longer than the mast of a television transmitter a few miles away! At this stage, we are not concerned about the real sizes of the Sun and the Moon, or about measuring the distances to them. All we need is the observation that the apparent sizes of the Sun and the (full) Moon each remain constant in time. This means that whatever their distances from the Earth, these distances cannot be changing to any great extent. Actually, the Sun and the Moon sometimes seem bigger when they are close to the horizon. This has nothing to do with distance – it is partly to do with the fact that light has to pass through a thicker layer of the Earth's atmosphere.

The Sun is the source of nearly all the light and heat that reaches the surface of the Earth. The Moon, by contrast, is much less bright and provides little heat as it mainly reflects light from the Sun. It can be seen more clearly during the night, although it is frequently above the horizon during the day. The most striking feature of its appearance is that, unlike the Sun, the Moon is not always seen as a full circular disc.

Either by studying the shape of the Moon over the next four weeks, or from previous experience and knowledge, try to plan out the changes that take place in the Moon's shape. Can you put them in order and add a timescale to your plan?

Commentary

The Moon undergoes a cycle consisting of lunar phases, as shown in Figure 113. The changes of shape correspond to the changes in the time of day or night when the Moon can be seen above the horizon (provided that it is not cloudy or obscured by bright sunshine). The whole cycle from one new Moon to the next is approximately 29.5 day–night cycles – a lunar month.

The shape of the darker areas seen on the Moon's surface (the 'Man in the Moon') do not change appreciably with time. Their relative positions on the face of the Moon also appear to be constant. They temporarily disappear as one part of the Moon progressively darkens, but they reappear in the same places when that part of the Moon brightens up again. The Moon appears always to show the same face to the Earth.

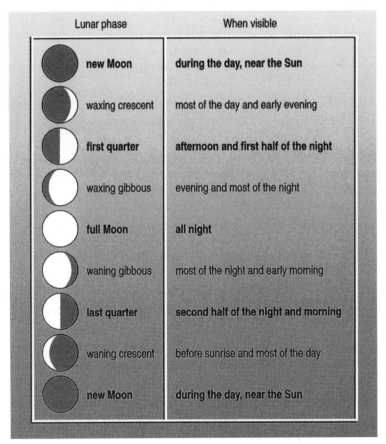

Lunar phase	When visible
new Moon	during the day, near the Sun
waxing crescent	most of the day and early evening
first quarter	afternoon and first half of the night
waxing gibbous	evening and most of the night
full Moon	all night
waning gibbous	most of the night and early morning
last quarter	second half of the night and morning
waning crescent	before sunrise and most of the day
new Moon	during the day, near the Sun

Figure 113 Phases of the Moon and the visibility above the horizon

The periodicity of events

In spite of their local variations, all the observations discussed earlier in this section indicate that there is a basic underlying regularity and an intrinsic order in the universe. Night always follows day, spring follows winter, the first quarter of the Moon follows the new Moon, and so on.

If you choose one particular event or situation, for argument's sake the full Moon, you will observe that after a sequence of changes this particular event or situation will be repeated. Moreover, the sequence of events between the two identical situations will also be repeated. A process in which an event is repeated at regular intervals is called a **periodic process**, and the time taken to complete the sequence once is called the **period** of the process. In everyday life, there are many examples of periodic processes, for example the rotation of a turntable and the swinging of a clock's pendulum.

So far we may have included the following in our evidence list:

▶ There is a periodic cycle of days and nights. The precise details of this cycle vary, depending on where the observations are made on the Earth's surface.

▶ There are longer-term, seasonal changes in the relative lengths of daylight and darkness within one solar day (the interval between two consecutive culminations of the Sun). The culmination point of the Sun occurs approximately halfway through the daylight period (noon), when it reaches its highest point above the horizon. These seasonal changes are related to the culmination point of the Sun and also depend on the place of observation.

▶ The Sun and the Moon are roughly the same apparent size. Their distances from the Earth do not change considerably with time, otherwise their apparent sizes would be observed to change.

▶ The Moon exhibits a periodic cycle of lunar phases and has some apparently stable features on its surface. It appears always to show the same face to the Earth.

Activity 5	Modelling the relationships of the Moon, Earth and Sun

We can now begin to build our model of the relationship of the Earth to the Sun and the Moon. To do this let's first look at the Earth and Sun. Can you, using your experience and notes so far, give explanations for:

▶ how we get day and night

▶ how seasons occur

▶ the different phases of the Moon?

If you are able to, complete this activity with friends. It may be useful (a) to compare intuitive theories and (b) to list the strategies you have used to elicit those theories.

Commentary

Observations made in the past may have been interpreted differently in the light of the accepted theory of the time. As new knowledge is formulated the theory may change, which results in a new way of thinking about familiar events. Sometimes supporting evidence comes a long time after theory – for example, information gathered during space travel has supported theories developed much earlier.

From their observations, scientists inform us that:

1   The Earth spins on its own axis (**axis of rotation**) in approximately 24 hours and this accounts for the day–night cycle.

2   The Earth's axis of rotation is inclined at about 66.5° to the plane of its orbit (or, to put it another way, its axial tilt is about 23.5°), remains fixed in space and points towards the star Polaris.

3   The Earth orbits the Sun following an approximately circular path and one complete circle corresponds to one seasonal cycle (one year).

What do we mean by the Earth's seasons?

Our concept of seasons rests on a number of annual cycles, synchronised with the year. In particular we think of the cycles of:

▶   day length

▶   altitude of the Sun at noon (its greatest altitude each day)

▶   weather

▶   foliation

▶   animal behaviour.

These are the main seasonal cycles. But what causes them?

Many people think that these cycles are caused by the variation in the distance between the Earth and the Sun. Is this one of your intuitive theories? This distance does indeed vary annually as the Earth orbits the Sun, because the Sun is not quite at the centre of the Earth's orbit, which is not quite circular. The Earth receives about 6% more sunshine at its closest point than at its furthest point. However, this theory has problems:

▶   It predicts that the Northern and Southern Hemispheres will have the same season at the same time, which is not the case – when it is summer in the UK, for example, it is winter in Australia.

▶   It predicts that when it is summer in the UK the Earth will be closest to the Sun; in fact it is closest in early January.

The Earth's seasonal cycles are actually caused by the tilt of the Earth's axis of rotation with respect to the plane of its orbit.

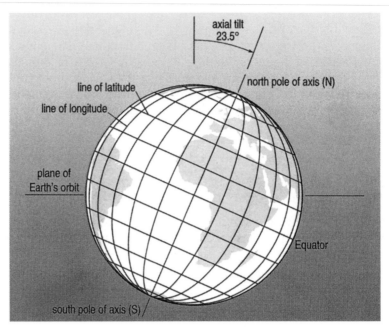

Figure 114 The tilt of the Earth's axis

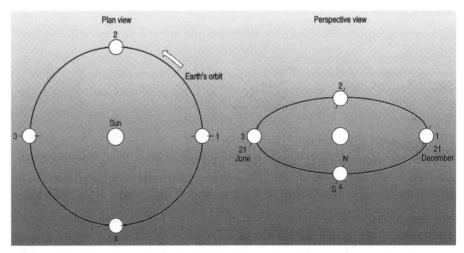

Figure 115 The direction of the Earth's axis with respect to the Sun (not to scale)

Figure 114 illustrates the tilt, and Figure 115 shows that the axis points in a fixed direction as the Earth orbits the Sun once a year. (Note that in Figure 115 the sizes of the Earth and Sun are *enormously* exaggerated). Figure 116 illustrates how the tilt of the Earth produces the seasons.

The main points to cover in an explanation of the seasonal cycles are:

▶ There is variation in day length; shortest and longest

▶ At any latitude (except at the Equator) there is a seasonal cycle in day length.

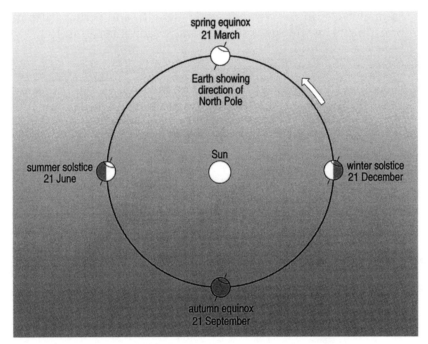

Figure 116 *How the tilt of the Earth produces the seasons*

- There is a seasonal cycle in the noon altitude of the Sun.
- When the noon altitude of the Sun is lower, the sunshine reaching the ground is more thinly spread as it has had to travel through a greater thickness of the Earth's atmosphere; i.e., the energy is spread over a bigger area and the atmosphere has a greater effect in absorbing and reflecting the energy (Figure 117).
- The lower the altitude, the shorter the length of daytime.

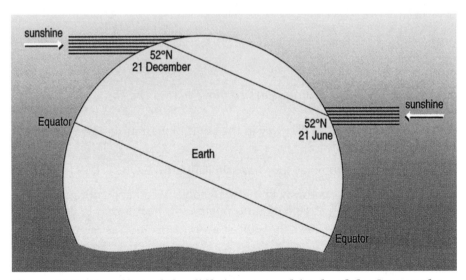

Figure 117 *The effect of the differing noon altitude of the Sun on the intensity of sunshine reaching the ground*

The seasonal cycles in the weather, in day length, and perhaps also in the noon altitude of the Sun, cause natural seasonal cycles in the biosphere, e.g. foliation, animal behaviour. We thus have our explanation of the seasonal cycles as shown in Figure 116.

Remember that there are seasonal cycles at all latitudes, but they may differ from those in the UK. For example, in most equatorial regions there is nothing like our spring–summer–autumn–winter, but some sequence of hot and less hot, wet and dry seasons.

The Sun's pathway	Activity 6

Figure 118 shows the pathway of the sun across the sky at different times of the year. Can you say which belongs to spring/autumn/summer and winter? Can you give reasons using information learnt in the previous notes?

Commentary

The spring and autumn pathways would be between the winter and summer pathways.

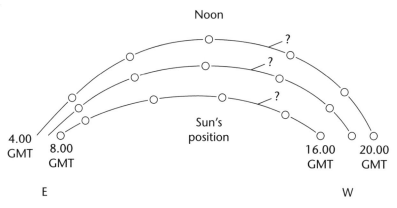

Figure 118 How the Sun appears to move across the sky

A   is summer. The Sun's pathway in the sky is highest in summer. We have shorter shadows.

B   is spring and autumn as they have similar pathways.

C   is winter – lowest pathway in the sky – cooler weather – light more affected by bigger stretch of atmosphere as its heat travels to Earth, and spreads out more widely over the surface.

The Moon and its relationship to the Earth and the Sun

The most striking observation about the Moon is the periodic cycle of its phases. The continuously changing shape and size of the bright part rules out any possibility that the light from the Moon originates in the Moon itself. It is very difficult to imagine any physical process on the surface of the Moon that could switch different parts on and off with such unfailing regularity and with such a sharp boundary between dark and light. On the other hand, the Moon's low overall brightness, the negligible rate at which it emits heat (compared with the Sun) and the shape of its bright crescent can be readily understood by assuming that the Moon is a spherical body that is illuminated by the Sun and reflects some of its light. But how is the Moon placed with respect to the Sun and the Earth, and how does it move?

We know that:

▶ The Moon is visible at different times during the day and/or night.

▶ The time at which the Moon is visible is closely related to the shape and size of its bright part (phases).

▶ The Moon is much less bright than the Sun and emits a negligible amount of heat.

▶ The complete cycle of lunar phases has a period of about 29.5 solar days.

▶ The Moon is visible, albeit at different times, for some part of each solar day (provided that it is not obscured by clouds).

▶ The Moon shows the same face to the Earth at all times.

▶ The Moon is always of the same apparent size.

▶ The apparent size of the Moon is about the same as that of the Sun.

▶ Eclipses of the moon occur relatively rarely (no more than twice a year).

Moon, Earth and Sun	Activity 7

Design a three-sphere model to explain and account for the observations relating to the Moon and its relationship to the Earth and the Sun.

Try to include the following features in your design:

(a) The Moon is a spherical body reflecting the light from the Sun.

(b) The Moon moves around the Earth in a circular orbit.

(c) The plane of the lunar orbit is slightly inclined with respect to the plane of the Earth's orbit.

Using your model, try to explain to a colleague as many of the observations, listed before this activity, as you can.

Table 15 Moon phases and time of day

Phase	Rises	In eastern sky	Highest in sky	In western sky	Sets
New	(Sunrise)*	(Morning)	Noon	(Afternoon)	(Sunset)
Waxing crescent	(Just after sunrise)	(Morning)	(Just after noon)	(Afternoon)	(Just after sunrise)
First quarter	Noon	Afternoon	Sunset	Night (p.m)	Midnight
Waxing gibbous	Afternoon	Sunset	Night (p.m)	Midnight	Night (a.m)
Full	Sunset	Night (p.m)	Midnight	Night (a.m)	Sunrise
Waning gibbous	Night (p.m)	Midnight	Night (a.m)	Sunrise	Morning
Third quarter	Midnight	Night (a.m)	Sunrise	Morning	Noon
Waning crescent	Just before sunrise	(Morning)	(Just before noon)	(Afternoon)	(Just before sunrise)

* Times in brackets indicate that the Moon cannot be seen because it is too close to the Sun in the sky.

Commentary

Table 15 and Figure 119 will help you to make sense of how the Moon moves around the Earth. It shows how we only see different sized bits of the Moon at different stages in its orbit.

Figure 119 shows how the phases of the Moon arise from its orbit around the Earth. The time interval between occurrences of the *same* phase (e.g. full) is, on average, 29.5 days (more precisely, 29.53 days).

You can see from Figure 119(a) that the Moon always presents the same face to the Earth: the Moon rotates on its axis in the same time that it orbits the Earth, and in the same direction. Moreover, whenever you see a full Moon, everyone else on the same side of the Earth will also see a full Moon. This applies to a new Moon and to every other phase of the Moon as well (see Table 15).

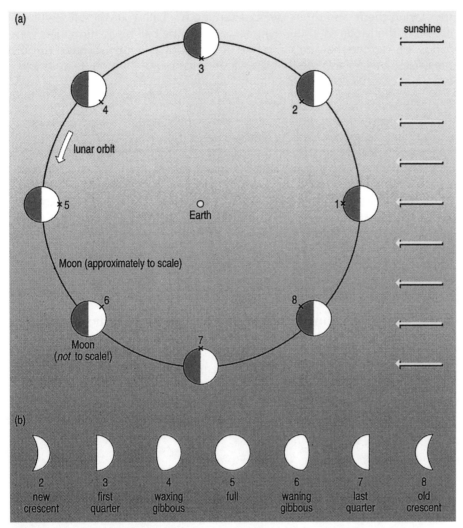

Figure 119 *The Earth–Moon system. (a) The Moon's orbit around the Earth, showing how the phases of the Moon arise. (b) The Moon's appearance from Earth (the Northern Hemisphere) in each of positions 2 to 8. In part (a) the x is always the same point on the Moon's surface, showing that the Moon always presents the same face to the Earth*

Modelling the phases	Activity 8

These ideas are complex, and you may want to continue to work on them by trying the following activity. You will probably find it more effective if you invite a friend to work with you and talk through the process as you do the activity.

In a darkened room using a bright light for the Sun and a wholly white ball for the Moon, mark a single dark spot on the ball. The person representing the Earth should hold out the ball, slightly above their head, with the dark spot facing them, and rotate without turning the ball. You will still see the phases of the Moon as in the diagram, and, as the ball is not turning in your hand, you can see that the same face of the Moon is always directed towards the Earth. You can also see that the Moon must be rotating once on its axis every time it orbits the Earth.

These ideas are not at all straightforward. Take time to consider them carefully and try devising different demonstrations and activities to enable you to think about the ideas in different ways.

It is worth repeating a point that we made earlier about the models that we use. We tend to devise models that focus on just one or two features of interest at a time while ignoring other features. So, when thinking about the phases of Moon at different positions in its orbit using a globe and a ball (or a human and a ball as in the first part of the activity) we usually ignore both the spin of the Earth and that of the Moon. If we want to demonstrate more features then we have to construct more elaborate models; however, it is often simpler and clearer to consider different ideas separately.

Easter, a very important festival in the Christian church, moves each year and this is related to the Moon. Easter is always taken as the first Sunday after the full Moon following the spring (vernal) equinox. It can be as late as one month after March 21 (e.g. Easter 2000 was on April 23).

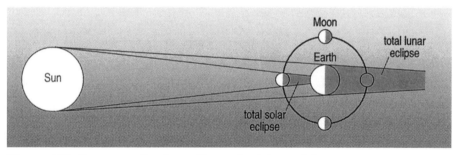

Figure 120 Lunar and solar eclipses (not to scale)

Eclipses

Figure 120 shows how total lunar and total solar eclipses arise. It would seem that there should be one of each per month, but the Moon does not orbit around the Earth in the same plane as the Sun and Earth, so eclipses are not as frequent. Lunar eclipses occur only around the time of a full Moon. Solar eclipses are seen only from certain parts of the Earth because of the difference in the relative sizes of the Sun, the Earth and the Moon. Eclipses are possible only at points B and D in Figure 121; and even then only when the Moon is in one of the positions indicated by the solid circles (●).

Having explored your basic ideas about night and day it is important now to consider the wider place of the Earth, Sun and Moon in the universe.

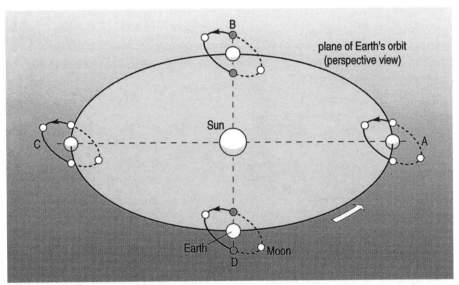

Figure 121 The relationship between the Moon's plane of orbit around the Earth and the Earth's plane of orbit around the Sun

The solar system and beyond

Look at the list of words below. They are words that we use often in everyday talk but what are their scientific definitions?

Write a sentence or phrases that say exactly what each is and then read the commentary that follows to confirm and develop your ideas.

- star
- galaxy
- comet
- meteors
- galaxy

- Milky Way
- solar system
- light years
- asteroids.

The Earth is one of a series of planets that orbit the Sun. The Sun is our nearest star and is at the centre of our solar system. The planets that orbit the Earth are shown in order from the Sun outwards and there is a simple mnemonic for remembering this order. There are several versions of this available – choose the one that helps you.

Table 16 Solar system – facts and figures

	Axial rotation	Time in orbit	Diameter in km	Km from Sun (in millions)	Miles from Sun (in millions)	Gravity (Earth = 1)	Mass (Earth = 1)	Density (Water = 1)
Mercury	My 56 days	88 days	4,878	57.9	36	0.38	0.055	5.4
Venus	Very 243 days	225 days	12,103	108.2	67.2	0.9	0.81	5.2
Earth	Easy 23h56m	365.25 days	12,756	149.6	93	1	1	5.5
Mars	Method 24h 37m	687 days	6,786	227.9	141.6	0.38	0.11	3.9
Jupiter	Just 9h 50m	11.86 yrs	142,984	778	483.6	2.6	318	1.3
Saturn	Shows 10h 14m	29.45 yrs	120,536	1426	886.7	0.9	95	0.7
Uranus	U 10h 49m	84.01 yrs	51,118	2871	1783	0.8	15	1.3
Neptune	Nine 15h 40m	165.79 yrs	49,528	4497	2794	1.1	17	1.6
Pluto	Planets 16h	248.43 yrs	2,284	5913	3666	0.04	0.002	2

In Table 16 there are some important facts about each planet such as its orbit, size, structure, etc. It is not necessary to learn these but such information is useful to have. An Open University lecturer in 2000 claimed he had identified another planet that orbits the Sun but it goes in the opposite direction. Such a claim it shows how our scientific knowledge is always being challenged and changed. Our solar system is just one of millions in our galaxy, the Milky Way galaxy.

Other features in our galaxy include the following.

Asteroids

Comets and meteors are often confused.

Asteroids are a belt of small planets that can be seen between Mars and Jupiter. They are about 450 million ku from the sun and orbit the Sun just like the other planets. They vary in size from a few metres to 1,000 metres across. The asteroid Ceres is the biggest.

Comets

These can be one of the most exciting and dramatic sights in the night sky. Comets are made up of ice and dust and travel through space, invisible to the eye most days. They become visible from Earth only when they approach the Sun in their orbit. The Sun's heat gradually causes the ice to melt and evaporate into gas and so release the dust. This cloud of gas and dust glows as it reflects sunlight. Comets travel at about 2,000,000 ku/h when close to the Sun. Comets often grow tails which are made of gas and dust that has been pushed from the core by a stream of particles from the sun.

Comets have been known about for hundreds of years. Halley's comet, probably the most famous, has been known for centuries. It is depicted in the Bayeux Tapestry that commemorates the Battle of Hastings in 1066. It will next be seen in 2062.

Meteors

Meteors are particles of rock that fall out of space and when they hit the Earth's atmosphere they begin to burn up. It is this that causes the bright streak in the sky. If they are small they will burn up before reaching the Earth's surface and fall as dust. But if they are bigger they may not burn up completely and fall onto the Earth.

In Arizona there is a crater 1,265 metres in diameter and 175 metres deep that is thought to have been caused by a meteorite that fell onto the Earth about 25,000 BC.

Our solar system and beyond

The universe is vast and understanding how large is quite difficult. To appreciate this we need to use models. A good model to use to understand the huge distances, just within our own solar system, is to think of the Sun as a 30 cm beach ball. The Earth would then be about the size of a pea and at the opposite end of an Olympic size pool. Pluto the outermost planet would then be 1.25 ku away!

Understanding the vastness of space is difficult for most of us as we cannot visualise 1,000 miles let alone millions and billions of miles. The scales of the model above help to give us some idea of how big distances are when we consider space.

Our solar system is a small part of the Milky Way galaxy (galaxies are groups of stars). This galaxy is a spiral galaxy that can be seen on very clear hot summer nights in the UK and Figure 122 shows where we are located in that galaxy. Our galaxy has an estimated 100 billion stars and we are only able to see about 6,000 to 7,000 without the use of a telescope. It is thought to be about 100,000 light years wide. (Light years are explained later.)

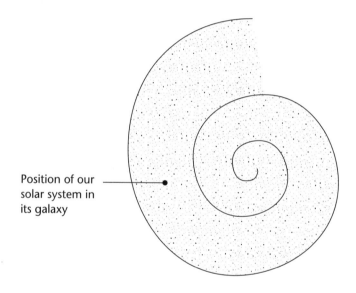

Position of our solar system in its galaxy

A spiral galaxy – billions and billions of stars

Figure 122 The Milky Way galaxy

The Milky Way galaxy is just one of billions of billions of galaxies in our universe and made up of billions and billions of stars.

Activity 10   What is a star?

Write what you think a star is.

Commentary

As you can see in Table 17 a star is a nuclear inferno. It is a ball of dust and particles that have collapsed under gravity and become very hot. When it reaches temperatures of 10 million °C nuclear fusion takes place when hydrogen is converted to helium in the core of the star. This gives out the light we see as a star.

Table 17 Stages in the life of a star

1 *New star*	A star begins life as a dense cloud of dust and gas that starts to collapse under its own gravity. The clumps of gas and dust grow hotter and hotter as they continue collapsing. At 10 million °C nuclear fusion reactions start and a star now exists.
2 *A steady star*	The star becomes a nuclear reactor and shines for billions of years by converting hydrogen to helium in its core. After 8 or 9 billion years the star is virtually unchanged. Reactions continue.
3 *Red giant*	This forms after about 10 billion years. The hydrogen in the centre runs out. This makes the core collapse and heat up. This causes the star's atmosphere to expand and cool. The star becomes a red giant.
4 *Hot white dwarf*	The red giant slowly loses its unstable atmosphere to show its collapsed core. The jettisoned atmosphere becomes a planetary nebula. The collapsed core survives as a very hot white dwarf.
5 *The star dies*	The white dwarf collapses to become a cold black globe.

If we consider that light from the sun, our nearest star, 93 million miles away, takes 8.25 minutes to reach us and that the light from the next nearest star, Centaur Proxima, takes 4.2 light years to reach us, we begin to get some idea of the vast distances in space. On our scale model of the solar system where we used a beach ball as the Earth, Centaur Proxima would be in Los Angeles, if you were standing in the UK. Using a model to explore the vast distances in space and their relationships is helpful for us to relate ideas and concepts. Because space is so vast we have to look differently at how we measure the distances. For this we use the notion of light years.

Light years

A light year is defined as the distance light travels in a calendar year and can be calculated by multiplying 365 (days) × 24(hours) × 60(minutes) × 60(seconds) × 300,000 (speed of light/second) and is equivalent to 94.6 billion ku. This means that light travels 94.6 billion ku in a year. From this you can determine how far our next nearest star Centaur Proxima is!

If you multiply the light years it takes by the distance it will travel in a light year you will see that our nearest star, other than the Sun, is 397.32 billion kilometres away.

$$4.6 \times 94.6 = 397.32 \text{ billion ku}$$

Some of the light we see from stars in the sky is from stars that no longer exist. Light travels 33,000 ku/sec and has taken hundreds of light years to reach Earth. These ideas are not easy to comprehend but are fascinating. They make you think about fundamental issues such as the meaning of life, our purpose and future. A major breakthrough this century, that extended our understanding of the universe and how it came into being, was made by Edwin Hubble, an American astronomer and cosmologist. He proved that certain nebulae beyond our galaxy were galaxies themselves and he classified galaxies into groups. He found that they were moving away from us. This provided some strong evidence that the universe is expanding. More recent findings have confirmed this.

We know that the universe is expanding so objects are moving away from each other. Much of space is actually empty.

Our knowledge and understanding of the universe is growing rapidly as technology and our scientific expertise advances. However, we are unable to travel as far in space as we would like. We need to be able to travel faster than the speed of light in order to reach stars within a human life span. 'Beam me up, Scottie' may never be a possibility.

Recent developments by eminent scientists have enabled us to explain more about space and the interrelationship of time, space and light. Many of the science fiction films that explore other worlds seem far from reality. But many of the ideas we now take for granted, such as the number of galaxies in our universe, were mere fantasies years ago. This branch of science is expanding (like our universe) rapidly. Black holes, pulsars and speculation on life on other planets are some of the exciting ideas to explore in the future.

In this section we have seen that:

- There is a pattern to the day and night.
- The seasons are caused by the Earth's tilt.
- The Moon has regular patterns to it movement.
- The universe is expanding.
- Distances are vast in space.
- Much of space is empty.
- Stars are nuclear infernos.

Primary Science Subject Audit

Introduction

This audit is designed to help you identify strengths in your science subject knowledge and highlight areas that you need to develop further. It is designed for use by people who are already teachers or on an initial teacher training course who need to evaluate their subject knowledge against the standards for primary science.

It is hoped that this audit will help you to identify better your own understanding in particular areas of science. It is important that you attempt all the questions. Answers are provided and will help you reflect on your understanding. It is impossible in this kind of document to cover all facets of each topic area, but the questions are designed to give you an indication of your understanding of that section.

Having attempted the audit, marked and reflected on your results, you need to plan a programme of study over a period of time that enables you to deepen your understanding of the identified areas. The plan needs to take account of the other demands made on you as a teacher or trainee. As the work is divided into small sections, it should be easier to break up your workload into manageable parts. Record your answers to the audit, your workings from the book and your reflections on your developing knowledge in a file. This is important as this can be submitted as evidence towards your claim for competence and Qualified Teacher Status (QTS). As you work through the subject study sections, it is important that you attempt the practical activities, answer the questions and record your findings.

Questions

The nature of science

What is science?

Scientific investigation

1   Which of the following questions or statements could lead to scientific investigation?

   (i)   Will it rain today?

   (ii) Which battery will last the longest?

   (iii) Why are you happy?

   (iv) What happens when you push this trolley?

   (v)   Which candle will burn the longest?

2　Choose one of the questions that could lead to an investigation that could include an experiment and plan how you might do it by considering the following questions.

(i)　What will you do?

(ii)　What equipment do you need?

(iii)　What variables do you need to consider?

(iv)　How will you collect the evidence?

(v)　What will you measure? How often?

(vi)　How will you record your results?

(vii)　How reliable will your results be?

(viii)　What are conclusions?

(ix)　What health and safety issues do you need to consider?

Materials

1　What are the following: an electron, a neutron and a proton? Where are they found?

2　What is the difference between an atom and a molecule?

3　What is an ion?

4　Name the three states of matter.

5　What is a physical change?

6　What is the difference between evaporation and condensation?

7　What happens when a chemical change takes place?

8　What is the difference between a mixture and a compound?

9　What is the difference between an element and a compound?

10　Approximately how many elements are there?

11　How are atoms or ions held together?

Forces

1　What is the difference between mass and weight?

2　What units do we use to measure (a) mass and (b) weight?

3　Why is your weight different on the Moon to the Earth?

4　What is gravitational force?

5　What is friction?

6　A plane is flying at a constant speed. Are there any forces acting on the plane?

7　What happens if forces are not in balance?

8 Which will reach the floor first if you drop a marble and a cannon ball at the same time?

9 Complete these sentences. To start a ball rolling quickly you need to give it a .... The bigger the ... the ... the ball will travel. To slow down or ... the ball a ... must act in the ... direction to movement.

Energy

1 What is potential energy? Kinetic energy?

2 What units is energy measured in?

3 What is the process called that captures the energy from the Sun and uses it to form sugars?

4 What do we obtain our energy from?

5 What happens to some of the energy during energy transfers?

6 What is the difference between energy and force?

7 Name a renewable energy source.

8 What does the law of conservation of energy say?

Life and living processes

1 What are the characteristics of all living things?

2 What are the functions of the circulatory system?

3 What do we mean by a balanced diet?

4 What happens to a piece of bread once you have eaten it? Describe the process in as much detail as you can.

5 How do plants make food? Can you explain the chemical process using a word equation?

6 What happens when you breathe in and out?

7 What are the main differences between plant and animal cells?

8 Drugs, alcohol, and smoking can affect health. What are the main harmful effects?

9 What is the difference between asexual and sexual reproduction?

10 What do they call the life cycle of an insect that goes through four stages?

11 What are the main secondary sexual characteristics that develop at puberty?

Continuity and change

1 What is a species?

2 What is a life cycle?

3 What are the four stages in the life cycle of a butterfly?

4 What is evolution?

5 How is the life cycle of a stick insect different from that of a fly or butterfly?

6 How is information about individuals passed on to the next generation? Include all the following terms in your answer: cell, DNA, gene, chromosome, meiosis and zygote.

7 Why do we look similar to our parents but not exactly alike?

8 What is a mutation?

9 Why are males affected by haemophilia?

Ecosystems

1 What do you understand by the terms ecosystem, habitat and community?

2 What is a primary producer within an ecosystem?

3 What do you call an animal that eats (a) plants, (b) other animals and (c) both plants and animals?

4 What do you understand by the term food web?

5 Why is the carbon cycle important?

6 Describe the water cycle.

7 What are some of the factors that could influence population size?

8 What do you understand by the term conservation?

9 Why do you think species are dying out more rapidly this century?

Electricity and magnetism

1 Which of the following are conductors of electricity: copper, chalk, paper, iron?

2 What is a material that does not allow electricity to flow through called?

3 What is flowing in a circuit?

4 What is resistance and what units is it measured in?

5 Why is it important to have a battery in a circuit?

6 What is voltage?

7 What is current and what units is it measured in?

8 Are the lights in a house arranged in parallel or series?

9 What is a magnetic field?

10 What happens if you put two north pole ends of a magnet together?

11 How would you make a simple electromagnet?

Waves and light

1 Visible light is part of the ... spectrum?

2 How are shadows formed?

3 Light travels in ... lines?

4 What happens when light is reflected?

5 How do we see?

6 We can see a book because light is ...

7 List the order of colours in the spectrum.

8 What is a lens?

9 A convex lens ... the light and a concave lens ... the light.

10 The primary colours for light are ..., ... and ... .

Sound

1 We hear when sound travels from a ... .

2 Sound is produced when something ... .

3 We can alter the pitch of a sound by altering the ... .

4 The loudness of a sound is changed by altering what?

5 What units do we measure noise levels in?

6 How fast does sound travel in air?

Earth and space

1 Is the Sun a star?

2 Which galaxy is our solar system in?

3 Name the planets in order from the Sun outwards.

4 What happens to the Earth during one day?

5 In the Northern Hemisphere why is the day shorter in the winter than in the summer?

6 How long is a lunar month?

7 Can you name the key phases of the Moon?

8 What is a star?

Answers

The answers given below are brief. More detailed information can be obtained about most areas in the main text. If you are unsure of your ideas or achieve less than half marks in any section you should work through that topic.

The nature of science

Science is a way of making sense of the natural world and involves the study and investigation of new and existing ideas. Science is more than just biology, physics and chemistry and is a co-operative activity involving a wide group of individuals from different scientific communities. Scientific knowledge is constantly changing and can be used in solving many problems.

Scientific investigations

1   Questions (ii), (iv) and (v) could lead to investigation and experiments.

2   (i)   Plan a systematic way of working that allows you to collect tbe information you need to answer the question.

    (ii)   Select suitable equipment to allow the test to give you useful data.

    (iii) You need to identify the dependent and independent variables and decide which one you are going to change.

    (iv)   You may collect evidence by making observations, by measuring and testing.

    (v)   What you measure will depend on what you are trying to find out and the activity needs to be designed to provide the relevant data.

    (vi)   You can use a table to record results or may, if you have access, use sensors connected to a computer so that readings are entered straight into the computer.

    (vii) Results will be more reliable if you repeat the experiment and obtain similar answers each time.

    (viii) Conclusions are the findings you make after completing the work.

    (ix)   At all times working in a safe environment with suitable equipment is vital. There are clear guidelines given in the ASE booklet *Be Safe* which is a must to read.

Materials

1   Electrons, neutrons and protons are the small particles found in an atom. An atom has the same number of electrons and protons.

2 A molecule is made up of more than one atom. It can be atoms of the same kind, or of different kinds, joined together.

3 An ion is formed when atoms gain or lose electrons.

4 Solids, liquids and gases are the three states of matter.

5 A physical change takes place when, for example, a substance changes from solid to liquid or to a gas or in reverse.

6 Evaporation is when a substance changes from a liquid to a gas and involves heating. Condensation is when a gas cools and changes into a liquid.

7 A chemical change results in a new substance being formed and involves the joining together of different elements or the splitting of compounds.

8 A mixture contains more than one substance but not in fixed proportions nor chemically combined. A compound consists of more than one element that are chemically combined and in fixed proportions within the compound.

9 An element is a substance that only contains one kind of atom and a compound is a substance made up of two or more elements.

10 About 100.

11 Atoms can be joined by sharing electrons as in covalent bonding or by ionic bonding which transfers electrons from metal atoms to non-metal atoms.

Forces

1 Mass is the amount of 'stuff' in an object. Weight is caused by the pull of gravity and will vary according to the size of the gravitational force acting.

2 Mass is measured in kilograms and weight is measured in newtons.

3 Your weight is less on the Moon because the Moon's gravity is a sixth of that found on Earth. This is because the mass of the Moon is about ⅙ of that of the Earth.

4 Gravitational force is the force of attraction between all masses.

5 Friction is a force. Friction always acts between surfaces that are sliding over each other, and causes objects to slow down.

6 Yes. Gravity, lift, air resistance and the propulsion force from the engines are all acting on the plane. When a plane is flying at a constant speed, the forces acting on the plane are balanced.

7 If forces are not in balance there will be a change in speed or direction.

8 Neither. The effect of air resistance is minimal.

9 Push, push, further, stop, force, opposite.

Energy

1   Potential energy is stored energy, e.g. a coiled spring has elastic potential energy. Kinetic energy is energy of movement. Anything that is moving has kinetic energy.

2   Energy is measured in joules.

3   Photosynthesis.

4   We obtain energy from the food we eat which contains stored chemical energy.

5   Most energy transfers involve some loss of useful energy. Most loss is dissipated as heat or sound. The less energy that is wasted, the more efficient the device is said to be.

6   Energy is needed to make things happen but this will only happen when the energy is transferred. Force is a push, pull or twist that starts, speeds up or slows down movement and can cause a change of direction.

7   Renewable energy sources include wind, water, waves, tides, solar and geothermal.

8   The law of conservation of energy says that energy can be neither created nor destroyed but is only converted from one form to another.

Life and living processes

1   Respiration, nutrition, excretion, sensitivity, movement, growth and reproduction.

2   The circulatory system is a transport system. It carries food, oxygen and other chemicals to all parts of the body, fights infection and carries agents that fight infection.

3   A balanced diet involves eating a range of foods that contain proteins, carbohydrates, fats, vitamins and minerals in appropriate quantities.

4   The food passes along the alimentary canal and as it does is broken down into smaller and smaller pieces. At various points along this canal digestive juices are produced containing different enzymes that act as catalysts to aid the digestion of the food. The food, depending on the content of the bread, is now in the form of amino acids, sugars and fatty acids and glycerol, and is absorbed into the body where it is used to provide energy for bodily activities and for growth and repair.

5   Green plants carry out photosynthesis. This means they are able to use energy from the Sun to make sugars from carbon dioxide and water.

Carbon dioxide + water $\xrightarrow{\text{energy from Sun}}$ glucose + oxygen

6 One of two sets of intercostal muscles and the diaphragm contract. This increases the volume of the chest as the ribs are pulled up and outwards and the diaphragm moves down. Air rushes in to balance the pressure from outside. Breathing out is the reverse with the volume being decreased as the ribs move in and down and the diaphragm moves up, thus air moves out of the lungs, as the pressure increases.

7 Plant cells and animal cells have a nucleus, cytoplasm, cell membrane and mitochondria. Plant cells have a cellulose cell wall, chloroplasts and vacuoles in them.

8 Smoking can cause lung cancer and heart disease. Alcohol can impair your judgement and affect your liver. Drugs alter your perception of events and can impair judgements. All of these are addictive and can have serious effects on personal life.

9 Sexual reproduction involves the joining together of a male and female gamete. Asexual reproduction does not involve separate sexes and exchange of genetic material. Offspring from asexual reproduction have the same genes as their parent.

10 The process is called complete metamorphosis. The insect goes through four distinct stages in the life cycle of egg larva, pupa and adult. Some insects hatch from the egg and look like a miniature adult and undergo up to five moults as they grow to reach adulthood. This process is called incomplete metamorphosis.

11 Girls develop breasts, hips and body hair. Boys develop body hair and the voice breaks.

Continuity and change

1 A species is a group of living organisms that can breed together and produce fertile offspring.

2 A life cycle is the stages an organism goes through from birth to death. Different plants and animals have different life cycles.

3 Egg, larvae (caterpillar), pupa (chrysalis) and imago or adult.

4 Evolution is the slow change of species over time.

5 A stick insect life cycle has three stages: egg, nymph and adult whereas a fly or butterfly has four stages (see 3 above).

6 Information about an individual is passed from generation to generation through sexual reproduction. The gametes (egg or sperm) are formed when the cells in the ovaries and testes divide. The number of chromosomes are halved through a special cell division called meiosis. The chromosomes, which are made up of genes, are found in the gamete from the parent. A gene is a length of DNA and carries the information and instructions for a particular aspect of each individual.

7 We do not look exactly like our parents because of the exchange of genetic material that happens during meiosis.

8 A mutation affects the functioning of the DNA and can affect more than one gene.

9 Males are affected by haemophilia because this is an inherited disease that is sex linked. Haemophilia is linked to the X chromosome. Males only have one X chromosome and if a carrier X chromosome is passed to the male, he will have haemophilia.

Ecosystems

1 An ecosystem is a community of plants and animals that live together in a particular habitat with all its specific physical features. A habitat is the particular place that an animal or plant lives in. Several animals and plants can share a habitat such as a pond. A community is made from the populations of different organisms that live in a habitat.

2 A primary producer is at the bottom of any food pyramid and is able to make sugars from inorganic substances through photosynthesis.

3 (a) herbivore, (b) carnivore and (c) omnivore.

4 A food web shows the food relationships between populations of organisms in a habitat.

5 The carbon cycle is important, as carbon is one of the key chemicals found in all carbohydrates and is essential to life.

6 Water from seas, rivers, lakes and plants evaporates into the atmosphere and as it rises it is cooled, forming clouds. As these clouds become heavy with water, they form rain, which falls onto the land and sea. The rainwater is taken up by the plants and fills up rivers and lakes and the cycle is repeated. Water is vital to all forms of life and care and protection of the water sources is important.

7 Factors that affect population size are birth, death, immigration and emigration, predators, conditions and competition for resources such as food, space, light and water.

8 Conservation is the careful management and protection of resources and the environment to help continuity.

9 Pollution and overgrazing are putting an enormous amount of pressure on resources that is destroying habitats. The overgrazing of just one animal in a habitat or ecosystem can destabilize the whole ecosystem and threaten other species as a consequence.

Electricity and magnetism

1 Copper and iron.

2 An insulator.

3 A current of electrons.

4 Resistance is a measure of how difficult it is for the electric current to flow through a circuit. It is measured in ohms.

5 A battery or cell is a source of chemical energy that causes a flow of electrons.

6 Voltage is a measure of the energy from a power supply given to a charge moving around a circuit.

7 The current is the flow of electrons and is measured in amperes (amps).

8 Parallel.

9 A magnetic field is a region where magnetic materials (like iron and steel) and wires carrying a current, experience a force acting on them.

10 Two north poles will repel or push each other away.

11 You would make a simple electromagnet by winding a coil of wire around an iron nail and connecting both ends of the wire to the terminals on a cell. A magnetic field will be found around the coil when the circuit is complete.

Waves and light

1 Visible light is a small band in the electromagnetic spectrum – see page 182 (Figure 91) for a diagram of the main bands we know about.

2 A shadow is formed when an object blocks light.

3 Straight

4 Light hits a surface at an angle and the ray is reflected off the surface at the same angle.

5 We see when light is reflected from an object into our eye. The light forms an image on our retina and a message is sent to the brain, which interprets what we see.

6 Reflected from it into our eyes.

7 Red, orange, yellow, green, blue, indigo and violet.

8 A lens is a shaped piece of glass or other transparent material that causes the light to bend as it enters and leaves the lens.

9 Converges and diverges.

10 Green, blue and red.

Sound

1 A source.

2 Vibrates.

3   Frequency.

4   Amplitude.

5   Decibels.

6   In air sound travels at 330 m/second.

Earth and space

1   Yes the Sun is a star – our nearest star.

2   The Milky Way galaxy.

3   Mercury, Venus, Earth, Mars, Jupiter, Saturn, Uranus, Neptune and Pluto.

4   The Earth rotates once on its own axis every 24 hours.

5   The length of day varies at different times of the year because of the tilt of the Earth. In winter, the Northern Hemisphere tilts away from the Sun and this gives shorter days.

6   A lunar month is about 29.5 days.

7   New Moon, waxing quarter Moon, waxing gibbous Moon, full Moon, waning gibbous Moon, waning quarter and new Moon.

8   A star is a nuclear inferno where hydrogen is converted to helium by nuclear fusion in its core.

Bibliography

Adey, P. (2002) 'Children's thinking and science learning', in Amos, S. and Booham, R. (eds), *Teaching Science in Secondary Schools* (Abingdon RoutledgeFalmer).

Alsop, S., Gould, G. and Watts M. (2002) 'The role of pupils' questions in learning science', in Amos, S. and Boohan, R. (eds), *Aspects of Teaching Secondary Science: Perspectives on Practice*, Abingdon, Routledge Falmer / The Open University.

Association for Science Education (2001) *Be Safe*, 3rd Edition, (Hatfield, Association for Science Education).

Carlton, K. and Parkinson, E. (1994) *Physical Sciences: A Primary Teacher's Guide* (London, Cassell).

Carre, C. and Ovens, C. (1994) *Science 7–11 Developing Primary Teaching Skills* (Abingdon and New York, Routledge).

COSHH (2002) Control of Substances Hazardous to Health Regulations 2002 (HSE).

Clugston, M.J. (1998) *The New Penguin Dictionary of Science* (London, Penguin Books).

Farrow, S. (1996) *The Really Useful Science Book: A Framework of Knowledge for Primary Teachers* (Abingdon, Falmer Press).

Goldsworthy, A. (1998) 'Learning to investigate', in Sherrington, R. *ASE Guide to Primary Science Education* (Cheltenham, Stanley Thornes).

Goldsworthy, A. and Feasey, R. (1994) *Making Sense of Primary Science Investigations* (Hatfield, Association for Science Education).

Harlen, W. (2000) *Teaching, Learning and Assessing Science* (London, Paul Chapman Publishing).

Hollins, M. and Whitby, V. (1998) *Progression in Primary Science* (London, David Fulton).

Jenkins, E. (1997) 'Towards a public understanding of science', in Levison, R. and Thomas, J. (eds), *Science Today* (Abingdon and New York, Routledge).

Littledyke, M., Ross, K. and Latin, L. (2000) *Science Knowledge and the Environment* (London, David Fulton).

Nott, M. and Wellington, J. (1993) 'Your nature of science profile: an activity for science teachers', *School Science Review*, 75(270), 109–12.

Ofsted (1996) *Inspecting Safety in Science: A Guide for Ofsted Inspectors in Primary Schools.* (London, CLEAPSS School Science Service).

Open University (1995) *Primary Teachers Learning Science: Workbooks 1–6.* Course 5624 (Milton Keynes, Open University).

Open University (1998) *Breakthrough to Science: Sight and Light* (Milton Keynes, Open University).

Peacock, G. (1998) *QTS Science for Primary Teachers* (London, Letts Educational).

Reiss, M. (2002) 'What is science?', in Amos, S. and Boohan, R. (eds), *Teaching Science in Secondary Schools: A Reader*, (Abingdon, RoutledgeFalmer/The Open/University).

Sherrington, R. (ed.) (1998) *ASE Guide to Primary Science Education* (Cheltenham, Stanley Thornes).

Wenham, M. (1995) *Understanding Primary Science: Ideas Concepts and Explanations* (London, Paul Chapman Publishing).

Useful Addresses

CLEAPSS School Science Service
Brunel University
Uxbridge UB8 3PH
Tel: 01895 251496

The Association for Science Education
College Lane
Hatfield
Hertfordshire AL10 9AA
Tel: 01707 267411

RSPCA Education Department
RSPCA Headquarters
Causeway
Horsham
West Sussex RH12 1HG
Tel: 01403 264181

Index

Added to a page number f' denotes a figure and 't' denotes a table.